Talent on Demand

Talent on Demand

Managing Talent in an
Age of Uncertainty

Peter Cappelli

HARVARD BUSINESS PRESS
BOSTON, MASSACHUSETTS

Printed in the United States of America

13 12 11 10 9

Library of Congress Cataloging-in-Publication Data
Cappelli, Peter.
  Talent on demand : managing talent in an age of uncertainty / Peter Cappelli.
     p. cm.
  Includes bibliographical references and index.
  ISBN 978-1-4221-0447-7
  1. Human capital—Management. 2. Employee selection. 3. Personnel management.
I. Title.
  HD4904.7.C325 2008
  658.3—dc22

2008001725

The paper used in this publication meets the requirements of the American National Standard for Permanence of Paper for Publications and Documents in Libraries and Archives Z39.48–1992

Contents

1

The Talent Management Problem

Talent management is the process through which employers anticipate and meet their needs for human capital. Getting the right people with the right skills into the right jobs—a common definition of talent management—is the basic people management challenge in any organization. Talent management often focuses on managerial and executive positions, but the issues apply to all jobs that are hard to fill.

The decisions you make about talent management will shape your organization's competencies and its ultimate success; from the perspective of the people who work for you, these decisions determine the path and pace of their careers. Talent management practices also can have a crucial impact on society. The lifetime employment model of the post-WWII generation, for example, provided the economic stability that created the American middle class.

Failures in talent management may be more recognizable than the concept itself. Those failures include mismatches between supply and demand: on the one hand, having too many employees, leading to layoffs and restructurings, and on the other hand, having too little talent, leading to talent shortages. These mismatches are among the biggest challenges that employers face. Over the past generation, corporations in particular seem to have lurched from surpluses of talent to shortfalls and back again. Something is wrong with this picture.

Talent management practices, especially in the United States, fall into two equally dysfunctional camps. The first and most common is to do nothing—making no attempt to anticipate your needs and developing no plans for addressing them. This reactive approach, which effectively relies on outside hiring, has begun to fail now that the surplus of management talent has eroded. The second strategy, which is common among older companies, relies on complex bureaucratic models of forecasting and succession planning from the 1950s—legacy systems that grew up in an era when business was highly predictable. These models fail now because they are inaccurate as well as costly. *Talent on Demand* describes a different, third way that is less risky than the do-nothing approach and more responsive than the 1950s models.

How Did the Talent Problem Arise?

Many observers assume that the management of talent is really about the internal development of human capital, but most vacancies in corporations now are filled from outside. Internal development practices—such as executive coaching, creating developmental assignments, establishing assessment centers, implementing high-potential programs, and succession planning—are also presented as new ideas. These techniques, along with other employee development practices that seem novel—forced ranking performance evaluation systems, 360 degree feedback programs, executive coaching—were all common in the 1950s. Except at a few large firms, such practices have been scaled back and in many cases abandoned.

It is not that these practices fail to develop talent but that they are too costly. The biggest cost is managing the unpredictability of the demand for talent. Internal development of talent collapsed in the 1970s when business forecasting failed to predict the downturn in the economy, and the talent pipelines continued to turn out talent under the forecast assumptions of booming corporate growth. The excess supply of talent, combined with no-layoff policies for white-collar workers, caused a bloating of corporate organizations. The steepness of the 1981 recession then led to white-collar layoffs and the end of lifetime employment as well as reengineering processes that cut the development practices and staff that created talent. After all, if the priority was to get rid of talent, why maintain the programs designed to create it?

From that point on, employers turned to the outside labor market to find the supply of talent to meet their business needs. Outside hiring worked well through the early 1990s, in large measure because it was drawing down the pool of laid-off talent. As the economy continued to grow, however, outside hiring drew talent from existing competitors, creating the problem of employee retention. Employers then further decreased investment in development when they saw employees walk out the door to take jobs at other companies.

I remember a conversation I had with a CEO in the medical device industry about a management development program being proposed by his head of human resources. He dismissed the proposal by saying, "Why should we develop people when our competitors are willing to do it for us?" By the mid-1990s, virtually every major employer asserted a goal of getting better at recruiting talent from competitors and getting better at retaining its own talent, an impossibility at the aggregate level. The older companies that still invested in development became known as "academy companies"—breeding grounds for talent—simply by maintaining some of the practices that almost all companies had followed previously.

But outside hiring as the solution to the talent management challenge began to hit an inevitable limit by the end of the 1990s after the longest economic expansion in U.S. history depleted the supply of available talent. Most employers began to realize that even when they hired experienced candidates, they were losing their own experienced employees out the back door, often to jobs elsewhere that looked a lot like those they were trying to fill with outside hires. Quality is especially hard to measure in outside candidates, and the high failure rate of outside hires, especially at the executive level, reminded employers that it's hard to pull off a just-in-time workforce.

Frustration with outside hiring peaked, and the problem of attracting the right employees and then retaining them went to the top of the list of business concerns:

- A 2003 Conference Board study conducted when the labor market was at its nadir reported that talent management issues ranked among three of the top five concerns for CEOs.[1]

- In a 2004 Conference Board study, 65 percent of the surveyed companies reported that talent management had become "dramatically or considerably more important" since 2001.[2]

- McKinsey & Co. interviewed CEOs and other business leaders around the world and found half worrying that their talent management practices were not aligned with business outcomes; more than half said that there was insufficient commitment to developing talent among line managers and insufficient time spent on talent management in general.[3]

- A 2007 survey by SEI's Center for Corporate Futures found that a concern about "difficulties in finding, retaining, and growing talent" ranked top in importance for international business respondents from a list of business challenges, topping factors such as the growing influence of China and India on business.[4]

- Another 2007 survey reports that 81 percent of U.S. employers have concerns about their supply of leadership talent that will affect their future business plans.[5]

Many, and arguably most, employers find this situation untenable. The frustrations of outside hiring are reinforced by the growing sense in the research and practitioner communities that competencies inside the organization are the key to success. Relying on outside hiring seems to fly in the face of the imperative that organizations should be engaged in knowledge management practices that capture and organize what they know about their operations to improve performance. At the same time, no employers are offering to return to the days of lifetime employment and forgo restructuring and layoffs. And as long as some competitors continue to rely on poaching outside talent, the ability of any individual employer to develop and retain talent is hampered.

A New Way to Think About Talent Management

We need a new way of thinking about the challenge of talent management. The first step is to be clear about the goal. Talent management is not an end in itself. It is not about developing employees or creating succession plans. Nor is it about achieving specific benchmarks such as limiting turnover to 5 percent, having the most educated workforce, or gaining any other tactical outcome. Rather, the goal of talent management is the more general and important task of helping the organization achieve its overall objectives. In the business world, that objective is to make money. And making money requires that you understand the costs as well as the benefits associated with your talent management choices.

Helping the organization achieve its goals begins with recognizing that the most important problem faced by virtually all employers is the need to respond quickly to changes in competitive environments. Employers now change strategies, structures, and operations quickly and repeatedly in response to customer demands, competitor innovations, regulatory changes, and other outside factors. The developments driving these responses are difficult to predict, and mistakes in responding—waiting too long to change or planning for circumstances that fail to pan out—are costly.

In this context, the fundamental problem for organizations is to manage *risk*, which we can think of as the costs associated with events that are uncertain or at least difficult to predict.[6] Business risk, driven especially by uncertainty about business demands, translates directly into risk for talent management. The greatest risks in talent management are, first, the costs of a mismatch in employees and skills (not enough to meet business demands or too much, leading to layoffs) and, second, the costs of losing your talent development investments through the failure to retain employees. These risks stand in the way of the ability of your organization to meet its goals.

The new way of thinking about talent management is neither the bureaucratic models of planning from the 1950s nor the free agency model of the 1980s and 1990s, both of which were rooted in unique and transient circumstances. This new approach represents a balancing of interests—between internal development and outside hiring, between the interests of employees and those of the organization. Fundamental to this new model is acknowledging the uncertainty that appears to be a permanent part of the business world and being able to respond and adapt to it. That acknowledgment means that you cannot rely on the assumption that drove the old models of workforce planning and talent management—the assumption that you can forecast away the uncertainty and plan years or decades into the future.

Fortunately, you do not have to invent a set of new practices for responding to uncertainty and risk. Many of the challenges in contemporary talent management are analogous to problems already analyzed in the field of operations research. For example, the issues in managing an internal talent pipeline—the ways employees advance through development jobs and experiences—are remarkably similar to those involved in moving products through a supply chain. In both cases, the significant challenges are to reduce bottlenecks that block advancement, to speed processing time, and to improve forecasts of need and thereby avoid mismatches. Other techniques from economics allow you to better manage the return on your investments in development, especially in an environment where employees have a market for their skills and your key concern becomes retention.

One of the great conundrums in business is that even though executives acknowledge the importance of employees in theory—"people are our most important asset, and we really mean that"—in practice they often disparage, or at least ignore, the management of people. It has been difficult for them to see how most human resource practices relate to the issues on which they focus: the business strategy challenges that define the direction of organizations and the ways they compete. Traditionally, internal talent development practices have been so long-term in their orientation that they are disconnected from the immediacy of contemporary business strategy decisions; the outside hiring model is reactive (after problems occur), becoming an execution issue that often disappoints not only because of its costs but also because it lags the need for talent.

This new way of thinking about talent management connects it directly to business decisions. In virtually every organization, people are the biggest component of costs and the source of the most important competencies, so it is crucial to adopt approaches to manage the risks associated with talent issues in helping your organization manage overall business risk. The ability to get the right people with the right skills into the right jobs in a cost-effective way makes it possible for an organization to adjust and respond in the strategy arena.

This approach to talent is strategic in the two most important uses of that term in business: it involves choices or strategies about managing human capital that must be made based on each organization's needs, and those choices also relate directly to business strategy. If done correctly, talent management feeds into the process of strategy formation by outlining the possibilities for those who are making business decisions.

The Current State of Talent Management

A recent survey reported that roughly two-thirds of U.S. employers do no planning for their talent needs.[7] For such organizations, every new need for talent presents a serious disruption. Every employee who quits represents a calamity, and every new demand for skills represents a crisis. A company that does no planning—does not manage its talent—basically waits for a need to develop or current employees to leave and then hunts for a solution.

A good illustration of the consequences of not managing talent is the apparent panic under way in many parts of the business community at the idea that the baby boom generation will begin to retire soon and its skills, knowledge, and competencies will be lost. Surely nothing was more predictable than the fact that a generation of individuals is growing older and will eventually stop working. Employees had been retiring from companies for generations without causing as much as a ripple in corporate planning. The reason for the panic now is that many organizations have just begun to realize that they have no arrangements for replacing these retiring workers, because outside hiring does not work for company-specific and legacy skills of the kind many of these older workers possess.

The only good news is that most employers are essentially facing the talent management challenge with a clean slate: they have little idea how to address the challenge. Unfortunately, the advice they are getting is to return to the practices of the 1950s. Foremost among these practices are long-term succession plans, which attempt to identify which individuals will move into what jobs, mapping out careers years into the future.

That approach is a mistake. The practices of the 1950s, including detailed talent pipelines and succession plans, no longer work because the business environment to which they were tailored no longer exists. The older models were based on the assumption that one could plan the future of an organization years or even decades in advance with reasonable certainty. Its human capital requirements could then be predicted with some certainty. A second crucial assumption was that a company's internal pipelines of talent, through which individuals advanced in roles and responsibilities, did not leak and that the supply of talent being developed would be available when it was needed. The title of William H. Whyte's classic book *The Organization Man* reflected the historically distinctive relationship between these candidates and their employers. They were tied to the organization over a lifetime in a way previously associated only with military or religious service.

Developing talent internally was an imperative in this earlier period because there was no alternative. Competitors used the same internal development approach, rewarding success with promotions and pay increases. Even if another employer wanted to hire talent from the outside, only those candidates who were failing to advance in their current organizations were interested in changing employers. This was a classic adverse selection problem, as they had to start in other companies at a much lower level. Because the failure to develop talent meant not having the players needed to run the organization, the costs of internal development were largely irrelevant, although internal accounting systems were so poor that it would have been difficult to assess the true costs of arrangements as complicated as developing employees in any case. Development practices, such as rotational job assignments, were so deeply embedded in the operating models of business that their costs were rarely questioned.

The current environment for talent management is fundamentally different because the two basic assumptions that underpinned the Organization Man model no longer hold. First, product markets are no longer predictable. The rise of deregulation of product markets in the late 1970s, increases in foreign competition in the 1980s, and changes in consumer tastes mean that it is now much more difficult to predict what will sell or, in the not-for-profit world, what constituents will demand. Customer demands change much more rapidly as new products from a larger group of competitors come onstream more quickly. The idea that a company can predict accurately what it will be making ten years from now—something that was common in industries as diverse as telecommunications, transportation, consumer goods, and financial services until the 1970s—has disappeared. The demand for talent follows directly from business and operating demands. So as business forecasts and plans have shrunk from ten years to five years to, in most cases, one year, the ability to predict the talent those plans demand also must be scaled back. Years-long programs for developing talent create a false sense of accuracy and no longer make sense.[8]

Second, the supply of internal talent is no longer easily predictable. The period of managerial layoffs beginning in the early 1980s made jobs insecure from the employee's perspective, but from an individual employer's perspective, the internal supply of talent was still reasonably predictable until labor markets tightened in the 1990s. Then more companies began outside hiring, and one employer's outside candidate became another's retention challenge. Talent pipelines hemorrhaged as employees embraced the overtures of executive search firms and other employers. It became difficult to predict what percentage of candidates who began a development program would remain when it ended. A company that has a 10 percent turnover rate among its managerial ranks—not an unusual level—will lose half the candidates in its management pipeline within five years. Does it still make sense to call that arrangement a pipeline, or is it better thought of as a sieve? Some number of employees will make it through to the end, but it is not clear exactly how many will drop out and when they will do so.

As if these two complications were not enough, another important change has occurred: pressure exists to show that there is a financial return associated with every set of practices. Internal accounting systems have gotten better at estimating costs, and the arrangements associated with earlier models of talent management, such as maintaining jobs for developmental purposes, proved to be costly following the reengineering trend. There is no trick to developing talent if you don't care how much money it costs. Because outside hiring provides an alternative to internal development, the latter must demonstrate its value just as does every other practice and form of investment.

At this point, if you're a thoughtful executive you throw up your hands: developing employees is too expensive and uncertain, and outside hiring has also become expensive and cannot meet unique organizational needs. What can you do? That is why you need to approach the problem in a different way.

As noted earlier, talent management should be about helping a business make money, finding the most cost-effective ways of meeting the organization's needs for talent. And the big challenge is uncertainty. The type of talent management that makes sense in this economic context does not pretend that it can eliminate uncertainty through better forecasting and planning. Talent forecasting cannot be any more accurate than the business forecasts on which it is based, and the latter are not very accurate. Because every plan involves commitments and commitments come with costs, long-term plans end up being expensive because they are often wrong. Rather than pretend to eliminate uncertainty, the better approach is to find ways to manage it.

A New Framework for Talent Management

I spent several years reading the best-practice literature in talent management and found I was learning nothing about how to solve this fundamental question of how to match the supply and demand for talent. What I got instead were largely discussions about developing individual leaders along with a rehash of talent practices from the Organization Man period. The insights I found came instead from a seemingly unrelated area: the field of operations research and supply chain management. These fields have made great strides in recent years in understanding how to solve problems that look very much like those facing talent management.

Those with economics training naturally think of supply-and-demand problems as something that markets solve, but the task of matching supply to anticipated demand exists first inside organizations. Few businesses simply produce as much as they can and then leave it to the market to sort out the price. Rather, they try to anticipate how much of which product or service they should produce at a given price to meet the estimated demand from customers. The talent management challenge is very similar. It involves the same steps: forecasting product demand is the equivalent of forecasting talent needs, estimating the cheapest and fastest ways to make products is the equivalent of developing talent, deciding which aspects of that process to outsource is the equivalent of outside hiring, and ensuring timely delivery relates to planning for succession events.

Of course, there are important differences between production models and talent management. The most important stems from the fact that people are not products, and, unlike products, they can walk away, taking your investments in them as they go. That difference complicates talent management by adding considerable risk to the option of internal development.

Virtually everything has changed about business since the 1950s, but it was not until about 2005 that it was possible to see employers experimenting with approaches to talent management that were different from those used in the 1950s. Few of those experiments and innovations were taking place at the older academy companies. Perhaps not surprisingly, it was newer companies, and often those outside the United States, that innovated, because they had no stake in the older practices.

Their innovations, along with the lessons on managing risk from supply chain management, led me to formulate four key principles for managing talent in the contemporary environment, where uncertainty is the major challenge. The first two principles address business risk and related challenges concerning the demand for talent; the second two address human capital risk and challenges associated with developing an internal supply of talent.

Principle 1: Make and Buy to Manage Demand-Side Risk

Risk has two aspects: the uncertainty of a given outcome occurring, and the costs of that outcome. It may be possible to reduce somewhat the uncertainty associated with business outcomes through better forecasting, but it is easier to make progress in managing risk by first understanding the costs of various outcomes.

For example, it is hard to forecast with accuracy how many units of some product will be needed, but it is relatively easy to know the costs of not having enough product and services to meet demand (losing opportunities as a result) versus the costs of exceeding demand (producing inventory). Cost effectiveness demands that we choose the amount to supply

that minimizes *both* costs. In other words, it is not enough to simply estimate the demand. You need to know what the costs will be when you are
wrong, as you inevitably will be in an uncertain world.

Talent management has the equivalent challenge, although it has rarely
been recognized as such. In the Organization Man period, the big worry
was falling short on internal talent because there was no other way to get
it. If a company did not produce enough skilled project managers, for example, it had to push inexperienced people into those roles or give up on
the projects and business those managers would have overseen. If the process produced an excess of talent, on the other hand, it was relatively easy
to bank it by creating a deep bench of capable candidates ready to step in
when needed. The candidates stayed put and waited for their opportunity
because they had nowhere else to go. Employers could predict business
demand reasonably far out and so were able to develop talent years in advance. They chose the level of talent to produce in order to ensure that
there would be no shortfall, because that was what produced the greatest
costs. Forecasts weren't perfect, though, so the only way to be sure that
there would be no shortfall of talent was to overshoot the estimates of demand. And why not? The cost of having excess talent was small. From the
employees' point of view, sitting on the bench wasn't much of a negative
because they were all but assured an opportunity for advancement at
some time in the future. And there was nowhere else to go.

The situation now is different. Producing too much talent has a greater
cost because candidates do not like sitting on the bench waiting for opportunities. Evidence presented in chapter 4 suggests that frustration with
advancement opportunities is among the most important factors pushing
individuals to leave for jobs elsewhere. Competitors can offer candidates
the chance to use their skills in more attractive positions, and the candidates accept those offers, taking with them all the investments in their
development. Before, it was possible to downplay those costs, but sophisticated approaches to cost accounting now make clear how substantial
they are. Overshooting therefore has big costs.

Producing too little talent, on the other hand, is less of a concern than
in the past because it is almost always possible to hire on the outside to
make up any shortfall in talent. Although the cost of outside hires typically is greater than the cost of candidates developed internally, that dif-

ference pales in comparison with the cost of losing a developed candidate to a competitor. Minimizing mismatch costs leads to a very different calculation now than it did a generation ago. The calculations may differ across organizations based on the nature of the jobs and the work being performed, but in most contexts, the costs of overshooting talent are now much greater than the costs of undershooting the demand forecast. Your goal therefore should be to structure internal development of talent so that it reduces the risk of producing an inventory of talent. Again, because forecasts are not perfect and the true demand for talent will surely vary from the estimate, the only way to be sure that the supply of talent does not overshoot actual demand may be to deliberately *undershoot* the best estimates of talent demand and make up any gap with outside hiring.

You now have an answer for the problem that the older internal development models no longer work and that outside hiring has hit its limits. Neither strategy alone is likely to work, but the choice is not "make versus buy." It is "make *and* buy." The modern approach to talent demand, therefore, involves striking a balance between internal development and outside hiring in a manner that minimizes the risk (and associated costs) of being wrong. Deciding how to strike that balance is a choice, a strategy judgment, that differs across organizations and operations depending on internal capabilities as well as the relative costs of overshooting versus undershooting talent needs. But the framework for thinking about how to do it is clear, and the techniques for determining the appropriate mix of internal development and outside hiring are straightforward.

Principle 2: Reduce the Uncertainty in Talent Demand

The second principle suggests ways to reduce the uncertainty associated with predicting the demand for talent. The problem is simply that the phenomena we would like to predict are more complex than contemporary forecasting techniques can handle: markets contain more competitors that innovate faster, businesses react to their competitors' strategies more quickly, and the options for doing business (outsourcing, joint ventures, acquisitions, etc.) are greater. All these developments make it much more difficult for organizations to predict where they will be in the future and what their needs for talent will be.

Traditional succession planning offers an important example of a talent management practice in which the drawbacks of having imperfect plans can be worse than having no plan at all. The idea of succession planning is to take the general talent management charge—matching supply to anticipated demand—down to the individual level. Succession plans try to forecast which individual will move into what ultimate role, typically many years in advance and across several job moves. The problem with these plans is that the organization chart is restructured with each change in strategy, reorganization, or change in top leadership. And many candidates in developmental pipelines leave to take positions elsewhere as others are hired into the organization. As a result, trying to predict who should fill which roles many years in advance is no better than tossing a coin.

But isn't a less-than-perfect, long-term plan based on imperfect forecasts still better than no plan at all? It may make the participants feel better, but no, a plan based on an inaccurate forecast can be worse than no plan at all. The reason is that every plan involves costs, not only the costs of developing the plan itself but also its commitments. Those commitments constrain your ability to respond when mismatches occur.

A good illustration of the costs of inaccurate plans comes from a common experience with succession plans: an important vacancy occurs, and the leadership looks at the candidate identified by the succession plan. But they decide to search on the outside market because they believe that the current needs of the organization and the job are now different.

Such outcomes are worse in several ways than having no plan. First, the candidates identified in the succession plans feel that they have been promised these positions and typically see a deep injustice if they don't get them. Second, to the extent that you have made investments in developing candidates, those investments are essentially wasted if the anticipated match does not take place. Third, the time and energy that go into this planning process restrict your ability to respond in other ways. Most companies must update their succession plans every year to keep up with the fact that jobs change and individuals leave. As a practical matter, how useful is a plan if it must be changed every year? What problem is it solving?

A better approach is not to assume that you can forecast and plan around the uncertainty in demand. Instead, it is better to take that uncertainty as given and find ways to adapt to it. One way is to use the principle of portfolios. In finance, the problem with holding only one asset is that its value can fluctuate a great deal, and your wealth varies a lot as a result. The way to protect against that uncertainty is to hold several stocks in the same portfolio in the hope that when some are down, others will be up, and the volatility in your overall wealth will be reduced.

To apply this to talent management, consider the situation in many large—and especially decentralized—organizations in which each division is held accountable for its own profit and loss and maintains its own development programs. Let's say that one of these development programs is trying to prepare managers to meet expected demand in that division in the next five years. The odds on any individual division doing this accurately are very poor for the reasons described earlier. The predictable result is that each division's program is likely to miss its target.

To the extent that the divisions truly are separate and face different business demands, the odds are high that they will miss their targets in different ways. Business and talent needs may be greater than anticipated in some divisions, less than anticipated in others. In practice this means that some divisions will end up with a surplus of talent and others will have a shortfall. If instead of operating these development programs separately, the organization had consolidated them into a single program, the unanticipated demand in one part of the company and an unanticipated shortfall in demand in another would cancel out, just as a stock portfolio reduces the uncertainty of holding individual stocks. Given this, as well as the duplication of tasks and infrastructure required in decentralized programs, it is a mystery why large organizations continue to operate decentralized development programs.

The notion of talent pools relies on a similar idea. With talent pools, you avoid developing employees to fit narrow, specialized jobs. Instead, you develop a group of employees with broad and general competencies that should fit into a range of jobs. Once the candidates are developed, you can allocate them to the actual vacancies, as opposed to your best guess as to where you think they will be years in advance. The fit between candidate and specific job may be less than perfect. But you can provide some just-in-time training and coaching to help close the gap.

A different approach to reducing uncertainty is to adjust the talent management process to rely on shorter forecasts. The longer a forecast, the worse it is; shorter forecasts always beat longer ones. Programs that can be restructured to rely on updated forecasts—for example, by breaking a long program into discrete parts, each with its own forecasts—will do much better. A good illustration comes from the functionally based internal development programs that some companies still offer. These programs often have common elements, such as learning general managerial or interpersonal skills. With a set of three-year functional programs, for example, you can break them into a first set, which teaches the common set of skills, and a second set, which teaches the function-specific skills. After employees complete the first set, you can reforecast the demand for candidates for each functional area and allocate the candidates across the final, function-specific aspect of the program. Instead of being a three-year forecast, the new forecast needs to go out only half as far because the new functional programs are only half as long. And as a result they are likely to be much more accurate.

The final two principles address the risks associated with the supply side of talent management.

Principle 3: Earn a Return on Investments in Developing Employees

A mix of internal development and external hires can help you manage the uncertainty of talent demand, but the problem remains how to develop employees in an environment where retention and other challenges make recouping investments in development a risky proposition.

One way to improve the payoff from development is to reduce the time spent in it, a practice that allows you to rely on shorter, more accurate forecasts and improve the odds that the investments will pay off. Lessons from supply chain management can help here as well. Consider the problem of bringing a new class of candidates into an organization. For those employers who hire people directly out of college, the entire pool of candidates comes in at once, typically in June. Let's assume that they go through an orientation program, take some classroom-based training, and then move into developmental roles. If the new cohort has one hundred candidates, then the organization must find one hundred developmental roles all at once, sometimes a challenge for an organization that is under pressure to, say, cut costs and restructure.

An alternative embraces the fact that many college graduates don't want to go directly to work from graduation. It is not difficult to split the new cohort, taking half in June and the other half in September. Instead of one hundred developmental assignments, now the program needs to find fifty in June and rotate the new hires through them in three months. The June cohort steps out of those roles at the end of the summer when the September cohort steps into them. Then rather than having to find one hundred permanent assignments in September for the June cohort, the organization needs to find only fifty, and so on. The more important advantage is that hiring forecasts can be shorter and more accurate. This eases the match with the first developmental assignment and then with every set of assignments along the progression of that cohort—for example, from test engineer, to engineer, to senior engineer, to lead engineer—throughout its career at that company.

Another way to address the financial return on development is to get employees to share the costs. Employees are now the main beneficiaries of investments in their development because of their ability to cash in on the open market with employers that do not have to worry about recouping the investments. It therefore seems reasonable and necessary to ask employees to help share the costs. In the United States, legislation prevents hourly workers from having to contribute to the costs of training that is required for their current job. There are, however, no restrictions even for hourly workers on their sharing the costs of developmental experiences that help prepare them for future roles.

The simplest way that individuals contribute to the costs of their own development is by taking on learning projects voluntarily, perhaps in addition to their normal work. Assuming that the candidates are more or less contributing their usual amount to their regular jobs and their pay hasn't increased, they are essentially doing these development projects for free. Several companies now offer promising employees the opportunity to volunteer for projects done with their leadership team, sometimes restricting them to projects outside their current functional area to broaden their experience. The employees get access to company leaders, a broadening experience, and good professional contacts, all of which will surely pay off later. But they pay for it. Similarly, tuition reimbursement programs in which employers pay college tuition and the employees attend classes on their own time offer another way to share the investment in development.

The most important approach to developing employees focuses more on the benefits than the cost side: to increase the value of employee contributions by speeding the process that gets them to jobs that add greater value to the organization. This approach requires that you spot talent and potential early and then give the employees opportunities to advance faster than they otherwise might. Identifying who is ready for more advanced work is the primary task for line managers, and that takes us to our final talent management task.

Principle 4: Balance Employee Interests by Using an Internal Market

The most important risk on the supply side of talent is that good employees will leave and take with them the investments you have made in their skills. Arguably the main reason that good employees leave is to take opportunities that are better than what they can find in their current organization.

Career decisions—making matches between individuals and jobs—used to be the most important task performed by the executives and managers in charge of talent management. *Chess masters*, as they were called, moved candidates around the equivalent of the chessboard of the organization chart. In the Organization Man period, the company decided which candidates were ready for which experience in order to meet its longer-term talent needs. Employees had little or no choice in the matter. If they refused to take the new position, their career advancement stopped.

Efforts to pursue this approach ran into trouble when labor markets tightened, especially for good candidates who could easily secure a job offer more to their liking. To improve retention, virtually all companies— 96 percent in a recent survey—have moved away from the chess master model to internal job boards that make it easier for employees to change jobs *within* the organization. If they want a new job, employers concluded, we should at least make it easier for them to find one within the organization.

Internal job boards, where employees bid on posted openings and through which virtually all internal job moves now take place, coincided with employers giving up on career planning. They effectively turned over the problem of managing one's career to employees. Employees, rather than the employer, now initiate job changes and drive career paths.

Although there are many benefits to this new approach, one drawback for employers is that they have much less control over their internal talent. Employees choose which jobs to accept and which paths to take based on their own interests and needs. Employees have relatively little information about how to make job and career choices, something that frustrates their planning, and their choices do not always align with the interests of their employer. For example, the supply of internal applicants for positions that offer the potential to develop experience and skills that are useful elsewhere—therefore improving the candidate's marketability— are plentiful. The supply is scarce for positions that are unique to the company, that develop legacy competencies where marketability is low. So the problem for employers is again a matter of managing risk: the risk that employees will not make career choices that meet the needs of the organization.

Programs that attempt to mitigate that risk by negotiating a balance between the employee's and the employer's interests in career advancement are one of the truly new developments in talent management. Some of these efforts involve simply providing information about career paths, descriptions of how individuals have advanced in the past. Others go much further, attempting to negotiate compromises between the preferences of the organization and those of the employee. It is fair to say, though, that most organizations have not yet thought through how to handle the challenge of managing a more open internal market for talent. Whether employers are willing to let it become a real market, where internal hiring managers are allowed to compete for internal talent by raising wages or making their jobs more attractive, is an open question.

Internal job boards provide a solution to at least one talent problem employers face, and that is to identify promising candidates for developmental jobs and experiences. The traditional approach was to ask supervisors to identify them. But with organizations operating as decentralized units with their own financial accountability, asking a local manager to identify top talent for development means asking the manager to give up an asset that is important to his or her unit's business success. Lots of anecdotal information suggests that local managers often hide their talented candidates or, worse, off-load those who are actually less promising. Internal job boards get around this problem by allowing individuals to nominate themselves for development opportunities. Local managers do not have the opportunity to hide talent, because the process no longer requires them to identify talent. Indeed, more than half of U.S. companies allow employees to bid and accept other positions in the company without the approval—or even the knowledge—of their immediate supervisors.

The self-nomination model also avoids the difficult problem of identifying who should get scarce developmental experiences. Most companies and organizations rely on efforts to predict the potential of candidates for success in future jobs. Doing so is fraught with peril, however, in large part because most assessments are not very accurate, and many rely on attributes that are not within the control of the individual. Telling people that they are not high-potential employees can be highly demotivating; telling them that the reason is their IQ, their personality, or something else they cannot change is basically telling them they might as well leave now.

Performance is certainly a more objective criterion for inclusion in high-potential programs. It is a much better motivator and causes fewer concerns about fairness. Self-nomination approaches can add another important feature to the selection process if you give only the most motivated employees an incentive to nominate themselves for development. The idea here is to tap in to knowledge that the candidates have about their own interests and abilities that they might otherwise not have an incentive to reveal.

If you think back to college, for example, students who wanted to impress teachers with their real interest and enthusiasm for a subject (and get good references in the process) signed up for the harder, more advanced courses. There was a cost to doing so—more work, or at least harder work—so students who were not really interested in the tasks were unlikely to take those courses. At the workplace, an example is the project-based development work described earlier. Employees who want broader experience and also want the desirable outcome of getting to know the leadership are willing to do extra work. Only those who are truly motivated are likely to sign on.

The best and most accurate screening devices, however, are simply to give people opportunities to try something and then see how they do. If you want to see who can lead a team, there is nothing better than giving various people the chance to try it. This process is objective, fair, and more accurate than anything else. The obvious downside is the cost of making mistakes: giving people the chance to fly the space shuttle to see whether they will be good at it is a dangerous and expensive test. So the key is to find those opportunities that are not costly but that approximate the experience of the more advanced job. Piloting a simulator is a great proxy for flying the space shuttle, but developing the simulator is very expensive. Leading a small team in charge of office space, on the other hand, may be a reasonable proxy for running a team for a client engagement. It costs next to nothing to set up, and it has little downside risk. Finding opportunities like these, in which candidates can fail quickly and cheaply, is a key element of developing talent and an important task for line managers in the talent management process.

How to Manage Talent on Demand

Organizations are ready for a paradigm shift in managing talent. The old planning models no longer work, and the drawbacks of outside hiring show that it alone cannot be the alternative. Most employers appear to be sitting on the fence, worrying about talent issues but so far responding to them only in an ad hoc way.

The problems of talent management are causing immediate pain to employers, although few internal accounting systems are sophisticated enough to calculate that pain with precision. The cost of having a good employee quit, for example, and against whose budget that cost should be allocated, are not questions that can be answered in most organizations. This inability reduces the incentives to improve talent management.

Even without hard numbers, though, you can see from the arguments outlined here why it makes sense to redesign your approach to talent management. New models that identify costs in other aspects of business have led to revolutions in those areas. For example, the costs of excess inventory were always there, but no one paid much attention to them until models of supply chain management made them easier to see; physical assets like real estate were always costly, but it took the accounting concept of economic value added to change how managers thought about and used those assets. There is every reason to believe that a similar paradigm shift will happen in the management of talent when we understand the costs of making mistakes.

Employees also have interests in a new paradigm because the current approaches do not provide reliable direction or even information that can help them manage their careers. More generally, U.S. society as a whole has an interest in better talent management, especially arrangements that can allow employers to invest in training and developing their own employees. The economy benefits from having highly skilled individuals, and there are many competencies, especially managerial skills, that can be learned only in the context of doing real work in real organizations.

The new way of managing talent described here is fundamentally different from what has come before it, first because it takes as its starting point organizational goals and not human resource targets. Its purpose is to help the organization perform, and it does that by managing the talent risks that are generated by uncertainty in business demand and the new, more open labor markets.

The new approach to talent management may help to resuscitate the development of managerial talent, something that risks being choked off because employers cannot envision how to make it work in the current environment. The lack of internal development of talent has increased the demand for outside hiring, which in turn causes retention problems elsewhere, undercuts the ability to develop talent internally, and creates a vicious circle that erodes managerial talent. The only way forward is to recognize these problems and adapt to the uncertainty that drives them.

There are many other important tasks that fit within this general framework for managing talent that are not addressed here. Among the important ones are the job of recruiting talent, which includes defining job requirements and finding appropriate candidates, a task that now requires managing networks of personal relationships, electronic sources, and other novel arrangements; determining the competencies that are important to develop internally and then the best approaches through which they can be learned; understanding and addressing what may be new interests and concerns among current and potential employees, especially work–life issues and how to balance them.[9]

Other issues include the array of new options, such as outsourcing and using contract or temporary workers, that make it possible to get work done without using employees; and of course the more glamorous task of picking which individuals should advance to what positions. Executing these tasks well matters a great deal, and much has been written about how to do so. But these tasks follow only after you have a general framework for thinking about talent, about how much talent to develop internally, and about how to manage the economic requirements of doing so. That is the purpose of *Talent on Demand*.

The arguments in the book begin in chapter 2 with an account of the history of talent management in the managerial and executive ranks. One of the lessons from this account is that the contemporary context may have more in common with the period before WWI, when outside hiring and informal networks were the norm, than the "traditional" practices that were dominant through the early 1980s. It is also instructive, and surprising to many, to see how many ostensibly innovative contemporary practices were created in the late 1940s. The main lesson, though, is that talent management practices have changed a great deal over time in response to business needs.

Chapter 3 describes how changes in the economy and in business practices undermined the logic behind the traditional, Organization Man model. Chapter 4 begins outlining the new principles for guiding talent management, especially the need to understand the costs of inevitable mistakes in forecasting demand. Chapter 5 then examines practices that can help minimize the uncertainty in predicting talent needs.

Considering the risks on the supply side begins in chapter 6 with a discussion of the financial problems employers face in developing talent and procedures that will help them recoup investments in employees. Chapter 7 considers innovations that are now well under way that change the way matches are made between employees and new jobs, reducing the risk of turnover but raising new challenges associated with long-term talent development. Finally, chapter 8 moves from the employer's perspective to consider the interests that employees and the broader society have in the talent management strategies that employers pursue. These interests clearly demand more attention than they are given here, but we must start somewhere.

PART ONE

Why Traditional Talent Management No Longer Works

2

The Rise of Talent Management

To get a clear sense of contemporary talent management challenges and ways to handle them, it helps to take a long-term view. How did companies provide the managerial and executive talent to meet the demands of the business in earlier periods, and why did those approaches change over time?

One surprising insight is that most current practices—forced ranking systems, 360 degree feedback, assessment centers, and so on—were well established by the 1950s. These practices were a response to the unique circumstances following World War II, circumstances that made long-term planning for talent and internal development possible as well as necessary. Although these practices continue to be advocated, even reinvented, the current business environment bears little resemblance to the post-WWII period, and that explains why the planning-based approach no longer makes sense. In many ways, the current situation bears more resemblance to the period before World War I than it does to the more recent past.

The Earliest Days of Talent Management

As business historian Alfred Chandler describes it, until the mid-1880s, the typical firm was simple—a single-unit operation that performed only one function, such as selling insurance or making soap.[1] These firms were masters at paring themselves down to what we would call in the 1990s their "core competencies"—those few tasks that they truly performed well—and either outsourcing or getting rid of everything else. The leaders of companies were their owners.[2]

Henry Ford was perhaps the archetype of the owner-manager who ran everything personally, even resisting management systems like accounting: "Put all the money we take in a big barrel, and when a shipment of material comes in, reach into the barrel and take out enough money to pay for it." Irritated about an accounting issue, Ford once went into the head office during lunch hour and threw all the accounting books into the street.[3]

It was possible to run these companies without professional executives or managers because many of the tasks that we think of as being central to a company's operations were outsourced. Such activities went well beyond acquiring parts and supplies. For example, at the turn of the twentieth century, companies like DuPont did none of their own sales or distribution. DuPont had 215 independent agents who managed relationships with merchants across the country. These agents were paid on commission and in many cases represented more than one company.[4] Some agents, such as those working for the McCormick agricultural implement company, were essentially franchisees and had enough business that they hired their own sales staff to work for them.[5] (The current practice of having auto dealerships operate independently from the companies they represent stems from this period.) Even production tasks were outsourced to contractors who hired their own workers, paid them piece rates, and managed them as they saw fit.[6] Some estimates suggest that as many as half of U.S. manufacturing employees in the early 1900s were employed contractors who typically operated inside their client's buildings.[7]

Because these companies had little hierarchy and because the founders typically ran everything until they got too old to be effective (and often past that age), the best career advancement opportunity for ambitious executives who were not family members was to leave the company where they worked and start their own business. Walter Chrysler and Charles Nash, for example, left their jobs at General Motors to start their own car companies; Henry Hyde left Security Mutual of New York to found Equitable. Several of the du Ponts left the original powder company to form their own companies; Lammot founded the Repauno Chemical Company, and Pierre left to form a railway company in Dallas before rejoining the family firm. Similar patterns can be seen today, especially in the high-tech industry, where executives often leave their firms to found similar, competing companies.

The Demand for Managers

Talent management did not become a serious concern until companies grew complicated enough to have real management jobs to fill. Most observers saw that happening first with the railroad industry, in large part because the early railroads were the largest and most complicated operations that had yet existed. Someone needed to have the discretion to implement decisions at the local level. These managers, called superintendents, were given responsibility for geographic sections of the railroad. They functioned much like the heads of operating divisions in later models of manufacturing, making a wider range of operating decisions than any executives other than owners. In some cases, superintendents were held to be legally and individually responsible for their decisions and were required to post bonds as protection against bad decisions.

In 1880 the Chicago, Burlington, and Quincy Railroad, a medium-sized railroad, had 191 executives divided across geographic and functional titles.[8] In contrast, a typical manufacturing company in this period with the same revenue might have two or three executive jobs. One of the developments that came with this expansion of executive positions in railroads was the creation of modern administrative titles and, with them, corporate hierarchies. Important jobs at railroad headquarters were given the title of vice president, a practice that spread in later decades to other industries.[9]

For an expanding railroad that needed a superintendent to handle a new region, an easy choice was to hire someone from the Pennsylvania Railroad, the largest and most sophisticated such operation in the world, just as contemporary employers poach talent from leading companies like Procter & Gamble. The poacher not only got an experienced leader but also learned and adopted some of the Pennsylvania practices. By the 1890s, job-hopping across railroad companies had become common.[10] The notion of a professional manager who could make a career by moving across companies was born.

When companies moved away from outsourcing and internalized their operations, they created a host of new managerial roles to oversee and coordinate those operations. With these new positions came talent management problems. The first question was what kind of employment relationship the company should have with these new managers. Perhaps because early white-collar employees tended to be family members and friends of the founders, it was a family-like arrangement. As historian Sandy Jacoby observes, "The employer had a gentlemen's agreement with his top salaried employees that they would not be dismissed except for disloyalty or (under extraordinary circumstances) poor performance."[11] That agreement expanded to cover these new managers as well.

Corporate Growth and the Need for Executives

These developments created more middle-management jobs, but for the most part, even large corporations like Ford Motor Company continued to operate with very few executives—typically the founder and a small team of two or three. That changed as companies grew large enough to have specialized functions. They needed people to head those functions at headquarters, and the jobs that resulted had enough authority and discretion to qualify as executive jobs. When the American Tobacco Company established an auditing function, for example, it also created an executive position to run that function. To run it, the company hired an auditor from the Pullman Palace Car Company. When the company created a leaf department to manage the buying of tobacco, it brought in someone who had been an independent tobacco buyer to head that function. Despite these new executive positions, the strategic decisions of the company continued to be made by only three men.[12]

The Standard Oil Trust, arguably the most important business enterprise of its day, generated a cadre of new executives in a different way. Because the organization was a collection of separate oil companies, its central tasks were run by the trustees of the companies through a series of committees. Each committee had a permanent staff of workers to support and execute the committee's work, and these staff members became middle management, handling the important tasks of coordination between the various committees. As the trust grew in size and complexity, the top trustees themselves eventually became full-time employees and executives in the company. The committee system remained, as did the staff jobs and their tasks of coordinating decisions.[13]

Much of the credit for the modern executive career in corporations, however, goes to Andrew Carnegie, who transformed the modern corporation by adapting many of the operating procedures of railroads to the manufacturing context.[14] Carnegie worked his way up from telegraph operator at the Pennsylvania Railroad and eventually became superintendent of its western division, the most important division in that railroad. He absorbed many of the railroad's elaborate operating principles, especially the notion that standards of performance could be created for every job and that every individual should be held accountable for his job performance. From the job of superintendent came the idea of an operating, or line, executive who had complete authority and responsibility for local operations. It was not a coincidence that the top job at a Carnegie steel mill and later at all steel plants would have the railroad title of superintendent.

Carnegie entered the iron and steel business as an investor, more accurately a speculator, but he soon began introducing operating principles from the Pennsylvania Railroad. Arguably his most famous executive, Charles Schwab, who would later head Bethlehem Steel, recalled that Carnegie had only one absolute rule: "Every man must have full responsibility for the complete performance of the work."[15] Because Carnegie eliminated overlapping responsibilities, it was clear who got the credit— or the blame—for performance.[16] The superintendents of Carnegie mills operated them almost as if they were their own.

Carnegie also believed in sorting talent based on performance. As Schwab observed, internal promotion was the norm: "There was no question of any man being brought in from the outside, and all the workers knew this."[17] The competition for advancement was internal, and this meritocracy meant that someone might overtake you from behind, much like the competitive environment in contemporary firms like GE. Almost without exception, Carnegie partners began as working men in the company. Comparing his management practices to those of his great financial rival J. P. Morgan, Carnegie noted, "Mr. Morgan buys his partners (outside hires), I raise my own."[18] Carnegie contributed to managerial careers by creating operating jobs with real responsibility and autonomy, but the innovation was to fill those positions from within based on job performance. It would be almost a generation before the rest of the corporate world caught on.

The next important step in the development of executive jobs was at DuPont, when Pierre du Pont took over the company and created the first multidivisional organizational structure; a separate operating division served each line of explosives, which was associated with a different market. The divisions operated with considerable autonomy, almost as separate companies, and each division needed a new executive at its head. DuPont acquired sixty companies between 1902 and 1907, and the leaders of the acquired firms, almost always their founders, became the executives in the new and larger merged operation. George B. Corless, Standard Oil's adviser on executive development, described that company's early approach to talent management as being similar: "Mr. Rockefeller Sr. recruited many of his executives by buying successful companies and then giving jobs to the former owners."[19]

This practice and the fluidity of these executive roles can be seen most dramatically at General Motors. The first president of GM was Charles Nash, who had come to GM from the Durant-Dort Carriage company. He left in 1916 to form a company of his own, Nash Motors (Rambler), backed by James Storrow, a Boston investment banker who had directed GM's finances. Among the other key GM executives were Charles Mott, who had founded his own axle and wheel company; Albert Champion, the founder of the sparkplug company; and Alfred P. Sloan, the founder of the Hyatt ball bearing company. All three had been acquired by Durant on behalf of GM. Henry Leland continued to build Cadillacs with considerable independence as head of that division within GM. Louis Chevrolet also came into the executive ranks of GM when his company was acquired. One of the few true inside executives in the company was Walter Chrysler, who was pulled up from one of the plants to become president of Buick. Like Nash, Chrysler would also leave to start his own car company.[20] The leaders of the Cadillac and Oakland (Pontiac) divisions were paid no salary, only a percentage of profits.[21]

The power of these executive roles expanded when DuPont's huge investments in GM eventually led to control over the company, and

Pierre stepped in as president in 1920. He set out to reorganize and modernize GM management based in part on the DuPont multidivisional model and on an organization plan put forward by Alfred Sloan that created larger central or staff functions. Sloan described the job description for these positions: "The responsibility attached to the chief executive of each operating division shall in no way be limited."[22] What was new about this model was that the staff operations, which included oversight of the divisions, became as important as the divisions. Who got these new and important executive positions? More outsiders: Donaldson Brown, DuPont's treasurer, headed the financial staff, and John Raskob, the former DuPont treasurer, handled outside finance; Norval Hawkins, hired away from Ford, headed sales and analysis; John Lee Pratt, head of DuPont's Development Division, took on the same function at GM.[23] And the operating committee of the corporation was du Pont, Sloan, Raskob, and Haskell, or, as Sloan described them, "four amateurs"—not only outside hires but also executives who had no prior experience in the car business.[24]

With few exceptions, such as the Carnegie Steel Works, it is difficult to see many examples where corporations reached into their own ranks and elevated people into these new executive positions. It is difficult to know why something did not occur, but we can speculate. Two explanations stand out. Most important is that the leap in requirements was huge between the middle-management jobs and the new executive jobs. There was no way to assess the capabilities of the managers and predict who could handle an executive role, a problem with a remarkably contemporary feel. Nor was there any way to develop managers who might have some but not all of the requirements for these executive jobs or to support them once they were thrust into those roles.

Business historian Thomas Cochran noted that even though many of the administrative problems of running large corporations had been solved by the time of WWI, one important issue remained unsolved: "how were men to be trained, selected, and inspired to undertake the task of coordinating and directing the enterprise as a whole."[25] Whether corporations could continue to grow and prosper with this ad hoc approach to talent management was unclear.

From Executive Jobs to Executive Careers

The notion that one could achieve a position of importance by working for a company, as opposed to starting one, was a new one in the early part of the twentieth century. To the extent that there was a true entry-level job that led to real possibilities for advancement, it was the office boy. These were essentially messengers and errand runners, and they were hired very young. An article describing practices for managing office boys in 1905 noted, "About 14 seems to be the best age" to hire them, complaining that older boys wanted more money. The businessmen interviewed noted that a big cause of unreliability among the office boys was that they would quit to go back to school.[26]

After WWI, companies began to establish entry-level positions in functional areas such as sales or engineering, hiring high school and college graduates and training them along the way. William H. Whyte describes his own experience as a new hire in the Vicks company's sales training program in the early 1920s.[27] New recruits were taken out in the field, given a short orientation, and expected to start selling Vicks products immediately. Thirty of the thirty-eight people in his cohort were dismissed soon after being hired. The young employees had first to prove themselves in a functional area before they might be given the opportunity for development and advancement elsewhere in the company.

A Different Direction

In 1926, Edward Plaut, president of Lehn and Fink Products, maker of Lysol and other cleaners, described an experiment that he began of hiring candidates with the intention of turning them into managers rather than functional specialists. The company looked for general leadership ability in college graduates as evidenced by their extracurricular activities, especially athletics. Once hired, the recruits were put to work in low-level jobs in various areas of the business, including manual labor, and were moved about every six months. In doing so, the company essentially discovered job rotation as a development device. The goal at the end of the training period was to have candidates who knew at least two functions well and who had demonstrated leadership qualities. So different was this arrangement that the company had to keep assuring the trainees that these assignments were only temporary and gave them pay increases with each rotation to get them to stay. In a telling phrase of things to come in U.S. industry, the president described the goal of the program: "We want organizational men first, specialists second."[28]

Augustus D. Curtis, president of Curtis Lighting in Chicago, took the notion of developing managers a step further. He noted that because his company was growing quickly, "we could not wait for the average young man who comes to us haphazardly to 'grow up with the business.'"[29] He created a training-based development program wherein new hires rotated through each of the company's ten departments and also received along the way a plan of one hundred lectures given by the department heads on aspects of their business. The goal, Curtis said, was for the trainees not only to learn about the functions of the company but also to see how the work of the departments fit together.

The Public Service Company of Northern Illinois, meanwhile, pioneered another innovation in management development in 1926: a high-potential program to identify employees who demonstrated the aptitude for senior management positions. Britton I. Budd, the company president, noted that in principle any employee—even manual workers—was eligible for the program. Good performance and evidence of leadership qualities were the criteria, and the program itself was designed to broaden the participants beyond their functional areas, in part by giving them exposure to the various departments. After completing the program, the participants went back to their old jobs and waited for management openings that would create the opportunity for them to advance.[30]

The General Electric Career Model and the Rise of the Organization Man

There were many such examples of development experiences in the mid-1920s, but most were small scale and ad hoc. A breakthrough in the modern executive career came at General Electric, where the scale of operations and the demand for talent were great enough to merit extensive investments in developing employees.

GE had been created by the merger of the Edison and Thomas-Houston companies in 1892. The first years of the new company saw a pattern of outside hires much like that practiced by the other corporations of the day. Its first president, Charles Coffin, a former shoe salesman and shoe manufacturer, had been hired into Thomas-Houston as its president when that company was created by merger. Its first research director, Willis Whitney, remained a faculty member at MIT while performing his tasks for GE; Charles Steinmetz, its most famous scientist and then head of research for decades, came to the company through the acquisition of the Eickemeyer Company, where he had been employed in a similar capacity. The individual companies within GE operated with considerable autonomy in this period, much like the car lines at General Motors.

Things began to change at GE when Gerard Swope became CEO in 1922. Having worked for Western Electric, Swope was also an outsider; he was hired after managing the sale of some Western Electric businesses to GE.[31] In what was a revolutionary approach to business organization, Swope liquidated some twenty independent companies that had operated under the GE umbrella and absorbed them into a new, common enterprise. To meet the demand for talent in the growing company, GE began to hire inexperienced workers directly from college not only for technical positions but also to fill management jobs. New arrangements were created to transform this raw talent into GE employees. In these new arrangements, we can see the roots of modern employee development practices throughout the corporate world.

The new hires were sent to GE facilities on a one-year program, either a business training track for the potential managers or a test engineering program for the technical jobs. (The term *test engineer* persists not only at GE but also across industry.) Both tracks had extensive classroom training and three-month rotational job assignments to expose the trainees to the important parts of the business. After the one-year assignment, the trainees essentially applied for jobs in functional areas of the business—marketing or accounting, say, for the business track, and electrical engineering or manufacturing for the engineering track. The evaluation of these employees was, in its day, a sophisticated process that was based on the assessments of three managers. Peer feedback in programs like these was an important part of the training and was used primarily to rub the rough edges off people who don't fit in.[32] Part of the evaluation was a secret rating of the employees' potential for higher managerial positions, a rating that the company used for promotion but was not revealed to the employees themselves. Promotions occurred almost always within the functional hierarchy and came relatively slowly. It was common to wait ten or more years.

GE also had some interesting informal arrangements for developing talent. The company had its own island on Lake Ontario, and in the summer its top executives as well as promising lower-level managers showed up for a week of camping that included socializing, indoctrination of new managers, and fun and games. These programs were seen as providing networking opportunities and, more generally, as a way to cross-fertilize thinking among the functional areas of the company.[33]

A Pause to Refresh Talent Management

The developments at GE and other companies were set back considerably by the Great Depression. The overall decline in business, which averaged about 25 percent, meant that companies had more than enough managers to meet their needs, and they had little inclination to invest in others. A few large corporations maintained some of the practices for developing managers, but the absence of candidates caused existing programs to wither, and the nascent practices never got beyond the experimental stage.

World War II ended the Depression and rekindled business demand and the demand for managers. There had been little management hiring and virtually no development programs for a decade, and as a result there was no new cohort of managers coming through the system. A study of companies that faced shortfalls of executive talent blamed the problem on the lack of development of managers in this period and, where there was development, on the practice of producing functional specialists rather than general managers.[34]

The demographic and experience imbalance caused by the lack of hiring from the Depression through the war continued to affect corporations long after the war ended. One consequence was that the ranks of senior executives initially grew older. George L. Bach, dean of the Graduate School of Industrial Engineering at Carnegie Institute of Technology, observed that although 56 percent of the top business leaders in the United States were more than fifty years of age in 1928, that proportion had risen to 64 percent by the mid-1950s.

A significant drawback of having an older executive cadre in the early 1950s was that the executives tended to die in office. One-third of managers age forty-five in this period were expected to die before age sixty-five, and separations due to death and disability accounted for as much turnover as did retirement.[35] Not only did companies lose a great deal of managerial talent, but also they lost it unpredictably. Without systems in place to identify successors and plan for succession, death and disability meant that companies faced continuous talent crises. Ben Moreell, chairman of Jones and Laughlin Steel Corporation, described how haphazard the succession process was: "When a great president retires, a vacuum is created. And into that vacuum is swept the nearest guy who has not had a coronary."[36]

A Serious Talent Shortage

The result of all this was noted by George Bach: "American Industry is grossly short of well trained executive personnel."[37] *BusinessWeek* observed that companies across the country were facing a "serious bottleneck" in the supply of top managers.[38] The shortfall had important implications for a range of business activities, many of which are familiar in the contemporary context. One observer noted, "A fairly high percentage of mergers are primarily due to the fact that the smaller companies, which are taken over by the larger companies, have never bothered to develop executive manpower to replace aging and ailing top management men."[39] And without a new generation of talent, they could not continue to operate independently.

The immediate response of employers, as in previous generations, was to try to raid competitors for talent. In the retail industry, one executive noted that "to go to another store for assistant buyers, buyers, and other executives" was the approach that had been "almost universally used" to fill vacancies.[40] An important consequence was the rise of the modern recruiting industry. A survey by the New York Association of Private Office Personnel Agencies—a group of staffing agencies that found candidates for employers—indicated that only 2 percent of employers used them in 1940; but by 1948, 28 percent of employers used them consistently, and 68 percent used them occasionally. These agencies maintained lists of people who were looking for jobs or looking to change jobs, but even these agencies typically were not good at helping employers find senior talent. Frank Zintl, head of the Executive Employment Service in Philadelphia, noted, "There is definitely a shortage of men in the $25,000 bracket," the equivalent now of the vice president level.[41]

The inability to find senior management and executive talent through staffing agencies led companies to turn to management consulting firms. These firms went a step further, searching for qualified individuals who were not looking to move but who might be persuaded to do so. The consulting firms charged daily fees of $50 to $300, a princely sum in those days. As an executive from Booz, Allen & Hamilton described it, "The man we are looking for is usually employed at present."[42] From this process, the executive search was born. The management consulting firms eventually spun off their talent search business: Korn/Ferry was created from Booz, Allen & Hamilton, and Heidrick and Struggles from McKinsey & Company, because of apparent conflicts of interest between their roles as advisers and as potential poachers of talent. (AT/Kerney was the exception, keeping its recruiting function until 2006.)

But the ability to hire talent away from competitors did not meet the demand for senior managers and executives. As *BusinessWeek* described the situation in 1949, "The normal result of a situation like this [the tight labor market], you'd think, would be a tremendous turnover rate among the second level of management, the rising men in their 40s and early 50s. They'd be leaving good jobs for better jobs, shifting from company to company, ending up in the places where they were needed most. Actually, it isn't working out that way. In manpower terms, the mobility of executive labor is very low."[43]

There were several reasons executives were not changing companies. First, pension plans locked people into place because they had onerous vesting requirements: benefits went up the longer one stayed with the company but were lost if one quit. Second, marginal income tax rates after WWII were as high as 90 percent, so executives at the top of the income distribution kept only 10 cents of every additional dollar they would earn from a new salary offer. Trying to use higher salaries to lure someone away was therefore difficult, because a huge increase in salary gave only a modest increase in purchasing power. Third, observers note that housing was in short supply right after the war, especially houses of the sort that mid- and higher-level executives and their families might want. Potential recruits often hesitated to change employers because of the difficulty of finding new housing. Finally, as the economy began to re-shape itself for peacetime, a great many executives saw opportunities for advancement in their own, growing companies. Was it worth the risks and costs of changing companies, and possibly locations, for the uncertain prospect of faster advancement?

So companies began to look in other directions for talent. A report on the shortage of executives in the early 1950s found that companies were hiring prodigiously from the military—retired generals, admirals, and other officers, including those that had already retired—to meet the need for executive talent.[44]

An even more popular and more important avenue was college campuses, especially attractive after the war when former GIs who already had some industry experience were completing their educations with the help of the GI Bill. As *Fortune* described the scene in 1948, "Corporate men who work the college circuit for likely executive material—'ivory hunting' in the trade jargon—complain that the market has never been so unruly. Prices are up at least 100 percent over 1941, and students . . . are having a wonderful time playing hard to get."[45] In a hiring frenzy not unlike that associated with the 1990s Internet boom, corporations sent their most impressive executives to recruit students, sometimes offering country club memberships and limousine services to lure recruits.

Learning from the Armed Forces

The difficulty of finding enough talent on the outside finally led companies, almost as a last resort, to look inside their own organizations and develop talent internally. This is where the war effort had its second major impact on corporate careers as companies looked to the armed forces for lessons on how to develop talent. Austin S. Ingleheart, president of General Foods, described how that company shaped its programs for developing talent. "During the last war, I spent some time in connection with the war effort, and was amazed at how the army could develop a program to develop men with the rapidity with which they did."[46] He found that seventy-five hundred of twelve thousand officers in the Army before 1938 had spent time at the War College, where they not only studied their own functional areas but also learned how the different functions fit together into a unified whole. The approach used at General Foods (and at most other companies) borrowed these lessons explicitly. It focused on broadening potential executives through exposure to the range of company functions.

It's interesting to see where the military got its lessons. When the war began, the armed forces immediately recognized the need for a huge expansion in the officer ranks to lead the rapid wartime buildup. As WWII began to unfold, the Navy took the lead by studying what it could learn from industry. The most significant outcome was a document, "Personnel Administration at the Executive Level," produced by the U.S. Naval Institute and based on the best management development practices drawn from fifty leading firms just before the war. The document begins by discussing how to survey existing talent (a "personnel inventory") and continues with how to develop promotion plans for each candidate, a process it calls "inventory control." These plans later became known as "replacement charts" and formed the basis of succession planning in companies. After the war, many employers used this Navy document as the basis for building their own development programs.[47]

The emerging science of personnel psychology received a tremendous boost from research conducted by the armed services, and the academic conversations among these psychologists spread practical lessons back to industry. For example, the practice of peer assessments of performance and potential began in the Navy during WWII. The Navy made extensive use of what it called "buddy ratings" in aviation squadrons: every member of a squad of officer cadets assessed every other member of the group to predict his performance in combat. The psychologists discovered that these assessments were more accurate predictors of actual performance than were the ratings of superiors because, the scientists surmised, the peers had more time to observe behavior and more realistic contexts for doing so.[48] These peer ratings became important in the early years of industrial development and were expanded to allow peers to assess their bosses as well.[49] They faded from the scene and then came roaring back in the 1990s, presented as something new, in the form of 360 degree feedback systems.

Another prominent example of wartime lessons was the use of forced ranking systems to assess individual performance. Before WWII, Army officers were assessed twice a year by their commanding officers. When the war broke out, the Army found it had to promote a great many officers to senior positions. But the assessments provided little guidance because they failed to differentiate among the candidates. So the Army experimented with a forced ranking system in which the commanding officers ranked their subordinates from best to worst to identify the candidates that should be promoted. The arrangement was tried with fifty thousand officers and was found to be not only far simpler but also more valid than the previous arrangements.[50] The technique was picked up by industry after the war.[51] Then, interestingly, the Air Force adopted it after the war, having seen it used in industry.[52] Forced rankings, like buddy ratings, would also fade from the scene until Jack Welch championed them at GE in the 1990s (they had been a lower-profile part of GE policies since the early 1970s).

Systematic assessment of job applicants also moved from the armed forces into the managerial world. Robert McNamara, secretary of defense in the Johnson administration and later president of the World Bank, describes his experience in being hired into the executive ranks of the Ford Motor Company after the war. Following a stint as professor at the Harvard Business School and important roles in the Army Air Corps during WWII, McNamara and ten of his wartime colleagues went directly into the executive ranks at Ford, a company that he describes as desperate for talent: "Of the top 1000 executives at Ford Motor Company, I don't believe there were 10 college graduates," he noted.[53]

Even though Ford itself was not run by college graduates, it relied heavily on military-inspired tests of academic ability after the war to make its hiring decisions, the same kinds of tests given in Officer Candidacy School. And even though McNamara and the "Whiz Kids," as they became known, had already been experienced wartime officers and were going to go directly into the executive ranks, before hiring them the company put them through the same battery of entry-level psychological tests that every management trainee went through. McNamara described the process: "They were going to give us tests, two full days of tests . . . intelligence, personality, you name it . . . This sounds absurd, but I remember one of the tests said, 'Would you rather be a florist or a coal miner?' I put down coal miner. The reason should be obvious to you." (The question was designed to identify "masculine" personality types—those who presumably would make the best executives—and in those days, the florist profession was seen as feminine.)

Among other innovations in career management in the 1940s was Studebaker Company's use of medical exams—in addition to IQ, vocabulary recognition, and math tests, vocational interest and aptitude batteries, and standardized interviews—to select employees.[54] The medical tests were justified on the basis that it made sense to make the substantial investments in employee development only for candidates who were likely to survive into middle age. McCormick & Company, maker of spices, created a "junior" board of directors made up of seventeen promising junior executives to give them the opportunity to wrestle with the same kinds of business problems that the real board of directors addressed. This technique, which became known as "multiple management," was adopted by a number of prominent companies.[55] McCormick also pioneered performance ratings by peers on this junior board.[56]

Back at GE

Many companies had innovative systems for developing managers in this period, but the most significant programs were at those companies that were large enough to be run on a large scale. Again, General Electric took the lead. GE's Manufacturing Leadership Program governed the development of trainees, executives, and everyone in between. It was based on a model of increasing job responsibility, classroom work and training carried out by line managers, and individualized counseling, what we now call coaching.

The first step was classroom training in manufacturing fundamentals. The number of recruits taken into the program was based on personnel audits and forecasts that predicted the number of future openings in the organizational hierarchy. Those who did well in the training progressed immediately into a program of job rotation that took them across jobs and to two or three plants. Their performance record from supervisors, interviews, and a series of psychological tests—IQ, vocational interests, Rorschach, and the Thematic Apperception Test—was used to judge their potential for higher levels of management.

The most promising candidates then went on to the Advanced Manufacturing Program, an eighteen-month high-potential program based on special project work, case study work, and recommended readings. The trainees had some say in their assignments and were given real responsibility along the way. Because the goal of the program was to give them an overall exposure to the manufacturing area, there was an effort to avoid specialization. They also received coaching about their performance, the areas where they needed to make improvements, and ways to do so.[57]

By 1950, GE itself began to change. The process that Gerard Swope had begun of seeing the company as a single entity with collective needs, as opposed to a series of independent and autonomous operations, reversed direction under the leadership of Charles Wilson. He introduced a new organizational model that attempted to balance the tension between central control and local autonomy that Alfred Sloan first described at General Motors. The GE version of the multidivisional firm moved back in the direction of local control, creating a large number of independent product departments over which the general managers in charge had almost complete freedom to operate. Each department had its own staff support as well as its own line managers. This more decentralized model was fully in place by 1955.

The transition to the new model created a great demand for general manager skills. Ralph Cordiner, who took over as president from Wilson, described his frustration with the shortage of these skills: "We cannot govern industry today with nothing but a group of specialists at the top, unless we are prepared to call a committee meeting every time there is a management decision made."[58] The complaint about an imbalance of functional talent and a shortage of broader skills has a contemporary ring. Like many other companies, and just as it had done after WWI with its first foray into general manager roles, GE responded initially by outside hiring. The typical white-collar employee hired during the transition period to the new model, 1951–1955, was fifty years old, suggesting that GE was hiring experienced employees.[59] Soon afterward, however, the company returned to internal development as the means for filling management jobs.

By the mid-1950s, the GE development model had advanced in important ways. One significant change was to eliminate the open-market "job shopping" that employees had enjoyed after completing the first year of training. Instead of individuals choosing their jobs, headquarters now made the decisions. Candidates were directed to the departments where the company had the greatest need and thought that they would be the best fit. Job ladders now included lateral moves, and it was possible to move across functional areas and across departments in the climb to the top. Such moves were more difficult in engineering but were still possible. The moves across departments but within functions—from engineering in lighting to engineering in engines—were even easier.

The company's initial goal for these lateral moves was to move talent to the place of greatest need, as manifested by growth and openings. From the perspective of the employee, the goal was to find a job ladder that provided more opportunity for advancement, especially to a coveted general manager job and from there into the ranks of corporate executives. To facilitate the movement of employees across functions and departments, the company required that hiring managers had to consider at least three candidates from outside the area when filling any management vacancy, and compliance with that requirement had to be documented. The company maintained "registers" of potential candidates interested in moving so that hiring managers could easily get qualified candidates if the managers could not come up with lists on their own.[60]

So deep was the management development process at GE that Ralph Cordiner required that succession planning for the company's top jobs extend three generations into the company: each top officer should be responsible for evaluating a second team of candidates—two or three people who were ten years younger than the current incumbents and who could be expected to take over those jobs in ten years. That second team, in turn, should evaluate a third team of candidates—two or three candidates ten years younger than the second team who could be expected to take over the positions currently held by the second team. This led to succession plans thirty years deep.[61]

In 1956, General Electric hired what was then a record eighteen hundred new college graduates, and 85 percent of them went directly into one of ten training programs. That same year, the company also created its Management Research and Development Institute, an off-site training facility for top executives. The facility was in Ossining, New York, a town that at the time was best known as the home of the infamous Sing Sing prison. The expression being "sent up the river" was used to describe the trip prisoners took from New York City up the Hudson River to Sing Sing prison, and GE's management trainees used to joke that they were also being sent up the river when they went to programs at the institute. Not appreciating the joke, the institute adopted the address of nearby Crotonville, New York, and it became known as "Crotonville."[62] Other companies developed similar centers, and their effect was to bring formal classroom training into the development process for both managers and executives.

Figure 2-1, taken from a GE management manual, documents the movement of employees up the management hierarchy, beginning with section heads, one step below the general management level. These movements were projected ten years in advance, and the plans were highly detailed— for example, that there would be precisely 193 individuals promoted from level 4 to level 3 over the next ten years. There were no outside hires at any of these levels. All the positions were filled internally from the level below.

The important point about the new GE model is that it placed control over the careers of individuals in the hands of the corporation at headquarters. The control by individual employees and local managers over jobs and career paths was sharply reduced when the company moved toward the corporate goal of providing the best talent to the most important positions across the corporation. On the management side, William H. Whyte described the essential difference that came with the new GE model: before, companies had training programs with the goal of developing candidates to make individual contributions. The new GE program, in contrast, was designed to develop candidates with the explicit goal of managing the work of others.[63]

The most sophisticated development programs were located in multidivisional industrial companies (like GE) where the demand for general managers was the greatest, but development programs were also an integral part of virtually all large companies. The extent of these programs in

FIGURE 2-1

The management hierarchy at GE in the 1950s

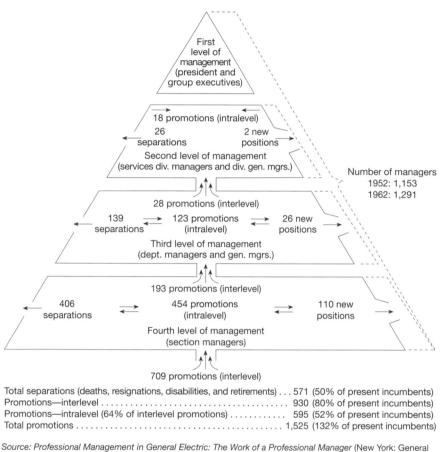

Total separations (deaths, resignations, disabilities, and retirements) . . . 571 (50% of present incumbents)
Promotions—interlevel . . . . 930 (80% of present incumbents)
Promotions—intralevel (64% of interlevel promotions) . . . . 595 (52% of present incumbents)
Total promotions . . . . 1,525 (132% of present incumbents)

Source: Professional Management in General Electric: The Work of a Professional Manager (New York: General Electric Company, 1954) 99.

retailing is perhaps the most surprising, because the flat organizational structure of retailing required few managers and because the skills of retailing management were not seen as particularly sophisticated nor unique across companies. But a 1953 study of fifty-one major retailers found that 80 percent had formal training programs for new executives, and 70 percent of those were longer than three months.[64]

These programs were limited to candidates younger than age thirty-four, and one-third of them required medical exams to ensure that candidates would live long enough to make good use of the investment. The companies screened carefully for admission; 28 percent conducted specific aptitude tests; 24 percent, IQ tests; and 22 percent, personality tests. The programs themselves included "action learning" (25 percent) based on special projects for the company, job assignments designed for development experience (33 percent), role-playing exercises (25 percent), and "personal conferences," the equivalent of coaching sessions (37 percent). Almost all the companies (96 percent) reported that they were committed to a policy of promotion from within, and 70 percent reported that the training programs were explicitly for advancement and promotion.

Sears, Roebuck and Co. pioneered the science of talent assessment. The University of Chicago helped Sears develop tests of management potential, and the company gave a standard battery of six ability and aptitude tests to ten thousand of its managers during the 1950s. Based in large measure on these tests, five thousand managers were placed in a "reserve group," essentially a high-potential group. "Once a man is put in the reserve group," *BusinessWeek* noted, "he has started up the ladder."[65] Five hundred of these managers were then selected for a "senior reserve group," an even faster track that pointed directly to senior management.

Sears also recognized that part of the cause of its talent shortage was the reluctance of senior executives to develop junior ones. It was asking a lot to have executives develop others to take over their jobs, so the company pioneered mandatory retirement policies to clear out the older executives and the career path. T. V. Houser, vice president of merchandising at Sears, said that retirement was made mandatory "entirely to keep the lines of advancement open."[66] Without those opportunities, he noted, the best young managers would leave for other companies: "The very minute they make a mark, some other company begins making overtures to them." Mandatory retirement was therefore introduced as a retention strategy.

1950s Best-Practice Models

By the mid-1950s, the importance of developing management and executive talent was clearly understood. The author of a 1953 *Harvard Business Review* article interviewed 204 corporate presidents and concluded that the biggest problem they faced was a lack of internal development of talent.[67] Studies of contemporary CEOs (see chapter 1) show that talent management issues are also at the top of their list of concerns. In the 1950s, part of the pressure to focus attention on internal talent came from the recognition that executive talent was now coming almost exclusively from inside the firm. Without improvements in internal development, the 1953 study observed, companies would be forced to go back to hiring top executives from outside. And the only places to find executives were smaller companies, where the skill set would be quite different from what was needed to run a large, complex corporation.

A 1955 survey of the Young Presidents Organization found that the worst business mistake its members made in the preceding year—the one that most hurt the company—was the failure to get the person they needed for a particular job. "In many companies where clerical, secretarial, sales, and production help are carefully chosen through batteries of tests and interviews," the study noted, "the top jobs are filled by guess, by gamble, and by hunch."[68]

The advice the authors of the *Harvard Business Review* study gave draws on the programs at companies like GE and seems remarkably similar to what is often proposed now, fifty years later: rotational assignments, a mix of staff and line experiences, the opportunity to run an operation, attendance at advanced management programs, and psychological counseling or coaching.[69] A great many companies appear to have taken that early advice. By 1955, a Conference Board study showed that 60 percent of companies with ten thousand or more employees had a program in place to develop executive talent. Twelve years earlier, in contrast, the Conference Board did not find enough companies with development programs to conduct a study on them.[70] A study by the American Management Association found that the size of personnel departments in proportion to the rest of the organization had been growing rapidly in U.S. companies in the 1950s—up 30 percent in 1955 alone compared with the preceding year.[71] And they were spending a lot of money on it. One oil company official noted that it cost $10,000—the equivalent of an executive's yearly salary—just to find out whether an individual had management potential.[72]

The rise of engineering as the field of choice for executive candidates created a new and somewhat different demand for employee development.

A study conducted at Virginia Polytechnic Institute in 1953 found that one-third of the largest corporations were headed by executives who had graduated with engineering qualifications; another at Columbia at the same time found that 40 percent of all the managers in industrial companies had been trained as engineers. In previous generations, the studies found, bankers and lawyers had been the most common fields for producing executives.[73] As one observer noted, engineers were "frequently bewildered" by executive positions because those jobs were fundamentally about overseeing people, a task for which they had no prior training. As a result, the movement of engineers into the executive ranks created a big demand for training and development in managing people.[74]

As companies addressed the need for management development, their programs became more sophisticated and more innovative. For example, Lockheed (now Lockheed Martin) developed a special reserve candidate pool drawn directly from college into a two-year training program designed to produce leaders with general skills that could be applied to any function if unpredictable demands developed, the equivalent of a modern "talent pool."[75] Monsanto was another innovator, pioneering interpersonal skills training and coaching in areas that we might now call emotional intelligence. They claimed to hire the best chemists and engineers, "some of whom are actually so brilliant," noted a company official, "they annoy everyone associated." So the company set up extensive interpersonal skills training and individualized counseling, provided in part by outside consultants, that went well beyond the typical executive coaching we see now.[76]

Standard Oil Company of California developed a sophisticated model for internal staffing and career development. It maintained a "Personal Experience Record" for all management employees that included a report on their experiences and skills and a new "Section 14, Concerning His Future," that made projections about a candidate's potential in management. Section 14 content included notations about the employee's shortcomings and the remediation that would be necessary to achieve his potential. The company's Office of Executive Development maintained these records on computer files. When a vacancy occurred, the officials processed the files to come up with a short list of candidates and recommendations that were then reviewed with the hiring department.[77]

Assessing Potential

An important goal for talent management in this period was to identify which candidates had the potential for advancement and were worth the investment. The development programs and experiences I've outlined required huge investments, which were lost if a candidate did not succeed. Companies like Procter & Gamble tried to predict who would get to the top ranks when hiring *entry*-level employees. As *Business Week* described it, "P&G picks its executive crop right out of college"; once chosen, the candidates had a predictable schedule for advancement from date of hire right into the senior ranks of the company.[78]

What did companies look at to predict who would succeed as a manager? Family background and extracurricular activities, especially fraternities and social clubs, featured prominently. The goal was to get at a candidate's "character." General Electric, one of the leaders in employee management, relied explicitly on what are now known as *trait-rating* psychological scales for assessing individual candidates for managerial development. We now think of these traits as representing personality, but at the time, they were described as character, the raw material that was crucial for executive leadership.[79]

My former colleague Ernest Dale was troubled by the reliance on traits and personality assessments in management, and he poked fun at it in 1957 by presenting *New York Times* readers with the comparison shown in figure 2-2 between two evaluation systems. One, he noted, came from a corporate personnel department, and the other was a report card from a local kindergarten. Could readers tell the difference?

The fact that they look similar was not accidental. Both were designed to assess character traits that were seen as central to one's potential. The only difference was that in one case, the candidates were middle-level executives, and in the other, they were starting a little earlier at age four. (The kindergarten report card was system B.)

Dale's study of corporate practices concluded that beginning around 1950, companies had begun to focus almost entirely on personality and character traits in assessing their managers and executives and that there was essentially no role for job performance in these systems. What concerned him was that assessments like these were rarely based on hard

FIGURE 2-2

Performance evaluation: Kindergarten or management?

System A

Rank candidates on a scale of Very Satisfactory — Satisfactory — Unsatisfactory

- Dependability
- Stability
- Imagination
- Originality
- Self-expression
- Health and vitality
- Ability to plan and control
- Cooperation

System B

Rank candidates on a scale of Satisfactory — Improving — Needs improvement

- Can be depended on
- Contributes to the good work of others
- Accepts and uses criticism
- Thinks critically
- Shows initiative
- Plans work well
- Physical resistance
- Self-expression
- Creative ability

science—few companies bothered to validate which traits actually predicted future career success—and they could be manipulated and biased relatively easily.[80]

In 1954, 63 percent of large corporations were using standardized tests of personality for hiring decisions, and 25 percent used them as part of their promotion process to assess employees' potential for leadership positions. Famed psychologist Alfred Binet (who helped create the Stanford-Binet intelligence test) proposed that the records of executives, including all their credentials, scores on aptitude and personality tests, and so on, be coded on a card that they could carry with them from job to job, like a passport. Westinghouse took up this idea and instituted the lyrically named "Management Development Personnel Code Card 24908" for all its executives.[81]

Careers and Career Planning

By the mid-1950s, the landscape of U.S. corporations had changed dramatically. If the corporate scene in the earlier part of the century was a dynamic landscape populated by entrepreneurs and new firms, the picture at mid-century was one of huge, stable enterprises run by professional managers. Some 40 percent of all the business assets in the United States in the mid-1950s were owned by about two hundred corporations. Manufacturers with more than one thousand workers in 1951 employed 34 percent of all employees, in contrast to 1909, when only about 15 percent of all employees worked in such firms.[82] Some 40 percent of all U.S. workers were employed by only one-half of 1 percent of all the enterprises in the country. These companies grew ever larger in part by mergers and acquisition, with roughly half of all the industrial companies in the United States being involved in a merger or acquisition every year.[83] Advancement in business meant advancing inside these large corporations. A survey of college graduate job seekers after WWII, the cohort that would come to populate the ranks of management in the 1950s, found that their number 1 interest was advancement prospects, followed closely by job security.[84] Large corporations offered both.

Careers advanced inside organizations because companies no longer brought in talent from the outside. The American Management Association surveyed employers about the extent of their outside or lateral hiring in 1956. It found that 15 percent of companies did no outside hiring at all at the executive level, 43 percent filled less than 10 percent of vacancies from the outside, and larger firms did less outside hiring. Note that "hired from the outside" meant only that the executive had been hired *at some point* from another firm and not necessarily hired as an executive. The AMA study noted that companies rarely pursued or poached an employee away from another company: "Some companies regard it as unethical and will consider such an applicant only when the man approaches on his own."[85]

Mabel Newcomer's study of corporate executives across the generations found that half the leaders of large businesses had been hired from outside their corporations in 1900, but by 1950 that figure was down to 20 percent. In 1950, 47 percent of executives in Newcomer's sample retired in office, as opposed to only 11 percent in 1900. Of those who retired in office, 40 percent had been with their firms more than forty years in 1950, in contrast to 21 percent in that category in 1925 and only 5 percent in 1900.[86] If one wanted to advance in a career, it had to come from within.

Although managers were much more likely to stay in the same company, they found themselves moving more frequently within those companies. The GE model described earlier of movement across functions to get to the general management position was now commonplace. Eugene Jennings noted how the norms concerning movement in the organization had changed: "The new generation finds that mobility brings competency whereas the pre-mobility generation believed that competency brought mobility."[87] Changing jobs was seen as the way to become competent, because the key competency was the broad understanding of the organization needed to become an executive.

The typical management job inside a company in the 1960s lasted only eighteen to twenty-one months before the employee moved on. The assumption was that 80 percent of the learning took place in the first 20 percent of the time in a job, so the way to maximize learning was to move people through jobs faster. Eighteen months was a guess as to the time when most learning took place.

Greater mobility also played itself out at the very top of the company: on the average, presidents stayed in their jobs about ten years in 1948 to 1953, but by the mid-1960s, five years was typical.[88] This greater turnover makes sense if we remember that the preceding generation of corporate leaders was made up of founders and owners who did not have to retire and could not be fired, at least without a huge fight. The new presidents, in contrast, were employees who were subject to mandatory retirement policies and had to leave to create the vacancies needed for the next generation to advance.

In the early 1950s, sociologists Norman Martin and Anselm Strauss took on what was at the time a novel question: what explained the career advancement of individuals inside a company?[89] They found clear pathways up the organization as well as paths that put careers on hold. The senior managers, typically with guidance from human resources, acted like stationmasters in a train yard, flipping switches that sent management candidates down different tracks.

Advancement within the executive ranks also became more predictable. When the head of the company had been replaced in the preceding generation, most of the management team went out the door, as is often the case now. The actions of the company rested heavily on the day-to-day decisions of the leader, and the new leader therefore wanted a staff that was loyal to him and would execute his own directions. By the mid-1950s, when the top guy left, it was much more of a nonevent. Virtually everyone else stayed in place because the company was now governed by rules and procedures, not by individuals, and the systems remained in place even when the head of the company did not. The company would operate in more or less the same way.[90] Newcomer's study of top executives found that the outgoing head of the company still played a key role in "naming his own successor" in the 1950s.[91] By the 1960s, even that influence had been taken away and transferred to a system of succession planning.

At the end of the 1960s, a study of management development practices conducted for the Committee for Economic Development found that the companies it examined saw talent management as a crucial issue. They were worried about the supply side, making good hires and developing them fast enough to meet the demand: "Most top managers believe that a shortage of executive talent exists and that consequently there is plenty of room at the top for a good man."[92]

The Legacy of the Organizational Man

After World War II, the practices of talent management based on internal development were solidly in place in most corporations. Figure 2-3 shows GE's 1973 statement of talent management principles. Based on practices that had been in place for almost a generation, this could have been a best-practice statement for virtually any of the large corporations of that period. GE still maintains something close to these practices, as do a handful of other large companies. But otherwise, practices like these disappeared almost completely within a decade.

The Organization Man model of internal development and lifetime careers was developed because of a unique set of circumstances on the demand side (stable markets made long-term planning possible, corporations grew ever larger, and the skills needed to run them were unique to each company) and on the supply side (outside hiring did not work, and talent therefore had to be developed internally).

FIGURE 2-3

Statement of the GE management development philosophy, 1973

- Assuring the development of managerial excellence in the company is the CEO's most important responsibility.
- Managers at all levels must be similarly responsible and must "own" the development system.
- Promotion from within—for its motivational value—will be the rule, not the exception.
- A key step in planning the development of managers is the review process.
- Managerial abilities are learned primarily by managing. Other activities are valuable adjuncts.
- Control of the selection process is essential in order to use openings developmentally.
- The company can tolerate and needs a wide variety of managerial styles, traits, abilities, etc.
- Several different managerial streams and development planning systems are needed to accommodate the company's size, diversity, and decentralization.
- Occasionally, it may be necessary to distort otherwise sound compensation practice and/or to change organization structure to achieve developmental results.
- Staff must add value in these processes, but their roles are secondary to the managerial roles.

Many pundits recommend a return to the practices of the 1950s, but even a cursory look at the contemporary business environment suggests that it is nothing like the 1950s. If anything, the environment looks more like the dynamic period around the 1920s, when long-term planning was difficult, authority and accountability were pushed onto individuals and not systems, and career mobility across companies was high. It is important to understand why the models from the 1950s fell apart in order to see why they will not come back as well as to get a sense of which practices will succeed in the very different contemporary business environment. We turn to that question in chapter 3.

3

The End of an Era

Among the most prominent companies in the world for developing employees was AT&T Corporation and its affiliated Regional Bell Operating Companies. AT&T was famous not only for the time and energy that went into planning employee careers but also for studying itself. By the mid-1950s, the company saw a number of manpower planning problems on the horizon. First, it predicted a demand for a large number of executives in the near future not only because the system was growing quickly but also because it foresaw a wave of retirements based on the company's internal demographics.

Second, like other corporations at the time, AT&T saw the need to hire more college-educated managers. Lateral hiring was not an option because there were no competitors from which to hire, and the traditional approach of promoting newly hired, college-trained managers up the ranks would take thirty years or more. So the company, like most other large corporations dealing with the same problem, created a fast-track, or high-potential, program for young managers. Those selected for the program were evaluated especially for their potential to be company executives.

In 1956, AT&T began a long-term study of managers and their development to understand which attributes predicted who would succeed. The company developed an assessment center that conducted a series of tests on management candidates: paper and pencil tests of personality and ability, interviews with psychologists, and especially simulations of important management tasks. The assessment center approach became

AT&T's best-known legacy in talent management. It developed its program by copying what the Office of Strategic Services, the precursor of the Central Intelligence Agency, had put in place during WWII to simulate intelligence activities and predict who would succeed in those tasks. Two years later, AT&T was using its assessment center to select first-level supervisors. By the mid-1970s, more than one thousand organizations in the United States had introduced similar assessment centers.[1]

Other companies were doing similar things, but what was different about the development efforts at AT&T was the scale on which they were undertaken. The organization was massive; it had more than two hundred thousand managerial employees by the end of the 1970s, and it included operating companies in every state as well as local offices in every city. The level of projected growth and the predictability of demand on the business side made it reasonable to make huge investments in management development.

Each operating company maintained a short list of candidates, called the "white book," which identified those managers who had the potential for executive jobs. For a candidate to make it into the white book required multiple sponsors from various business contexts as well as passing grades from the assessment center. Managers in the white book became the subject of an enormous amount of attention from the Bell system. The operating committee of the local Bell company reviewed the career plan of every senior executive and all its fast-track employees at least once a year. And each year the AT&T operating committee reviewed the career plans not only of its top executives but also those in the white books of its operating companies.

An important part of the development path in the Bell system was getting staff experience at the AT&T corporate offices. Headquarters picked a few people at the district manager level inside the operating companies and brought them to New York City for a temporary, two-year assignment. The idea was to give them a small task over which they could have ownership and that also had implications for the entire system. An example would be something like coordinating protocols for the Yellow Pages across operating companies. The task mattered, but the real goal was to give the candidates experience in coordinating ideas and information, negotiating a set of solutions, and implementing the results across the entire system to give them an understanding of how the national telephone system worked. (In later years, this approach was rediscovered and labeled "action learning.") Then the candidates rotated back to their operating companies with the stamp of having had development experience with AT&T.

The Decline of Internal Development at AT&T

Despite having a huge investment in arguably the most sophisticated arrangements for developing management talent, AT&T began to dismantle that model, and did so earlier than most companies. Two events proved crucial. The first was the discrimination case brought by the federal Equal Employment Opportunities Commission against the company, a case that was settled by a consent decree in 1976.

The government argued successfully that the company's career advancement and assessment systematically discriminated against women and minorities. Initially, the company used its sophisticated assessment system to identify women and minorities who could be pulled up faster into the management ranks. But the consent decree eventually called into question many of AT&T's career management practices, especially its system of assessment, because, as with practices at other companies, it was designed to predict a person's ability to learn and succeed at training and development, and not job performance per se. Job performance was the criterion that the law required. The many companies that looked to AT&T as a role model thought that if this company—with its resources and its PhDs working on assessing employees using the latest, cutting-edge techniques—could be taken down for discrimination, what chance did their own planning and advancement programs have?[2]

The second and more important event that turned back AT&T's interest in managerial development was a 1985 consent decree that ended the government's decades-long antitrust case against the Bell system. The decree eventually separated local phone service and the operating companies from long distance service and AT&T. The operating companies would no longer be the feeders for talent into AT&T. The new arrangement also meant the eventual end of regulated prices and the ability to pass costs, including development costs, to ratepayers through the regulatory system.

The beginning of competitive markets for long distance service meant a very different business model for AT&T.

When Hal Burlingame took over responsibility for human resources at AT&T in the 1990s, what struck him was that even though the consent decree had been in place for several years, "the practices were so deeply embedded that the system didn't recognize the change. We were still preparing people at AT&T to become presidents of the operating companies, as if the white books still existed."[3] In fact, the business requirements for leaders were now quite different. "We had a whole new set of tasks to address and a new kind of manager to develop. We had to learn what it meant to be a general manager with profit-and-loss responsibility, not just a functional manager. We had to rethink what it meant to develop these new people."

The question was how to find these general managers where none had existed previously. One approach, as GE had found sixty years earlier, was to go outside, and for the first time, the company began to recruit managers and executives from other companies. But "hiring managers were sometimes terrified of a new skill base coming in," Burlingame notes, and it was not always possible to get them to accept outside talent. The other approach was simply trial by fire: take capable managers who had not yet had anything like the relevant experience, put them in these new roles, and support them as well as possible with coaching and other kinds of help.

The fast-track programs, in which candidates either advanced immediately or washed out, were discontinued because they wasted too much talent. The new version of the high-potential program—the Leadership Continuity Program—no longer trained candidates directly from college campuses, because the need for new managers and hiring were down sharply. Candidates were now selected from the current workforce based on job performance rather than predictions of potential. The internal and external classroom-based development programs also were stopped. Instead, the new program relied on job activities, which were cheaper and faster to deliver. Job rotations slowed as well. Burlingame notes, "We wanted to not move them around so much and not across every phase of the business. We wanted them to see what they were doing longer, to live through a full cycle of their activities. With fewer layers protecting them from below, they had to learn to really run things."

Two other developments adversely affected long-term talent management and career planning. First, the constant restructuring and realignment of business operations rearranged job and promotion ladders, in most cases severely disrupting them. A candidate might be anticipating promotion to the head of his area, but then businesses would be consolidated and the position eliminated. By the 1990s, these changes became so frequent and so significant that it was no longer possible for the existing career structures to function even with frequent adjustments. It was essentially impossible to forecast talent requirements with any accuracy.

The second development coincided with the general trend in corporate restructuring to downsize and flatten operations. The resulting new structures removed many steps from the remaining job ladders and further eroded clarity about career advancement. "Even where the programs remained," Burlingame says, "people wondered what their future was and what career growth was available to them." The steps in the career progression became leaps, because the job requirements for the next level could be dramatically, rather than incrementally, greater.

Doug LaPasta had been a consultant to AT&T in the 1980s and remembered working on the design of performance appraisal systems with a staff of fifteen or so AT&T psychologists in a special unit dedicated to appraisals. He came back to the company in the mid-1990s and was again asked to help with appraisals. "I was in the same building I had been in before," he says. "The appraisal unit was completely gone, and the new HR people in the building weren't even aware that the company had ever had an appraisal unit."[4] In 2006, AT&T was purchased by Cingular Wireless. Although the AT&T name remains in place, its pioneering models for managing talent disappeared along with the company.

The Decline of Internal Development at IBM

A more publicized change in direction occurred at IBM. Walter E. Burdick, its legendary executive vice president of human resources, was arguably the person most responsible for its famous lifetime model of career development. The joke at the time was that IBM stood for "I've been moved." "We had no qualms about putting a person into something that they hadn't done before—they were bright people," Burdick notes.[5]

IBM hired from twenty or so of the best colleges, and the divisions were evaluated on how many of their hires came from those schools. Candidates were brought into functional tracks, given specialized training in that function, and then evaluated within two years to make the big move into line management, supervising a group of about twelve people. Management training followed, as did evaluation by the business units for the candidate to be nominated for advancement based on job performance. The division presidents evaluated those nominees and decided which ones to send up to the company's Management Committee. It is remarkable in contemporary terms to think that the operating committee of a huge multinational company spent the time to map out the development of these four hundred fifty or so candidates EACH YEAR, most of them younger than age thirty. Supervisors themselves were evaluated in part on their ability to develop their subordinates.

Burdick explains, "There was a big debate in the company as to how important it was for advancement to be multifunctional. [Former CEO] Tom Watson really wanted multifunctional, and the big exchange was between engineering and marketing." The idea behind a multifunctional experience was to develop candidates by giving them a broad experience that would help them see the overall corporate picture when they advanced to senior leadership jobs.

Each move meant significant increases in salary and responsibility, lots of additional training—including two weeks at "Charm School," as it was known, at the IBM Sandy Point center for newly promoted managers—and interaction with senior executives concerning the strategies and policies of the corporation. (Burdick notes that the decision to build IBM's famous training and development center in the Armonk, New York, headquarters was to save time for the senior executives, who had been traveling to Sandy Point, Long Island.) Perhaps the best known of IBM's development practices was the requirement that each manager receive forty hours of formal training on managerial issues each year.

IBM was relentless about moving its managerial talent, and each move up the ladder involved relocation. "The person who was being moved was not involved until the offer was made," Burdick says. "A higher-level manager in concert with an HR person made the decision as to the best place for them to be assigned." The candidate could then be asked what he was interested in, "but they knew that being willing to move was necessary to chase a higher career." At its peak, IBM relocated seven thousand of its fifty thousand managerial employees every year. The company laid out and managed the careers of managers all the way to retirement. Like Sears a generation earlier, IBM required that all officers retire at age sixty to help open opportunities for internal advancement and to make career planning more predictable, reducing the disruption caused by early retirement.

Between 1985 and 1993, IBM pushed a quarter million employees out of the company, breaking its tradition of lifetime employment, and hired one hundred thousand new ones, many of them experienced hires at the management and executive level. Hiring executives from outside the company "would never have happened earlier," Burdick says, but it soon became commonplace. Outside hiring was driven by the need for IBM to obtain new competencies to respond to new markets. Development opportunities became less pervasive, as did relocations. Lou Gerstner described his amazement when arriving to take over IBM at discovering the scale of the AA (administrative assistant) developmental jobs at IBM.[6] Bright, up-and-coming managers shadowed middle and senior executives for years as part of their career planning. Programs like those did not survive Gerstner's restructuring efforts. During his tenure, company observers began to worry that the path to the top was faster for outside hires and that having a multifunctional background was much less advantaged than having a purely functional orientation.

Donna Riley, head of talent planning for IBM, notes that its career planning has been scaled back considerably since 1985 to reflect the greater uncertainty in business planning. Career paths used to be so deep that "we would identify five possible successors for each key leadership job." Now, career planning is much more immediate: "We ask candidates to identify what they would like their next two positions to be, and then to identify two alternative moves. We put those in our database to help with planning."[7]

Decline in the Traditional Models of Talent Management

The experience at AT&T and IBM played out at most companies. John Kotter describes the collapse of management development at a major

New York bank in the early 1980s. Line managers in this system were responsible for identifying talent and nominating employees for development experiences, tasks that line managers there and elsewhere often saw as time-consuming and burdensome. Downsizing followed the recession of 1981–1983, and top management's attention shifted to questions of strategy and restructuring. Line managers balked at doing the work of assessing talent when they had more pressing demands, and especially when the business was getting rid of managers. They appealed to the executive leadership, which agreed that these development tasks were a low priority in the current environment. Line managers stopped doing them, and that was the end of the program.[8]

Citibank had one of the most sophisticated management and executive development programs in business. But when Sandy Weill took control, he saw little value in those processes, succession planning in particular. He made staffing decisions for executive jobs by relying on loyalty and the ability to deliver financial performance in one's previous position.[9]

The Opinion Research Corporation identified the percentage of executives who thought their companies were good or very good at developing talent. By the mid-1980s, only 27 percent believed that their talent management practices were even adequate, let alone good. The worst practices, in their view, were rewards for developing talent in others, guidance for managing one's own career, and arrangements for lateral transfers within and across divisions, in that order. These practices had been at the center of the older system of talent management through internal development.[10]

By 2004, an IPMA-HR survey of employers found that 63 percent did no workforce planning of any kind; presumably this meant that these employers dealt with every vacancy as if it were a unique, surprising event. (Recall that 96 percent of large companies had a dedicated manpower planning *department* in the 1950s.) A Society for Human Resource Management (SHRM) survey a year earlier found that 60 percent of the companies surveyed (all SHRM members) had no succession planning of any kind. In the preceding generation, virtually every company of any size conducted sophisticated workforce planning and then succession planning for the management and executive ranks. In professional service firms, where human capital is the only real asset, studies show that planning for talent is even less common. Only about 19 percent of public accounting firms, for example, have any planning for succession events.[11] A survey of CEOs at large companies found that only 25 percent had any kind of talent planning past two levels below the CEO, that is, past the senior vice president level.[12]

It is not that companies abandoned succession planning and other practices and moved to new approaches. Instead, they appear to have abandoned the systematic approach of managing talent.

Part of the decline in the traditional models of talent management may have had to do with the ossification of the planning process itself. Libby Sterbakov, vice president for talent at Pitney-Bowes, describes her earlier experiences at Digital Equipment Corporation (DEC), one of the leaders in talent management in the 1970s and early 1980s. "[DEC founder] Ken Olsen was intensely interested in the talent review process, but then the process got mechanical, and the leadership was turned off," Sterbakov says. "Filling out the forms on each leader, completing the books of talent, became more important than the conversations around the table." Donna Riley reported a similar decline in engagement at IBM when the talent management programs became heavy on administrative requirements. As it became seen as a staff function of human resources, the leadership of companies lost interest in it, and the importance of the function declined.

The most important reason that the existing talent management practices came apart, however, was not that they failed in their mission of producing talent. They collapsed because of their costs.

How the New Economy Crushed the Organization Man

The principle of internal development was that companies invested in the development of employees and later secured the benefits of that investment through the employees' enhanced performance. The size of the investment could be thought of as the difference between what the company was spending on the program—not only the direct costs of training and the administrative costs of running the program but also the compensation costs while candidates were in it—minus what the managers produced during the program.

These investments were huge because they extended over decades and involved candidates in virtually full-time development experiences. The programs helped stabilize the supply of talent in the pipeline, or, in contemporary terms, they helped retain employees. Even now, the evidence indicates that longer job ladders with more promotion steps are associated with lower rates of turnover.[13] These programs also offered employees and the employer stability with respect to earnings and compensation costs. Evidence suggests that wages remained higher than those in the outside market in economic downturns but also did not rise as high in economic upturns.[14]

If a company took college graduates and developed them over a period of twenty years to fill executive roles in marketing or sales, it had to be sure that the need for the competencies that were being developed would be there in twenty years. If the need was no longer there, then that huge investment in development might be wasted. Accurately making that forecast required knowing what the company would be doing years and even decades into the future. That is where the system began to fall apart.

The Failure of Forecasting

Lawrence Klein, of the University of Pennsylvania, won the Nobel Prize in economics in 1980 for his work over the previous decades in developing the techniques for forecasting the state of the economy, a recognition of the prominence of forecasting and related planning efforts in the economy. Every major corporation engaged in long-term plans for its businesses, which in turn were based on long-term forecasts of the economy.

What made the period from the 1950s through the early 1970s a golden age for talent management was also what made it the golden age for economic forecasting: demand and business requirements could be accurately predicted well into the future. Government regulations restricted the level and nature of competition—in particular, in communications, transportation, and finance—and that restricted new entrants, price cutting, and other aspects of what we now think of as normal competition. The goal of these regulations was in part to facilitate long-term investments at the company level, investments that were seen as crucial to making the economy more efficient and effective. The number of industries in which competition was effectively regulated away was, by contemporary standards, amazingly high.[15]

At the same time, foreign competition in U.S. markets was almost non-existent. In manufacturing, domestic competitors often operated as an oligopoly, avoiding competition based on prices and generally keeping competitive pressures on the back burner. In the auto industry, for example, news stories every autumn began by noting, "General Motors today announced its annual price increases for the new models. Ford and Chrysler were expected to follow." There was little price competition.

Unions standardized labor costs by negotiating common contracts across employers, effectively removing labor costs as a source of competitive advantage. In the auto industry, the United Auto Workers contracts guaranteed a 3 percent wage increase every year (plus inflation) to match what had been predictable productivity increases in the economy. Production workers suffered layoffs during recessions but were called back when business picked up. Companies carried white-collar and managerial employees during these downturns, avoiding laying them off. IBM argued, with some justification, that the employment security it offered facilitated what was (by contemporary standards) low-level restructuring of operations brought on by unforeseen market changes.[16] There was little pressure to maximize shareholder value, at least by contemporary standards, and executives had much greater discretion to devote resources to such goals.

Larry Lapide, director of MIT's Center for Transportation and Logistics, described the situation from the perspective of a large corporate employer: "Up to the early 1980s, large-scale manufacturing companies with strong brands ruled the roost and 'pushed' products out. If they made something it would sell. So manufacturing plants made big production runs of items to keep production costs low, recognizing that everything they made would automatically sell or, if not, the marketing folks would easily get customers to buy what was left over."[17]

Talent management plans, known at the time as "manpower planning," were a crucial part of business planning. The goal was to ensure that the supply of workers, managers, and executives met the requirements associated with forecasts of business demand. Manpower planning models had their roots in the War Manpower Commission, which required businesses to report on their current staffing levels and requirements for the future because shortfalls in skilled workers could derail production and the war effort. The first of these models were based on "replacement planning tables," which simply reported the number of incumbents in each position, organized according to the internal promotion structure and showing which workers were in line to move to the next position in the table.

By the mid-1960s, a study of personnel departments found that 96 percent had a dedicated talent planning function.[18] Virtually every company had an executive ("the manpower planner") who headed that area. The most crucial job in the HR organization—and some would argue the most powerful job in the company—was the position informally known as *chess master*. The chess master decided how executives would move around the chessboard represented by the company's various assignments. The favored few found themselves with plum jobs at corporate headquarters; those out of favor saw the moving van come to take them to the greenfield plant in East Nowhere.

The tools for workforce forecasts were remarkably sophisticated. TRW, for example, adjusted top-down estimates based on marketing forecasts against those generated by line managers to reach a precise figure. North American Rockwell's estimates included adjustments for employee time spent in training programs.[19] Jim Walker described the forecasts of the American Oil subsidiary of Standard Oil Company as extending out ten years.[20] This figure may have been typical.

Estimates of demand for talent were then matched against estimates of supply. The assumption was that the supply of talent was an internal function within the control of the company.[21] Planners began by estimating the internal supply of candidates for each position in the future, assuming the current rate of hiring and advancement. They then adjusted the supply pipeline to ensure that it matched future demand. Because the supply for all except entry-level jobs came only from within, managing that supply involved adjusting the rate at which candidates progressed from job to job in the firm.

Serious modeling of the movement of employees within organizations was based on the work of mathematician Andrei Andreyevich Markov, who developed procedures for understanding the movement of items from one state to another, in this case the movement of individuals from one job to another in a promotion hierarchy. The models calculated the rates of movement according to variables such as company growth rates and the attributes of the individuals in each position, such as average tenure.[22] As models began to accommodate the variety of arrangements possible for advancement (such as "flexible" hierarchies, in which workers could move across functional silos), their complexity—and the amount of mathematics required to describe them—expanded considerably.[23]

The peak of workforce planning was probably a late-1960s model called MANPLAN, which attempted to model the movement of individuals within a career system by including individual behavior and psychological variables such as worker attitudes and aspirations, the practices of supervisors (appraisals, compensation arrangements, practices for employee transfers), the group norms in the workplace, and labor market outcomes. These factors at the individual level were then aggregated at the company level to produce overall estimates. Arguably nothing more sophisticated has been created since.[24]

Workforce planning (and the related practices of succession planning and employee development in general) began to fall apart when the ability to forecast the overall level of demand in the economy eroded after the oil shocks of the mid-1970s, first in 1973 and then in 1979. Gross national product, which had been forecast to grow at about 5 to 6 percent in real terms as it had during most of the 1960s, actually declined in 1974, in 1975, and again in 1980. The 1970s became known as the decade of "stagflation": low economic growth despite inflation.[25]

Talent management arrangements ran into trouble because of the long lead time inherent in a system of internal development. The number of managers who were ready for director positions, for example, was set in motion by hiring and development decisions made ten years or more before, based on forecasts of much higher demand. Overshooting demand by only a few percent soon added up. A 3 percent overage per year led to having one-third too many managers in the pipeline at the end of a decade.

What were organizations to do with all those excess managerial candidates, especially in the context of lifetime employment for white-collar workers, a practice employed by virtually all companies? The immediate concern was not the cost of excess employees but the consequences for their motivation when there were not enough promotion opportunities.

Commenting on the decline in corporate growth and the resulting slow-down in opportunities, Sandra Beldt and Donald Jewell noted at the time that this situation created a problem for companies in which promotions were the most significant reward and the source of motivation. They found that "the need to continue promoting people has been met in many companies by creating positions, [but] often such positions have a title without commensurate responsibility and authority."[26] In other words, companies added management and executive jobs, and the bureaucracies of the corporations began to bloat.

The recession that began in 1981 was the worst downturn in business activity since the Great Depression. Gross national product declined by 2 percent in 1982 alone. At the same time, companies found themselves carrying a huge burden of excess talent produced by their internal development systems. It also brought to a head a number of even more significant changes in the business environment, changes that also had a profound effect on talent management practices.[27]

Changes in the Nature of Competition

Growing competition in product markets further weakened the traditional talent management model by sharply increasing the uncertainty associated with planning. The economic deregulation of product markets was the most noticeable change, beginning with airlines in 1978 and followed by other transportation industries, communications, and banking and finance. The end of the cold war had a similar destabilizing effect on the large section of the economy represented by the defense industry.

Jim Williams spent a career in talent development in large corporations like GE and IBM. "I noticed the change away from the lifetime employment models," he notes, "around the time that communism fell, when we tried to convert the defense businesses into the rest of the operations."[28] The defense divisions of companies like GE and IBM operated on project models; teams of employees stayed with a project—say, a weapons system—for the life of the system, perhaps ten years or more. When the cold war wound down and much of the defense business dried up, the human assets that had been cultivated and maintained for these military projects became a liability.

The dominance of large employers, which had been the leaders in talent management, also began to erode. The one hundred largest employers in the United States, the United Kingdom, France, Germany, and Japan accounted for about 8.4 percent of all the employment in their respective countries in the 1970s. By 2002, it had fallen to 7.7 percent. Only thirty-four of these largest one hundred firms were new to that list between 1955 and 1972, reflecting considerable stability. From 1972 to 2002, in contrast, the number of new entrants jumped to sixty-four. The dynamics of the economy are also revealed by the fact that retail companies jumped from eight on the list in 1972 to forty in 2002, while the percentage in manufacturing fell from 71 percent in 1972 to 30 percent in 2002.[29] Within the United States alone, government data collected at the local level suggests that the proportion of all employers with more than five hundred employees fell from 28 percent in 1970 to about 20 percent by the mid-1980s.[30]

Rising foreign competition also brought new competitors with new products and ideas, contributing to greater volatility in markets. Nothing illustrates the rise of global competition within the United States more clearly than the overall level of spending on imported merchandise, which rose by 300 percent from 1990 to 2004 (the overall economy grew about 40 percent in the same period).[31] In practice this meant that foreign companies had a much bigger share of the U.S. product market, adding to the number of players in each industry and increasing the number of innovations in products and marketing, thereby giving consumers many more choices. In automobiles, for example, in the early 1970s essentially three large domestic producers captured almost all of the product market; now, foreign companies have half the U.S. product market (see figure 3-1).

Greater levels of competition contributed to the second major change in the competitive environment: shorter production cycles with more-rapid changes in business strategy. Technology companies like Hewlett-Packard and medical companies like Medtronic reported that about 90 percent of their profits came from products less than one year old. As products change, the competencies needed to produce them can change as well. In the pharmaceutical industry, for example, the change from physical chemistry to biotechnology as a basis for new drugs created a demand for a new set of research and development capabilities and led to

FIGURE 3-1

Foreign-owned firms now account for more than half the U.S. car market

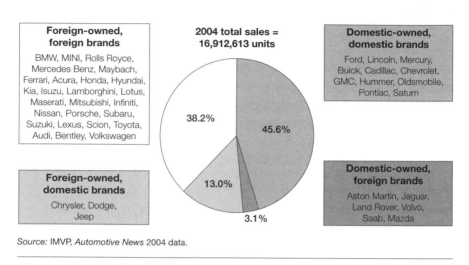

Foreign-owned, foreign brands
BMW, MINI, Rolls Royce, Mercedes Benz, Maybach, Ferrari, Acura, Honda, Hyundai, Kia, Isuzu, Lamborghini, Lotus, Maserati, Mitsubishi, Infiniti, Nissan, Porsche, Subaru, Suzuki, Lexus, Scion, Toyota, Audi, Bentley, Volkswagen

2004 total sales = 16,912,613 units

Domestic-owned, domestic brands
Ford, Lincoln, Mercury, Buick, Cadillac, Chevrolet, GMC, Hummer, Oldsmobile, Pontiac, Saturn

Foreign-owned, domestic brands
Chrysler, Dodge, Jeep

38.2%

45.6%

13.0%

3.1%

Domestic-owned, foreign brands
Aston Martin, Jaguar, Land Rover, Volvo, Saab, Mazda

Source: IMVP, *Automotive News* 2004 data.

the redundancy of another set. Takahiro Fujimoto of the University of Tokyo calculates, for example, that the lead times in product development in the auto industry declined from thirty months in the beginning of the 1990s to as little as twelve months now. Business strategies also are adjusted as new competitors enter markets.

Employers do not have time to develop the new skills they need internally when dramatic changes in products and strategies happen so quickly. So they turn to outside hiring to get those new skills. They also turn to outside hiring to get the managerial skills and experience to facilitate changes in their administrative operations. One way to think about these developments is that product life cycles have now become considerably shorter than the time it would take employees to retool their own skills significantly.

These changes contributed to a different model of doing business, what Lapide describes as "a change in focus . . . from 'selling what you make' toward 'making what you will sell.'"[32] To do this, you must figure out in advance what customers want. Zees de Baat, a forecaster in the fashion industry, reports that twenty-five years ago, even seasonal collections were sold on a "forward-order basis," meaning that companies did not begin production until orders had been placed. Little in the way of forecasting was required with those arrangements, and the same designs were sold sometimes for several years. Now, however, new collections come out six to ten times a year, as opposed to twice a year as in the past.[33] Ordering in advance is essentially dead.

Forecasting is much more difficult in this new environment. Here is one simple example: with companies selling more products tailored to different niches, they must now develop forecasts separately for more products—each of which has its own error rate—across more markets in which demand varies. Having more new products also complicates forecasting because forecasts rely on historical data, and new products have little with which to work. The more important problem is that these forecasts are not very accurate. The average error rate of forecasts at the level of the individual product is now about 33 percent only one year out.[34]

Changes in the Boundaries of the Firm

Changes in the boundaries of the firm, such as mergers and acquisitions, divestitures, and outsourcing, also disrupt planning for talent management. These changes often lead to dramatic and disruptive changes in the structure of the firm, causing turnover of executives and employees and altering the competencies and skills required for operations.

In the 1980s, based on academic research, companies were persuaded that divesting unrelated businesses and acquiring new ones with appropriate synergies could raise shareholder value. When a company is merged or acquired, as many as half the managerial and executive positions become redundant, and the incumbents are virtually always let go. Organizational structures are reconfigured, and their job ladders are broken, as are the career paths of those on them. Mergers and acquisitions have hit record levels not only in the United States but also worldwide almost every other year since the mid-1990s.

Divestitures are the flip side of acquisitions. The divestiture wave was driven originally by research in the 1980s showing that the financial performance of corporations improved when they shed unrelated businesses. The conglomerate wave that developed in the 1950s and 1960s was designed to stabilize corporate earnings by putting together unrelated businesses, with Gulf and Western as the prime example (oil, motion pictures, and everything in between). If investors wanted a diversified portfolio, the argument went, they could buy stocks in the separate companies. Divesting unrelated businesses and focusing on a common core of operations brought back the original volatility, and that made long-term workforce planning much less reliable. There is also a strong argument that at least some of the financial gains associated with these changes came from breaking the employment relationships and implicit contracts associated with lifetime employment, pension obligations not yet vested, and so on.[35]

Mergers, acquisitions, and divestitures disrupt any sophisticated efforts to manage talent. Debbie Seidman observed during her years as a human resources executive on Wall Street that the shift away from internal development coincided with the rise of mergers and acquisitions. "Companies that were thinking about growing through acquisitions don't necessarily want to do talent development," she says, because they don't know what set of employees they will inherit when the changes are taking place.[36]

The Rise in Outsourcing

Virtually any function can now be outsourced, and an enormous market has developed to outsource and "offshore" functions that were previously performed inside companies. Staffing agencies also lease employees having a wide array of skills, even CEOs, so that labor costs can be transformed from fixed to variable. Why bother developing an internal workforce when it may soon prove cheaper to outsource it?

This overall change in the business environment has meant that business strategy, and strategic planning in particular, as a planning function is no longer relevant. The idea that businesses can plan their strategies far in advance is far more the exception than the rule. Instead of planning, strategy is now much more of a reactive task, reacting to new circumstances and options that come from the environment: the CEO sees an opportunity for an acquisition, a market dries up unexpectedly or a competitor introduces a substantial innovation, an economy goes into a recession—these developments and others like them are almost impossible to predict, and they demand new responses and new strategies. In the process, the old "strategic plans" go out the window.

Jan Rivkin of Harvard Business School notes that for almost all the companies that conduct strategic planning it is a calendar-driven exercise ("time to generate a plan") that is more about negotiating a consensus of business proposals than articulating a true direction for the company. He also asserts that the real strategic process approximates an adaptive process that responds to options that present themselves from the evolving business environment.[37]

Stanford's Kathleen Eisenhardt studied the factors that enabled firms to respond quickly to changing circumstances. She concluded that the large firms with traditional and apparently sophisticated strategic planning departments were considerably slower than smaller firms, precisely because the large firms relied on forecasts and plans. It took a lot of time and energy to create the plans, and they were almost always wrong. The most adaptable and fastest-moving firms did not attempt to make long-term forecasts and plans but instead relied on real-time data and then responded to the changes they were seeing.[38] Adaptation and responsiveness trumped planning.

Within human resources per se, planning has had a similarly checkered record. A study of downsizing arrangements, for example, found that employers that had the most-sophisticated and most-detailed plans for workforce reductions actually had the worst outcomes. The more-detailed forecasts and plans turned out to be wrong in more significant ways than less-detailed plans, creating greater annoyance among employees and management.[39]

Evidence of the Collapse

Facing an internal glut of talent, the sharp recession of 1981, and changes in the economic environment, employers moved aggressively to break lifetime employment arrangements with their employees. As late as the end of the 1970s, survey evidence from the Conference Board indicated that management's priorities in setting employment practices were to build a loyal, stable workforce. But a decade later, that priority had shifted to increasing organizational performance and reducing costs.[40] The most powerful evidence in this regard is another Conference Board survey, in which more than two-thirds of the large employers in the sample reported that they had changed their practices and no longer offered employment security; only 3 percent said that they still offered job security to employees.[41]

The most important manifestation of this new relationship was downsizing. The term *downsizing* was at first a euphemism for layoffs, but it later came to mean something different. Whereas layoffs had been seen as a temporary response to downturns in business resulting from recessions focused on hourly workers, downsizing was a permanent reduction in jobs, and it did not appear to differentiate between levels in the organization. The U.S. Bureau of Labor Statistics did not even measure permanent job losses (as distinct from recession-based and temporary losses) until after 1984 because of the assumption that workers who had lost their jobs would get them back when business recovered. Similarly, the level of *contingent work*, defined by the Bureau of Labor Statistics as jobs that are expected to end soon, was not measured before the 1990s. Contingent work by this definition remained roughly constant at about 4.3 percent of the employed workforce through the late 1990s, even as the overall unemployment rate fell and the labor market tightened.[42]

The American Management Association (AMA) surveyed its member companies about downsizing during the 1990s. It found that the incidence of downsizing increased virtually every year through 1996 despite the economic expansion of the 1990s. Roughly half the companies reported downsizing, and 40 percent had downsized in two or more years over the previous six.[43] Other surveys report roughly similar rates. The scale of these job cuts was unprecedented in a period of economic expansion. The rate was about the same in 1993–1995, a period of significant economic expansion and prosperity in the economy as a whole, as compared with the 1981–1983 recession, the worst downturn since the Great Depression.[44]

White-collar and managerial employees experienced the most fundamental change from this new approach, because they were the ones with the most protections to lose. There has been a sharp rise in unemployment for white-collar employees compared with other groups, as well as increased risk of job loss for individuals.[45] This is certainly among the strongest evidence that whatever special protection this employee group had in the past is gone. White-collar and managerial employees faced much the same insecurity and instability as production workers, a profound change that undermined what had been the very basis of the distinction between white-collar and blue-collar workers.

That distinction stems from the New Deal–era Fair Labor Standards Act, which is based on the assumption that production workers needed legislative protections that white-collar workers did not because the latter were protected by firms. White-collar employees who kept their jobs also saw internal careers evaporate as job ladders shrank; moreover, restructuring disrupted the remaining promotion tracks, and external hiring for senior positions blocked advancement. Employers abandoned virtually everything about the old system, even the rhetoric about their responsibility to employees.

Figure 3-2 shows the downsizing experience of the most stable workers: those who had been with their employers for more than twenty years. It compares the experience in the steepest downturn in modern times— the recession of 1981–1982—to the period of the most rapid growth in a generation: 1999–2000. It is no surprise that the displacement rate for blue-collar workers is roughly twice as high during the recession as during the boom. What is remarkable is that there is almost no difference in the rate of layoff for white-collar workers in the two periods. Reengineering (discussed next) and restructuring generally explain why white-collar job losses remain high even in a booming economy.

After the 1981 recession, companies began to find new ways to get work done with fewer people, a process that became known as *reengineering*. Work systems that empowered employees, such as cross-functional teams, eliminated supervisory positions and widened spans of control. Information systems eliminated many of the internal control functions of middle-management positions, and decentralizing operations through the creation of profit centers and similar arrangements further reduced the need for central administration. Corporate hierarchies flattened in the 1990s.[46] As headquarters were deflated and power was decentralized, the need for managers was reduced.

Once the option of outside hiring became credible, then it became possible, indeed obligatory, to question the costs and benefits of internal

FIGURE 3-2

Downsizing of long-tenured workers

*Displacement rates of long-tenured workers twenty years and older
by occupation group of lost job, 1981–1982 and 1999–2000*

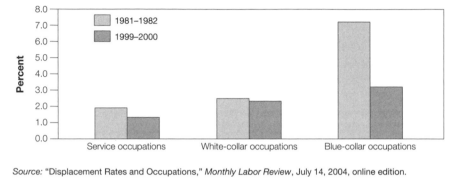

Source: "Displacement Rates and Occupations," *Monthly Labor Review*, July 14, 2004, online edition.

development. At the same time, the squeeze on company costs was growing from what became known as the *shareholder value* movement: pressure from shareholders to maximize profits. Institutional investors now
held so much stock even in large companies that if they disapproved of
management practices they could not dump their stock without depress-
ing its price. As a result, they pressured corporate executives of underper-
forming companies to improve their stock prices, forcing CEOs out of
their jobs if they failed to do so. Legal decisions made maximizing shareholder value the singular goal for directors of public companies and the
executives they managed, and also made shareholders the only stake-
holders to whom companies were legally accountable. New financial instruments such as junk bonds enabled hostile takeovers of companies
that were not maximizing shareholder value. Investors and analysts seem
to be persuaded that cutting jobs raises shareholder value even though
the hard evidence on that point is decidedly mixed. New accounting
techniques, such as economic value added, sought to maximize shareholder value and punish holding fixed costs, including the fixed investments in employees.[47]

   The combined effect of these changes was that firms were under pressure to squeeze out costs. A prime target was employee development. Few

companies had the internal accounting information to demonstrate that their human resource programs paid off, let alone show the value of an entire system of developing employees. But they did identify costs, and employee development now became a cost center. With no way to show that development paid off and with outside hiring as an attractive option, the programs were scaled back with each round of cost cutting.

Outside Hiring

To the extent that there was any systematic thinking about talent management in the 1980s to mid-1990s, it was directed at outside hiring. The just-in-time approach to talent extended to leadership positions, especially when companies were looking to change direction or strategy. New strategies frequently require competencies that do not exist internally, and companies understandably look outside to find employees who have those competencies.

CA, a New York–based technology company, grew rapidly in the 1990s, arguably too quickly to make use of systematic internal development practices. CEO John Swainson reports that when he arrived in 2004, when CA was already a midsized company with about sixteen thousand employees, the response to any vacancy was, "We'll hire someone into that role."[48] The company sought outsiders to fill its openings, he explains, in part because it did not have a clear sense of its own internal talent—who was capable of doing which other jobs.

The extent of outside hiring in the United States is significant: 2.7 percent of the U.S. workforce changes employers each month, and about 30 percent, each year.[49] A recent study by Taleo, an employment software firm, found that in the large companies that use its software, roughly two-thirds of all job vacancies were filled by outside hires. A survey of recruiters in the late 1990s found a sizable increase in the proportion of employers that sought experienced workers for entry-level jobs, those positions that traditionally were filled by new college graduates.[50] My examination of proprietary surveys of employers finds that they report a greater interest in outside hiring to meet skill needs.[51]

Anecdotes about employers poaching talent from one another are legion. Townships on the New Jersey shore in the late 1990s hired lifeguards away from one another during the summer; nurses receive job ads faxed into operating rooms; a Gulf state in 2007 attempted to hire the entire urban planning department away from the Singapore government. For another example, see "Teams for Sale."

An important development accelerating outside hiring for lower-level and traditional positions has been the rise of nondegree credentials provided by nonacademic organizations (such as Microsoft) that certify skills and proficiency in technical areas. Millions of these credentials have been issued, easily outpacing the rate of academic degrees. The consequence is to increase the ease with which individuals can move across organizations by certifying that they can perform tasks central to standard jobs with a high level of proficiency.[52]

At the executive level, boards and CEOs often bring in outsiders precisely to change strategies and practices. Evidence from Deloitte Consulting suggests that the average U.S. employer spent about fifty times as much to recruit an average middle manager with a salary of $100,000 as they spent in total training their average employee.[53] One interesting proxy for the growth of outside hiring is the fact that the revenues from corporate recruiting firms that perform outside searches tripled during the mid-1990s.[54]

Teams for Sale

The following ad appeared on eBay (item number 3868319541): "An award-winning, clear-thinking, bottom-line-focused creative-services organization is now immediately available to rock your bottom line." It was placed by a team of employees leaving PeopleSoft, who wanted to be hired as a group. (Unfortunately, the winning bid was only $108.30.)[a] Furthermore, *Harvard Business Review* offers advice on how to execute these "lift outs" of entire teams of employees from competitors.[b]

a. Jena McGregor, "Engineering the Great Escape," *Fast Company*, December 2005, 103.

b. Boris Groysberg and Robin Abrahams, "Lift Outs: How to Acquire a High-Functioning Team," *Harvard Business Review* (December 2006).

We now have an employment services industry that manages this outside labor market, putting together workers and employers. It includes temporary help, professional employer organizations (which take on the legal obligations of an employer but not their day-to-day management), and employment placement agencies of various kinds.[55] This industry itself employed 3.6 million people in the United States in April 2004, with revenues exceeding $100 billion.[56] The size of the executive search business within that industry is hard to estimate, because there are many small and privately held companies. The best estimates suggest that revenues are about $11.5 billion worldwide, with more than half generated in the United States.[57] Hunt-Scanlon consultants report that in 2003, the combined revenue of the twenty-five largest U.S. search firms was $1.2 billion. In the United States between 2001 and 2003, more than half (54 percent) of companies relied on executive search firms to fill executive-level jobs paying more than $150,000.[58]

Greater use of outside hiring, then, was both a cause and a consequence of the decline of the traditional model of talent management. Outside hiring reduced the need for internal development and caused retention problems that made it too expensive to justify internal development. Once the internal development models were gone, companies had no choice except to hire from the outside.

This is perhaps most noticeably so at the executive level. Studies of large, publicly traded firms that had historically relied on internal succession found that outsider CEOs became especially prominent—approximately 25 percent in the 1990s.[59] A different study, also of large firms, reported that outsider CEOs represented 30 percent of all CEOs by the late 1990s and that the rise of outside hiring of CEOs was related to the rising demand for managerial skills that translated across organizations, as opposed to company-specific skills.[60] Worldwide turnover of CEOs in the twenty-five hundred largest publicly held corporations broke records in 2004 and 2005, with more than 15 percent of CEOs leaving, a figure 70 percent higher than in the preceding decade. The region with the highest turnover of executives was, perhaps surprisingly, Japan, at slightly less than 20 percent. One-sixth of all the departing CEOs did so as a result of a merger or acquisition. Reports suggest that about one-third were pushed out because of failure to meet performance targets.[61] But these estimates are likely to be wildly understated, because companies go to great lengths to cover up the real reasons executives leave.

Figure 3-3 compares the careers of the top ten executives in the *Fortune* 100 companies—the largest companies most wedded to models of internal development—in 1980 and in 2001. The figure shows sharp declines in the percentage who had been lifetime employees, and even sharper declines in tenure—in part because executives were now advancing more quickly.

But these overall declines mask some interesting patterns, particularly the difference between the very oldest firms—the twenty-six who were listed in the *Fortune* 100 in both 1980 and 2001—and the rest, as shown in figure 3-4. In the oldest firms, there appears to be little, if any, difference in the important outcomes associated with attachment to the firm. The top executives were just as likely to be lifers and to be with the firm just as long in 2001 as in 1980. These are the academy companies, such as

FIGURE 3-3

Decline in lifetime employment for top executives

Descriptive statistics for top executives. Career patterns 1980 and 2001, full sample

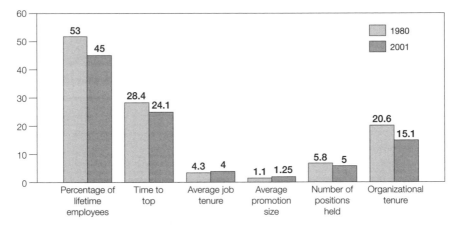

Source: "The Path to the Top: Changes in the Attributes and Careers of Corporate Executives, 1980 to 2001," *Harvard Business Review*, January 2005, 25–32.

FIGURE 3-4

Lifetime employment for top executives in older firms

Top executive attributes and experiences in 1980 and 2001 for the twenty-six companies in both the 1980 and 2001 samples

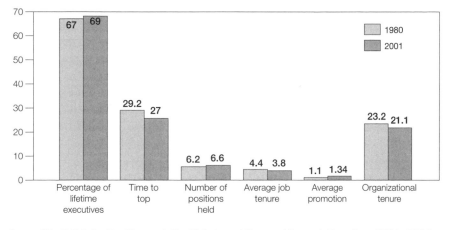

Source: "The Path to the Top: Changes in the Attributes and Careers of Corporate Executives, 1980 to 2001," *Harvard Business Review*, January 2005, 25–32.

General Electric, Exxon, and IBM—the companies still using talent management practices from the 1950s.

Of course, if the overall pattern across all big companies is changing but nothing is changing among the oldest subset of companies, then the changes in the newer companies must be huge in order to drive movement in the average. Indeed, that is what we find. When we compare those companies younger than thirty years with those older than thirty years, even in the *Fortune* 100, we see stark differences: only 17 percent of the top ten executives are lifers in the younger companies, compared with 52 percent in the older companies. Average tenure in the younger companies is about nine years compared with eighteen in the older ones. This suggests that the newer companies and the growing companies have experiences that are not at all like those of the academy companies. Even in academy companies like GE and IBM, we know that their practices have changed considerably, especially the end of lifetime job security and the expansion of outside hiring. Those practices have not yet affected the very top executives, perhaps because their careers began decades earlier.

Outside hiring of executives is particularly important for talent issues, because the new leaders often bring with them their own team of managers, blocking succession to all the executive roles that are filled from the outside. This process undercuts the development programs whose goal was to fill those executive positions. Outside hiring of executives also shifts the attention of managers to networks of potential employers outside the firm as they get the message that the way to get ahead involves outside hiring. When top executives come from the outside, they also are much more likely to make changes in the direction of the firm and, at lower levels, in policies and practices. Turnover of executives therefore means turnover of business direction and practices. Long-term planning suffers when strategies are changed. The turnover of human resource executives is especially important for talent management, because new executives are more likely to change whatever programs are in place for talent management, perhaps to put their own stamp on them.

Virtually every lateral hire is pulled from another employer and typically is unexpected from its perspective. The departure causes retention problems that we discuss more thoroughly in chapter 4, but the basic issue is that when employees quit, their current employers lose their investment in those employees. Additionally, any development or succession planning that includes the employee is disrupted.

Online Job Searches

By increasing the flow of information about jobs, online recruiting has helped boost the movement of individuals across jobs. This no doubt has positive outcomes for individuals, but it exacerbates the problem of planning for talent issues by increasing the challenge of retention. Online job search began with the explosion of personal, career-related information that is available on the World Wide Web, making it easier for employers to find possible candidates who were not necessarily looking for a new job. Many people have their resumes posted on their personal Web pages, but more important for recruiters are objective sources of Web-based information, such as industry associations or—better yet—those associated with individual employers that report information about workplace achievements.

Some of these search techniques can be somewhat sinister, such as "flipping the URL," which means getting inside a company's internal Web pages to look for information such as "employee of the month" awards or other indications of competence. In the search for these so-called passive applicants (in contrast to those who are actively looking and applying for jobs), Internet recruiters during the tight labor market of the late 1990s were aided by a slew of new resources, such as sites that paid participants for confidential leads and references about colleagues who might be interested in moving. Some companies were creative in finding ways to get potential applicants to reveal their abilities. Cisco Systems, for example, was well known for techniques such as holding contests online with prizes oriented for Internet engineers, in part as a way of identifying creative potential employees among those who responded.

Online information solved what had been the basic problem of outside hiring from the days of the first search firms: the issue of adverse selection. Like the Groucho Marx joke about not wanting to join any club that would have him as a member, recruiters want only the best candidates, and they tend to be ones who have no reason to move. In part, it's because they are loyal, and in part it's because their current employers appreciate how good they are.

Census data in figure 3-5 show that slightly more than one in every ten individuals aged sixteen and older used the Internet between January and October 2003 to search for a job. On a typical Monday—the peak time for job searches—Monster.com reports that in 2004 about 20 million people were searching for jobs on its Web site, and there are thousands of job boards where resumes and job openings are posted.[62] Proprietary research suggests that about two-thirds of the people searching job boards are passive candidates. Some estimates suggest that as much as 10 percent of the time individuals spend on the Internet is spent searching for jobs.

The number of executives who say that they have their resume posted online jumped from 52 percent in 2000 to 75 percent in 2002. A comparison of more than twenty-five hundred users in 2003 and 2004 of BlueSteps, a

FIGURE 3-5

Searching for a job on the Internet

Percent of civilian noninstitutional population who used the Internet to search for a job, by selected characteristics, October 2003

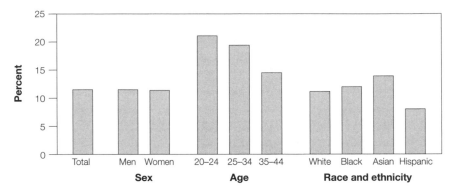

Source: "Job Search Via the Internet," *Monthly Labor Review* online edition, http://www.bls.gov/opub/ted/2005/aug/wk1/art05.htm.

career management service for senior executives on the Association of Executive Search Consultants Web page, showed that the salary bracket between $200,000 and $300,000 had the greatest number of executives who had posted their resumes (29 percent).[63]

It's easy to see the retention challenge posed by online recruiting. In the past, employees who got angry with their bosses or companies might feel like quitting but would calm down before typing up their resume, identifying the right contact information for potential employers, mailing off an application, and receiving a reply. Now they can post their resumes on a job board in minutes and be contacted by potential employers within twenty-four hours.

One implication is that employers need to be much more active in heading off the issues that push employees to think about moving, because once employees look, there is no time to respond. Even if employees don't leave, receiving all this information about job opportunities is likely to change them in a variety of ways. Research on organizational commitment (see the discussion in the next section) has demonstrated that having more job choices reduces the commitment that employees have to their current jobs, and online recruiting makes it much easier to get many job offers quickly.

Declining Attachment Between Employers and Employees

The churning of employees based on layoffs and outside hiring shortens the length of time that the employee and employer are together and increases the uncertainty of those attachments, thereby complicating the task of talent management. About two-thirds of all job changes take place because an employee quits, almost always moving immediately to a new job. Most observers are surprised to find that roughly 40 percent of U.S. workers have been with their current employers less than two years, a figure that has changed little in recent decades.

If we compare the 1980s with earlier periods, we find that the average amount of time that a typical employee spent with an employer was similar; layoffs were higher, but quits were lower because jobs were scarce. Data from the mid-1990s show declines in average tenure, especially for managerial employees but even for the workforce as a whole.[64] The largest declines in tenure are for older white men, the group historically most protected by internal labor markets. For example, for men approaching retirement age (fifty-eight to sixty-three) only 29 percent had been with the same employer for ten years or more as compared with 47 percent of the same group in 1969.[65] The percentage of the workforce with long-tenure jobs (ten years or more) declined slightly from the late 1970s through 1993 and then fell sharply through the mid-1990s.[66] The rate of dismissals also increased sharply for older workers with more tenure, doubling for workers aged forty-five to fifty-four.[67] The finding that tenure declined for managerial jobs is especially supportive of the arguments for the erosion of internal career systems.[68]

Figure 3-6, drawn from the Current Population Survey of the Bureau of the Census, shows the changes in tenure across the economy as a whole through the 1990s. This chart includes all workers; managers and corporate employees in general represent only a small part of this number, perhaps less than 10 percent. Although tenure for men declined noticeably, tenure for women has not declined and indeed appears to have increased,

FIGURE 3-6

Changes in job tenure in the 1990s

Median tenure for employed men and women twenty-five and older, selected years, 1983–2000

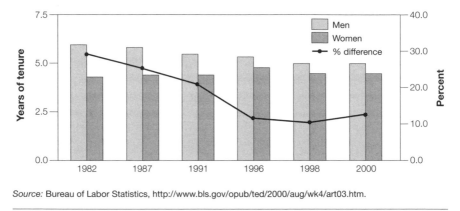

Source: Bureau of Labor Statistics, http://www.bls.gov/opub/ted/2000/aug/wk4/art03.htm.

because women are now less likely to quit their jobs when they have children, in part because of new legislated protections.[69]

Changes in tenure for men are more dramatic when we examine the changes within age groups. Because older men quit jobs less frequently, the aging of the workforce over the past decade or so should have worked to *increase* average tenure in the workforce as a whole. Comparing levels within age groups over time controls for that effect. The striking point again in figure 3-7 is that tenure is declining the most among those older age groups that historically have had the greatest attachment to their employers, especially the cohort closest to retirement.

The most persuasive evidence of a change in the employment relationship comes from studies that follow a cohort of individuals over time. A recent longitudinal study of workers born from 1957 to 1964 indicates how unstable jobs are even for those we think of as in the "prime age" workforce. Between the ages of eighteen and thirty-eight, this group of younger baby boomers changed jobs every two years.[70] When these workers were well into middle age, a large percentage of them were still experiencing the same level of job instability and insecurity. Of those who started a new job in the 1990s, for example, 40 percent saw that job end

FIGURE 3-7

Changes in job tenure of older men

Change in median years of tenure, 1983 to 1998, adult men by age

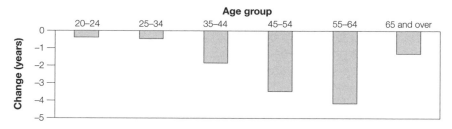

Source: Bureau of Labor Statistics, "Median tenure declines among older men, 1983–2000," http://www.bls.gov/opub/ted/2000/aug/wk4/art05.htm.

Median years of tenure with current employer, men aged fifty-five to sixty-four, 1983–2000

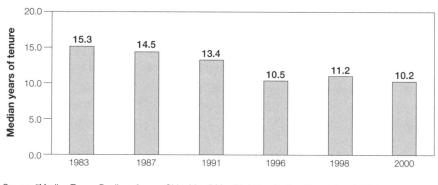

Source: "Median Tenure Declines Among Older Men," *Monthly Labor Review*, September 1, 2000, http://www.bls.gov/opub/ted/2000/aug/wk4/art05.htm.

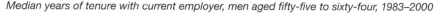

in less than a year; only 30 percent who started a new job saw it last more than five years.[71]

The most powerful of these studies compares the experience of young men from 1966 to 1981 to a later group from 1979 through 1994. In the earlier period, about 16 percent of workers had stable job histories, as defined by having one or two employers over their careers; in the later period, the percentage fell to 11 percent. In the earlier period, 15 percent of the workforce had seven or more employers, a figure that rose to 21 percent in the later period. When we compare equivalent workers, the odds on leaving a job—being dismissed or quitting—after two years was 43 percent greater in the latter cohort.[72] Another study indicates that members of the more recent cohort experienced considerably greater changes in their jobs and occupations than did those in the preceding generation even when they remained with the same employer.[73] A third study finds workers in the more recent period changing industries and occupations more frequently than in the preceding generation.[74] Collectively, they suggest the instability that makes it difficult to recoup long-term investments in employees and in career planning.

One of the important attributes of the old system of internal talent management was that compensation was organized to form distinct and clear hierarchies associated with promotions. The technique of *job evaluation* described the tools used to fashion wages across jobs so that senior positions in promotion ladders always paid more than lower positions, thereby encouraging upward mobility. One of the facts about wage growth was that individuals did better by staying with their current employers than by moving, because staying put increased the possibilities for promotion. The steady progression of wages based on seniority or tenure was one of the hallmarks of internal systems. But by the early 1990s, there was no longer any advantage to inside moves as compared with those across employers.[75] The apparent decline in the return to tenure with the same employer is further evidence of the decline of traditional pay and employment relationships.

Researchers studying the semiconductor industry, for example, found a decline in the wage premium paid to experienced workers. Among the explanations are that new technical skills are becoming more important and that those skills are learned not inside the firm but outside, typically in higher education.[76] In aggregate data, the returns to seniority—that is, tenure with the same employer—have collapsed in recent years, by about $3,000 annually from the 1970s to the 1980s for workers having ten years of seniority.[77]

Another way to describe this effect is that the costs of voluntary job changes dropped dramatically. Workers who changed employers every other year saw almost the same rise in earnings in the late 1980s as did those who kept the same job for ten years.[78] Further, the probability that employees who quit will find jobs that offer a large pay raise has increased by 5 percent while the probability that those who are dismissed will suffer a large decline in their pay has risen by 17 percent over the preceding decade.[79] These results suggest that a good, lifetime match between an employee and a single employer is becoming less important in determining an employee's long-term success. By default, what must be gaining importance are factors outside the relationship with an individual employer—factors associated with the outside market.

Pension plans have been the aspect of compensation benefit with the most important implications for the employment relationship, because they represent a continuing obligation to employees even if employment ends (at least for vested employees). Although overall pension coverage has declined over time, more important has been the shift in the nature of pensions from *defined benefit* plans, whereby workers earn the right to predetermined benefit levels according to their years of service, to *defined contribution* plans, whereby employers make fixed contributions to a retirement fund for each employee, especially 401(k) programs, in which employees contribute directly to their retirement funds.[80] With this shift, the employer no longer bears the risk of guaranteeing a stream of benefits. The employee does. And employees need no longer stay with a company to gain access to their retirement contributions. The employer's obligations to the employee end with employment, signaling a move away from long-term obligations and relationships. In 1980, 84 percent of full-time workers in the United States were covered by a defined benefit pension plan. But by 2003, the figure was down to 33 percent.[81]

Finally, it is worth noting that a growing percentage of the workforce is not employees at all. In 2006, for example, 7.4 percent of the workforce was independent contractors, up from 6.4 percent in 2001.[82]

Little In-House Development of Talent

Direct evidence about the extent of employee development, even of training, is poor in the United States, and there is little consistent information about how it has changed over time. What we know suggests that training is not very extensive: only about one in four young adults aged twenty-two to twenty-nine received any training provided by their employers in a five-year period from 1986 to 1991; those who received training got about thirty-six hours of training per year, a little less than one week.[83] The average annual amount of training on management issues received by employees was 1.6 hours in 1995.[84]

Most employers report that they offer some training, although how many workers get it is another matter. Only about 17 percent of employees report that they had some formal training over the course of a year in the mid-1990s. The training that is provided seems oriented to the employer's unique needs, as opposed to developing skills that are transferable.[85] There is some evidence that employers are making substantially fewer investments in new hires now compared with the past, particularly in the extent of training for new jobs.[86] According to *Training* magazine's periodic survey of employer training in 2003, training expenditures had declined 6 percent over the preceding year and were lower than the nominal level in the mid-1990s, not counting the additional effect of inflation.[87] At the level of production workers, apprenticeship programs to teach craft skills—once a central part of employee development in the United States— appear to have declined so much that the U.S. Bureau of Labor Statistics no longer reports information on them.

The big concern is that employers will back away from even the limited investments they now make in employees because of concerns, first, that changes in direction, strategy, and so on make it difficult to know how long the employee competencies will be needed and, second, that declining employee tenure will make it more difficult to capture returns on those investments. We have some evidence about the effects of changes in technology on training, and possibly because new technology requires new skills from workers, it has not led to a reduction in training investments.[88]

Data on training outside the United States are somewhat better. A 2002 study of skills in the United Kingdom produced a critical assessment of employer-provided training and development, which had declined following the end of a statutory system wherein employers had to contribute a fixed percentage of their wage bill every year to training. Commenting on employers' interest in training, the head of the Sector Skills Development Agency identified the key issue: "It's how quickly employers can get a return that counts."[89] The annual survey of employers concerning the skills of their employees in the United Kingdom found about the same percentage offering training as in the United States (65 percent) but also found that about 25 percent of all vacancies persisted because of a failure to find workers having the right skills. In about 25 percent of those cases, the employers blamed their own failure to train and develop employees; no doubt a more objective assessment could put the figure much higher, given that 35 percent do no training whatsoever.[90] U.K. business leaders assert that their biggest concern in the area of skills is with management and leadership development.[91]

Consequences for Talent Management Programs

The changes just outlined have had a profound impact on talent planning and talent management practices. An interesting 1984 study surveyed large and midsized employers on their talent management practices and compared the results to a similar survey that had covered practices in the late 1970s, roughly six years before. There was a sharp decline in sophisticated programs for forecasting talent needs. The percentage of employers that used statistical regression models to forecast talent needs declined from 30 percent to 9 percent; the use of sophisticated Markov chain models fell from 22 percent to 6 percent; and operations research tools in general declined from use in 23 percent of employers to only 4.5 percent. The authors found a statistically significant decline in the percentage of companies that had succession planning practices in place in the two periods, supporting the evidence presented earlier. The biggest problem companies saw in doing succession planning effectively was a lack of precision in their business plans—inaccurate forecasts. But 66 percent of employers still had them in 1984.[92] By 2005, a similar survey found that only 29 percent of employers had succession planning programs.[93]

How are employees reacting to these changes? Some observers suggest that the economic decline associated with the 2001 recession has made employees more interested in job security, less interested in job-hopping, and more interested in staying with a single employer. A national probability survey of employees conducted in 2003, when the job market was at a low point, asked what would be required in compensation to get them to leave their current job and take an equivalent position elsewhere. The results of conjoint analysis, shown in figure 3-8, suggest that even in

2003, large proportions of employees were willing to leave for small amounts of additional compensation. Especially noteworthy was their short-term orientation: a $1,000 bonus would move as many employees to a new job as would a potential salary increase of $6,000 in five years. This orientation reflects a lack of trust that a current employment relationship will pan out in the future.

There is a great deal of concern among employers about the perceived loyalty of the next generation of workers. As noted in chapter 2, a study of college graduate job seekers reported that their number 1 concern in an employer was career advancement, followed closely by job security.[94] Surveys of college graduate job seekers conducted more recently report that their number 1 interest in an employer now is to provide a good reference for a position elsewhere—still career advancement, but in a very different manner.[95]

I surveyed 486 members of the Wharton MBA class of 2006 about their employment experiences; most had worked for five or six years before entering the MBA program. What was striking about the results was less the respondents' own footloose view of mobility—on average, they said they would wait less than ten months for opportunities to develop if their

FIGURE 3-8

Compensation that would motivate employees to leave

I would change jobs for . . .

I would leave for . . .	25% of workers		50% of workers		75% of workers	
	Units	Dollars	Units	Dollars	Units	Dollars
Stock grant face value	50 shares	$500	100 shares	$1,000	1,000 shares	$10,000
Vacation days	7 days	$652	10 days	$1,400	15 days	$2,769
Bonus opportunity	$1,000	$1,000	$5,000	$5,000	$10,000	$10,000
Salary increase	10%	$3,750	20%	$7,500	35%	$15,000
Potential salary in five years	$6,000	$6,000	$15,000	$15,000	$35,000	$35,000
One-time retirement contribution	$5,000	$5,000	$20,000	$20,000	$50,000	$50,000

Source: Sibson & Company, 2003.

prospects for advancement appeared to be blocked—than their percep-tion of career prospects with their most recent employer. The average or-ganization they worked for had twenty thousand employees, so most were large enough to have sophisticated talent and career planning practices. The students themselves are among the highest-performing and most ca-pable employees one could imagine. Yet when asked a straightforward question—"Could you identify the next step up in the organization for you if you had stayed with your previous employer?"—30 percent said that they had no idea what it would have been (see figure 3-9). Even more re-markable is how few thought they could have become leaders if they had stayed with their last employers. (It is unlikely that the low response stems from undue modesty on the part of the MBA students.) The best explana-tion is that these organizations did not promote from within for these jobs, even for these exceptional candidates.

More revealing of attitudes toward loyalty was a study of the behavior of executives in the financial services industry.[96] Here the question was how many of these executives would be willing to take the invitation from an executive search firm to become a candidate for a position else-where. In this context, the executives learned relatively little about the potential position before responding, so their answers reflect their attach-ment to their current organization. We found not only that a majority (52 percent) of the executives said yes and were willing to begin the process of becoming a candidate and leaving their current organization, but also that the willingness to say yes actually increased the higher up an individ-ual was in the hierarchy. The lowest-level employees in the study with

FIGURE 3-9

Wharton's students' views of their most recent jobs

- Percent who could identify the next promotion: 69%
  - 30% had "no idea"

- Percent who thought they had a good chance of getting that promotion: 69%
  - 31% said "no"

- Percent who thought they could become a leader if they stayed with their company: 63%
  - 37% said "no"

- Percent of their executives who came from within: 40%

- How long they would wait for opportunity: 10 months

manager titles said yes about 39 percent of the time; executive vice presidents said yes about two-thirds of the time (see figure 3-10).

The fact that current executives seem just as footloose as MBA students when it comes to changing employers suggests that generational differences are not the main factor in the lack of loyalty to current employers. Current executives as well as those of the next generation are not willing to be the loyal Organization Men (and now women) of the preceding generation, who waited for the company to plan their careers. This development complicates the talent management challenge for employers, because it means that their internal supply of talent is not stable, reliable, or predictable.

Talent Management Now

The evidence explains why the talent management models of the 1950s broke down and no longer work. If we cannot make long-term plans with respect to business needs, it is next to impossible to do so with human capital. In response, employers have moved toward human capital models that rely heavily on the outside market. They have effectively moved from a model of planning to a model of shopping for talent. Unfortunately, the shopping model also has plenty of drawbacks. Searching for candidates takes time and money, and it means that you must rely on the supply of talent that happens to be available in the market at the mo-

FIGURE 3-10

Percentage of executives willing to consider becoming a candidate for a position at another employer

Current position	Percentage willing to be a candidate
CEO	55.2
EVP	64.7
SVP	54.1
VP	46.8
Other	49.8

Source: Peter Cappelli and Monika Hamori, "Executive Loyalty and Job Search," working paper, Wharton School, Center for Human Resources, Philadelphia, 2006.

ment. Tom Clardy, vice president for human resources at the TV shopping giant QVC, describes their talent challenge now: "The biggest problem we have is that the big retail companies no longer have management development programs. That had been a great source of talent for us."[97]

The fundamental problem employers face in the modern competitive business environment is managing uncertainty. In the next chapter, we begin to construct a new approach for managing talent that addresses the challenge of finding cost-effective ways to anticipate and deliver the talent you need in the context of highly uncertain operating environments.

An International Comparison

It is interesting by way of comparison to see what has happened to talent management practices in other countries. In the United Kingdom and especially in Europe, for example, legal constraints make it difficult to lay off and dismiss employees. That, in turn, makes it difficult to use outside hiring as a talent strategy, and this might keep the focus more closely on internal development.

The use of three practices—career planning for individuals, succession planning for organizations, and high-potential, or "high-flyer," programs—seems higher than in the United States, although the variation across countries is extraordinary, as figure 3-A indicates. Only about one-third of companies in the European Union (EU) countries have formal career planning; more of them, perhaps 40 percent, use succession planning. Germany tops this list, with roughly two-thirds of employers using succession planning. The use of high-potential programs is considerably lower, less than 30 percent; Spain tops this list, with almost two-thirds of employers having them.[1]

The country whose economic circumstances and legal framework are the most similar to those of the United States is the United Kingdom. Here during the 1990s we see slight declines in the incidence of succession planning and high-potential programs and a slight increase in career planning. The 2006 U.K. training and development survey conducted by

Careers and human resource management—a European perspective

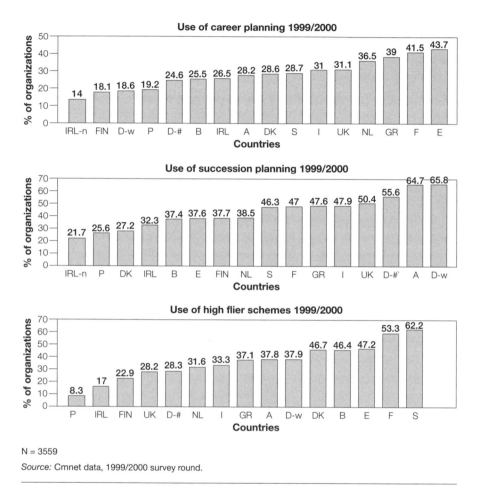

N = 3559

Source: Cmnet data, 1999/2000 survey round.

the Chartered Institute for Personnel Development reports that 60 percent of U.K. employers have no formal plan for developing talent, similar to the United States, and that 49 percent report no talent management activities.[2]

Assuming that the countries of the European Union make greater use of traditional talent management practices, particularly planning-related practices, than does the United States, it raises the fascinating and open question as to whether the EU countries lag behind the United States in the sense that many of the changes in the way U.S. business operates may eventually come to the EU and undermine these practices as well; are the EU countries ahead of the United States in that it will (as argued next) eventually have to reestablish talent management practices? Or are they simply on a different path because of different regulatory practices and economic circumstances?

A comparison with the experience of Singapore offers additional insights. Singapore's approach to talent management begins with Lee Kuan Yew's memoirs, in which he noted that for "a small resource-poor country like Singapore, with two million people at independence in 1965, talent is a defining factor."[3] He describes his interest in and appreciation of the management practices used by multinational companies operating in Singapore to develop their own pools of talent. The most important of those practices, at least for the government, concerned the selection and development of leaders. Lee applied many of these talent management principles to the running of the country.

Yet even the companies with the most systematic talent management practices seem to have a difficult time holding on to talent. Estimates of managerial turnover in Singapore suggest that it has averaged around 30 percent for at least a decade. Most companies lose a great many managerial employees in whom they have made substantial investments. Where they go is also clear. There is almost a pipeline that takes employees from the large firms that invest in talent to the smaller firms that do not. It's not clear how much of this is a "push" in the form of employees who feel their advancement prospects are blocked, or a "pull" from smaller firms that need skills and cannot develop them internally in an efficient way. But there is no doubt a well-beaten path from the pre-executive ranks at large companies into the executive ranks of smaller ones.

The surprise is the extent to which the companies in Singapore appear willing to reinvest in programs of internal talent development. Virtually all these companies still talk about talent management as if internal development is the norm and outside hiring will remain the exception. Some talk explicitly about rebuilding lifetime careers. An explanation suggests that the current arrangements work for Singapore even though they may not work for the individual companies. The larger companies have the scale and the resources to develop managerial talent. The fact that they lose much of that talent to smaller companies represents something of a subsidy that helps the rest of the economy.

Why do the larger companies continue to do it? It is because the government wants them to do so. Through its influence on boards of directors, especially at the listed companies, and then spread through social norms, the government ensures that this transfer of talent continues because it benefits the broader economy and society.

The example of Singapore points out a more general concern about talent management in larger countries like the United States. There, much the same transfer of talent from large corporations to smaller firms has taken place. The entire Silicon Valley high-tech economy can be traced to executives who left large corporations to begin start-ups. Similar events are occurring in the biotech industry as well as entrepreneurial companies across the economy. As the corporations reduce their efforts to develop talent, the pool of individuals having managerial competencies diminishes.

The pool is so big in the United States that it took quite a while to notice any change. When the economy began to take off in the 1990s, however, the complaints about a talent shortage began to surface. As described earlier, there is no shortage of people nor of college graduates. The most significant complaints are focused at the managerial and executive levels, even from executive search firms, which report difficulties in finding candidates who are prepared for advanced positions. The rise of business education provides something of a substitute. But the work-based competencies associated with talent management programs are difficult to duplicate. In this sense, the concern about the decline of talent management has implications that go beyond the individual firm to the economy as a whole.

PART TWO

A New Model of Talent Management

The Four Principles for Matching Talent Supply and Demand

4

The Make-Versus-Buy
Decision

Chapter 3 lays out the talent management challenge facing employers: it is extraordinarily difficult to forecast business needs and even more difficult to estimate needs for talent. At the same time you can no longer be certain that the talent you have in your organization and in your development pipelines will stay put. Despite this uncertainty, employers must find ways to make sure that they can meet the future demand for talent. Mistakes lead to expensive talent shortfalls or layoffs. To find a solution to that challenge, we can borrow lessons from operations research.

One way to understand what talent management means in practice is to think about how things would work if there were no systematic effort to manage talent, apparently the situation for a large segment of the business community. Failing to manage your talent is the equivalent of failing to manage your supply chain. In the simplest business contexts, it may be possible to get by with no supply chain management. In my home office, for example, I do not manage my office supplies very carefully. When I run out of paper in my printer, I look to see whether I have extra on the floor. If not, I could stop what I'm doing and go to the store. But instead, I go downstairs and take it from my wife's printer. When she runs out, then we go to the store and buy more. In the meantime, of course, what I've done is to push the problem off to her. The cost of having to stop work and go to the store seems small enough that I don't bother to plan.

The same issues play out with human capital, but here the equivalent of running out of paper is a much greater problem. When an employee quits or even when she retires—assuming that no one was paying attention until the retirement party was planned—the costs of not having someone to do the job can be significant. Clients can be lost when key contact employees leave unpredictably; work can stop or must be outsourced to expensive vendors until new employees with specific skills come on board.

A typical attempt to solve the problem of an unanticipated vacancy begins when the boss looks around and says, "Do we have anyone here who can take over the work?" If so, we move him in and hope he will figure out how to do the job. The vacancy we've now created in *his* job often becomes the problem of another manager, just as my paper shortage leads me to take printer paper from my wife. But a single vacancy can generate a chain of "bumping" problems as the first vacancy kicks off a series of internal moves, and you find yourself having to go to the store for a new employee.

Diane Rothbard Margolis's account of corporate life in the 1970s described the central role these bumping problems played in shaping careers.[1] An executive in the company she studied reported that a single vacancy there triggered five additional job changes.

Each of these kinds of internal moves creates the possibility for something to go wrong, most likely candidates moving into roles for which they are not prepared. Performance suffers. The candidates can become dispirited and quit.

Today when a vacancy occurs, we are more likely to hire from the outside labor market. An appeal of outside hiring has been that it prevents bumping problems. Outside hiring is the equivalent of running to the store when we run out of paper, though, and it comes with its own problems. Work in the vacant job stops or at least slows until an outside search is completed, and that can take time. Outside searches are expensive, as when employers pay search firms to help them. And outside hiring blocks prospects for internal promotions, aggravating retention problems among current employees.

The Limits of Outside Hiring

Because outside hiring has become popular, it is worth spending a moment to think more carefully about its natural limits. Outside hiring took off in the mid-1980s because in comparison with earlier approaches, it was breathtakingly simple: managers and executives could be brought in precisely when vacancies occurred, "just in time," without the fancy developmental arrangements of earlier generations. There was no need to spend time and money teaching skills and competencies. Nor was there a need to maintain developmental positions to teach people how to become managers. Those jobs could all be reengineered out of the system. Because the expenses of development had been borne by previous employers, these were *sunk costs*, in accounting terms. All a new employer had to pay was the market wage for managers, and with a strong supply available, the market wage was depressed to a level far lower than the cost of internal development. Matching supply with demand was easy, as long as the external labor market was flush.

But outside hiring in this fashion created the problem of employee retention, exacerbating the risks and costs of internal development. Organizations that invested in the development of candidates risked losing them to other employers that did not train and therefore could afford to pay more. In the language of economics, this is a classic example of an *incomplete contract*: the initial employer fronts the investment with the intention of recouping it through the employee's improved performance.

Employees participated in this arrangement, putting in the effort associated with development and securing the benefits of advancement. But it was not an explicit contract, and when employers started to break that arrangement with layoffs, employees began to question why they should not also exploit it. If employers can lay off managers when circumstances demand, why should employees not be able to move on when it benefits them? And, of course, employers created the retention issue because they were the ones offering jobs and hiring candidates from other companies.

Lessons from IT

An interesting window into how the world might look when employers abandon systematic attempts to manage talent and rely instead on just-in-time hiring comes from the world of information technology (IT). The rise of IT jobs played a significant role in the economic expansion of the 1990s, and IT skills are now crucial to the success of most companies.

Given that, what is remarkable about IT jobs, and especially those in companies producing IT products, is how little most employers do to manage their talent.

The early days of the IT industry were dominated by large companies with traditional models of talent management—IBM in particular but also companies like Hewlett-Packard, Sperry, and Univac. A new generation of companies located on Route 128 in Boston led the growth of the industry in the late 1970s and early 1980s: Wang, Data General, and especially Digital Equipment Corporation. Their practices for managing talent were also traditional, with elaborate planning models based on internal development.

The Silicon Valley firms that exploded on the scene in the 1990s took a new and different approach that relied on hiring the skills from the outside when they were needed, luring talent by offering stock options and exciting projects. A large proportion of the talent for these companies came first from larger, traditional companies like Fairchild, Hewlett-Packard, and IBM. The Silicon Valley companies eventually beat out the more traditional companies in the product markets, especially those around Route 128. A large part of their success has been attributed to their ability to use outside hiring to move quickly. It is also fair to conclude, however, that their ability to hire talent away from competitors without having to make up-front investments in development played a key role.[2]

The triumph of the Silicon Valley companies brought the outside hiring model to the rest of the IT industry. When the supply from older, traditional companies began to dwindle and as required IT skills changed, employers increasingly targeted university and college IT programs. At this point the drawbacks of a just-in-time strategy of talent management became clear: employers are at the mercy of a volatile labor supply, and a quick review of the evidence since the IT boom illustrates the risk.

Real wages for college graduates entering IT jobs reached a peak in 1986 and then began to decline, coinciding with the downsizing of IT departments and the 1991 recession, which hit IT especially hard. There appeared to be an *oversupply* of IT workers in this period, especially for the high-end jobs. Companies could hire more or less whatever skills they wanted on the outside market.

The number of students graduating with IT degrees and majors actually declined through the mid-1990s in response to the poor market for IT jobs through 1992. This smaller cohort of graduates entered the labor market just as the IT market improved and then exploded, leading to a red-hot labor market in the mid-1990s; high wages were a hallmark of that era. Employers had a hard time finding the talent they needed. In this period only about half of IT professionals had even bachelor's degrees in an IT-related field, and only about 10 percent of workers in programming positions had a bachelor's degree of any kind. The importance of nondegree, technical credentials in the IT field exploded and may have been an even more important source of IT skills than higher education. The major accrediting organizations in the work of information technology, many of which were IT companies like Cisco Systems and Microsoft, have now awarded more than two million credentials certifying skills to individuals in the workforce. Some companies paid for their employees to receive these credentials, but the trend over time was for employees to acquire them on their own, often from for-profit proprietary training schools.

Employers complained loudly about the difficulties of finding the talent they needed and asked for public policy relief in the form of expanding immigration as well as higher education programs. Employers also discovered that outside hiring by other firms created retention problems at their own firms. Turnover rates of software engineers in these companies averaged about 40 percent per year, and employers turned to a range of elaborate rewards and "employer of choice" programs to try to keep the talent they had.[3]

As wages and opportunities rose, the number of students majoring in IT-related fields rebounded sharply, rising by 40 percent in 1996–1997 and 39 percent in 1997–1998. These new graduates began to pour into the labor market a few years later. Unfortunately, the tech market deflated rapidly in 2001, just about the time that many of those graduates entered the labor market, creating a surplus of talent and falling wages. When employers must rely on colleges and universities for their talent, the problem is that the supply is not within their control. It responds to signals from the market but with a time lag.

The flip side of a model in which new talent is brought in when organizational requirements change is that old talent must go out. Retraining in IT occupations is virtually nonexistent, and IT employers churn through employees when requirements change. The number of openings that resulted from employees leaving not only companies but also the programming occupation *exceeded* the number of net new positions in programming in the 1990s. The National Survey of College Graduates found that although 52 percent of civil engineering graduates were still in that field twenty years after graduation (typically in their early forties), only 19 percent of computer science graduates are still in that field twenty years later. In computer programming, 36 percent of all graduates have left that field and are working in other occupations.

A study by George Mason University found that IT workers overall were twice as likely to have changed careers as were those in other occupations. This kind of turnover in part explained two facts: that there were few opportunities for retraining when skills became obsolete, and that there were no paths for advancement in these jobs. Programmers stay programmers until their skills are obsolete. Then they move on to something else.

Avron Barr and Shirley Tessler, who ran the Software Industry Study at Stanford University, suggested that, at least at the leading companies, management believed that the key to developing the software competency of their firm was simply to bring in more-capable employees, and not necessarily to manage them better.[4] Professor Denis M. S. Lee, who studies work issues associated with high-tech employees, observed that virtually all of the management efforts with respect to IT workers were directed at getting them in the door; after that, there was nothing.[5]

The focus on hiring recent grads has some negative implications for older workers. Many studies of the IT labor force contain stories about employers' preferences for younger employees and, in some cases, actual practices to secure that result. In an *Information Week* survey of IT managers, only 2 percent reported that they would hire a worker with more than ten years of experience.[6] Another survey, this one by *Network World*, found that only 13 percent of the respondents aged twenty to thirty said that they would hire anyone older than forty.[7]

The returns to greater experience in the IT workforce have been declining over time, suggesting that greater experience is less valued now. Even when unemployment was quite low for IT workers, the duration of unemployment has been rising since 1998. This is consistent with the view that older workers, who are the most likely to be unemployed, have been experiencing a harder time finding new jobs. Among electronic and electrical engineers who were laid off, a group that may map only partially to the IT sector, only 4 percent reported that it was fairly easy to find a new job in the tight labor market of 1998; 76 percent thought that age was an important hindrance in their job search, and older respondents reported significantly more difficulty.[8]

Lessons from Other Industries

Outside the IT industry, most employers seem to have concluded by the end of the 1990s that a strategy of relying on outside hiring to address talent needs was not working, and some began to think about the alternative of building an inventory of talent internally, completing the historical cycle from internal development to outside hiring back to internal development. The Co-Operative Group, a London-based conglomerate with fifty thousand employees, reports that it had been using outside search firms to fill as many as 80 percent of its executive vacancies. Based in part on the uncertainty of quality hires from the outside, CEO Martin Beaumont describes a sharp shift in the company's intentions: "Our goal is to get to the point where 70 percent of those appointments are internal," a virtual reversal of its previous position.[9]

Observers of the human resources scene in Canada describe the same pattern: the admired companies in the 1980s were those that moved away the fastest from the Organization Man approach toward something like a "hands off" and just-in-time model of development. Now, companies are recognizing that it is in their self-interest to be involved in employee development.[10]

It seems as though the ideal solution would be to have a plan that could anticipate vacancies before they occur and have internal candidates ready to fill them; in this way, you would avoid the problem of having to tap an uncertain pool of outside talent whenever a vacancy occurs. The detailed planning and internal development of candidates was designed to do exactly that, and yet it came crashing down after 1981. Outside hiring doesn't seem to work, but neither does the old model of internal development.

The New Problem of Talent Inventory

We typically think of supply and demand creating their own balance, but that happens only in an open marketplace having many suppliers and buyers. Before that happens, individual producers try to estimate demand and then deliver a supply that just meets it at the desired price. If producers undershoot demand, they lose business opportunities. If they overshoot demand, they are stuck with inventory.

In operations research, this challenge is often illustrated as the classic news agent problem: if you were a news agent trying to estimate how many newspapers to order for the customers who will come by your stand tomorrow, how would you do it? The reason this problem is hard becomes clear when we get past the fact that our forecast of demand will never be perfect and we begin to factor in the costs of making mistakes: we could have too few papers and lose opportunities for sales, and we could have too many papers and be stuck with useless inventory.

In the world of talent management, it is possible to have too little talent, and it is also possible to have too much, the equivalent of a human capital supply closet. A simple example of excess supply occurs in organizations that experience variations in demand for their services, such as baggage handling at airlines, where the volume of work varies with flight schedules. Employers sometimes staff such operations to serve peak demand, effectively carrying excess staff in the other periods. In that context, the costs of excess supply are clear: paying employees who are underused except in peak periods. Most employers try to reduce such costs with a just-in-time workforce of part-time workers, temporary help, and other flexible staffing. The challenge for talent management is similar but more complicated because the variability in demand—and in supply—is much more difficult to predict.

This uncertainty is particularly expensive for the internal development of talent. The costs of training are significant, but the biggest costs stem from having an excess supply of talent because it can now walk away, taking your investment. When an employee is sitting on the bench, being paid a salary and waiting for a vacancy to occur, she can start thinking about leaving, especially if another employer offers her the option of using her skills now. Nothing is more likely to signal that it is time to move on than being ready to take on a new role or assignment and having to wait for it to appear. The worst situation would be sitting on the bench in a traditional succession plan waiting to step in if the boss gets hit by a truck, gets fired, or otherwise decides to pack it in. This process is frustrating, especially for ambitious candidates, because they have no control over their advancement, and there is no timetable for it. One of the best remedies is for the individual to get some control over the situation, and candidates do that by looking for opportunities elsewhere. When they find them, they leave.

Evidence for this comes from the 2006 global employee survey conducted by the consulting firm Towers Perrin. It surveyed eighty-six thousand employees across countries in the developed world, asking about issues such as what attracts employees to organizations, what causes them to stay, and what drives their engagement with the organization and their willingness to work hard. Around the world, 15 percent of the respondents said that they were actively trying to leave their current employer, and 43 percent said they were open to learning about opportunities elsewhere. Only a minority were committed to staying put.

Among the most important factors driving employee retention, especially in the United States and Europe, were opportunities to develop and advance in their careers. Such opportunities were also the leading factor in employee engagement in all countries. To put it differently, the lack of development and advancement opportunities was the biggest factor explaining why workers were not engaged in their jobs.[11] Lack of engagement is also a major predictor of employee turnover.

Studies by the consulting firm Watson-Wyatt suggest an even more ominous finding. One of the best predictors of turnover was whether an employee had recently received training. Those who had were more likely to leave, presumably because they were hired away by competitors.[12] Other studies confirm that executives who feel they have been made to wait longer for promotions are more likely to quit.[13] Recall as well the survey of Wharton students cited in chapter 3, which found that they would wait only an average of ten months for opportunity to develop before concluding that advancement was blocked and that they should move on.

Scott MacMeekin, CEO of Bossard Trans-Pacific, a Singapore-based manufacturing company, outlined his concern about the limits of deep benches: "My belief is that if there is a guy good enough to be running the company effectively, they would resign because they would already want to be senior . . . If he is capable, someone will pick him off."[14] Peter Johnson, CEO of Inchcape plc, a London-based automotive company, described the most talented executive candidates as ambitious. "You develop them over a two to three year period. They're ready for the bigger job. The bigger job isn't available, then you lose them, and very often they go to your competition."[15] The Economist Intelligence Unit, which interviewed CEOs about these talent management questions, concluded that one of the common issues companies now face is that "executives who believe their career is blocked are more likely to leave, and they have a larger number of companies from which to choose."[16] The best way to drive up turnover among promising managerial talent, therefore, is to develop them and then make them wait for an opportunity to use their new skills. For another example, see "HR Talent at GE."

The Economics of Management Oversupply

To see why the excess inventory in talent management is now a problem and why it matters to the cost and efficiency of human capital, it is important to understand the economics of management development. To maximize the contributions of candidates, it is important to have them in positions that use all their training and development.

Figure 4-1 illustrates a typical arrangement. The curved line represents the value employees contribute over the course of lifetime careers; it is initially very low, rising sharply in part because of investments in their training and development, and then tapers off as they approach retirement. The straight line represents the costs of employing them. The ini-

HR Talent at GE

General Electric is famous for developing talent internally. Observers often point to the fact that many former GE managers and executives have ended up in leadership roles in other companies.[a] For example, one report lists seven GE human resource executives who left from 1998 to 2000 who now head HR in other companies. Another way to look at this situation, of course, is that it represents an excess inventory of talent: a company recruits and develops enough leaders to staff not only its own roles but also those of other companies.

Whether the associated costs are worth the benefits, which include the ability to attract high-quality talent, is an important empirical question. Academy companies like GE have always asserted that they kept the best talent themselves and let their weaker executives "go play for our competitors." That may have been true in the past, when outside hiring was not commonplace and the candidates who left had been passed over internally. Now, however, candidates who are sitting on the bench get calls offering them senior roles now; why wait for opportunity? In that environment, the candidates who leave are not necessarily the weak performers. They may simply be those who are in the most hurry.

a. Robert Rodriguez, "Filling the HR Pipeline," *HR Magazine*, September 2004, 78–84.

---

tial costs are driven by the prevailing wages in the outside labor market at the time they are hired. After that point, the company manipulates wage levels to ensure that senior jobs associated with promotions always pay more than lower-level jobs.

Crafting a wage profile that maps compensation to positions in the organizational hierarchy is known as *job evaluation*, and it is one of the standard functions in human resources. The Hay Company of compensation consultants and its famous Hay System, which represented a job's position in the pay hierarchy through the assignment of *Hay points*, was the best-known embodiment of this arrangement. In the Organization Man period, this system was used by virtually every large corporation in the United States and most of them around the world.

FIGURE 4-1

The ratio of value produced by employees to the costs of employing them

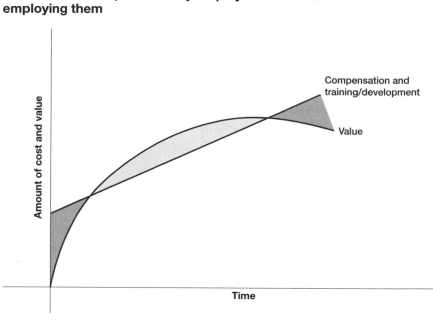

In the first years on the job, the employer was investing in the employee, and the costs far exceeded the value the new hire contributed. In the next period, perhaps after three to five years, the employee's performance increased rapidly, faster than the increase in compensation costs, which were fixed by the job evaluation system. During this period—represented by the middle shaded area in figure 4-1—the employer recouped the investment. At the very end of an employee's career, the employer paid out more than the employee contributed because of seniority-based pay increases and a leveling-off of performance, represented by the shaded area at the right. Corporations used the Hay point system and the other job evaluation models to administer the internal wage profiles for jobs past the entry level so that wages rose mainly with promotions and stayed below the level required to earn returns on investments in development.

Figure 4-1 also explains what happened in the 1970s when there were no longer enough roles to occupy the supply of managerial candidates. A generation of middle- and upper-level managers never got into the middle shaded region because the envisioned opportunities failed to materialize. Business growth slowed, but talent continued to come through the pipeline rapidly, based on plans laid out decades earlier with much rosier growth projections. Employers found places to "park" the excess candidates, maintaining a deep bench of talent for any possible succession event. That talent had to be paid, of course, and therefore represented a continuing stream of losses.

It is reasonable to conclude that a crippling inventory of excess talent was almost inevitable, given the earlier assumption that the mission of development was to ensure a deep bench of talent without much ability to track the costs of doing so. And in fairness to the development function, it would be more than a decade before we began to understand the costs associated with product inventory, let alone an inventory of talent.

The model came apart in the 1980s when employers began to hire experienced workers. A new employer could pay trained candidates more than the employer who had trained them because the new employer did not have to recoup the investment. To retain their employees, those who provided training faced the no-win choice of either raising wages and eroding their ability to recoup training investments or holding the line and risking loss of their talent.

Most employers chose to raise wages, at least in the short term, and the move toward market-driven pay helped undercut the economics of the old model, particularly at the managerial and executive levels. The extraordinary rise in executive compensation plays a special role in contributing to the difficulty of financing managerial development programs. The net return on the investment consists of the difference between the value that executives produce and what it costs to employ them. As compensation costs rise, the net return falls.

To illustrate, the compensation for the average U.S. CEO of a publicly held company in 1993 was $1.3 million. By 2003 it was $2.5 million, an increase of 7.1 percent per year, or more than double the increase in wages over the same period. Estimates of the average compensation for other senior executives suggest that they make, on average, about 40 percent of what their CEOs earn and their pay has increased at roughly the same level. An additional $1 million, net of inflation, is now moving out of the firm to the CEO each year as compared with a decade ago, along with an additional $400,000 for each other executive.[17] If those funds had remained in the firm—if compensation had remained lower—it would have been part of the return that firms were earning on their executive talent. Another way to describe this change is that executives now capture more, perhaps most, of the benefits of employers' investments in their development. The transfer of funds to executive compensation reduces the return on developing those executives and erodes the benefits of executive development.

The Need for a Change

Now you can see more clearly why the earlier models no longer fit the current environment. In the Organization Man period, falling short in the development of talent was a huge problem, because there was no good alternative to filling vacancies from within. In the current environment, recouping big investments in development can be difficult if human capital needs change and especially if employees leave—two common developments. You can also see the problem of doing no internal development and relying on outside hiring. That model leaves employers at the mercy of the labor market, creating big shortfalls and other costs whenever labor markets tighten.

What's needed is a way to address both the problem of oversupply and the traditional problem of undersupply. Neither internal development of the traditional kind nor outside hiring alone will solve the problem.

The Make-or-Buy Choice

Beer has been described as the cause of and solution to all of life's problems.[18] Something similar could be said for outside hiring in the context of talent management. Hiring laterally has caused many of the talent problems that employers now face, especially retention. But it can also be at least part of the solution to managing uncertainty.

Outside hiring has changed talent management by providing an important benchmark for internal development. Internal development must at least pass the test of being more effective than external hiring. (Some evidence suggests that outside hires perform better than internal candidates, but the reason may be that employers set the standard when hiring outsiders to meet or exceed the quality of their internal candidates.)[19]

Employers have a choice, but it is a mistake to think that the choice is "make versus buy"—either developing your talent internally or hiring it from the outside. The better option is to do some of both. Choosing the mix is crucial to meeting talent management challenges, especially the fundamental tasks of managing uncertainty.

Interesting evidence on the extent to which employers already think in terms of the make-versus-buy decision comes from research on employer-provided training. When the unemployment rate rises and surplus labor is readily available, the rate at which employers train their employees falls off. An explanation is that it is easier to hire new talent in downturns and cheaper to develop them from within when labor markets are tight.[20]

In certain jobs and circumstances there really is no option. Some companies have proprietary technology and competencies that cannot be learned elsewhere or have a culture that is so strong that outsiders struggle to find their way. On the other hand, sometimes the organization requires new skills that do not exist internally and can be obtained only by lateral hires. Some companies must hire laterally to change the culture. In the nuclear power industry, for example, it was common for a company that has safety issues to be directed by the Nuclear Regulatory Commission to hire new managers—often from the Navy, which has a superb safety record—to change the culture of the operation.

Beyond such situations, organizations can choose. In recent years so many companies have shifted to outside hiring that they have caused a collective problem by depleting the talent pool. What is in the interests of individual firms may cause a collective problem for the economy, and that may eventually turn this problem into a public policy issue.[21]

It may seem reasonable to ask why any employer with a choice should develop talent internally given the apparent infrastructure and costs involved. The short answer is that it can be cheaper. The cost advantage comes in part from eliminating the costs of searching for, hiring, and transitioning outside talent. In addition, you gain potential performance advantages because candidates who are promoted from within may be more committed and loyal than outside hires and because the promise of promotion is a great retention device. Organizations that manage their talent well should have a better idea of the abilities and potential of internal candidates than of outside hires; if they don't, they are seriously mismanaging their operations. That should make for fewer mistakes and better performance. And it may be possible to pay internal candidates less than outside hires for the same work, at least when they are given the opportunity to take on significant tasks sooner than they would elsewhere.

One can think of the financial differences between internal development and external hires as follows: in the former, a large percentage of the costs are paid up front in the form of development costs. Compensation costs tend to be lower for managers developed from within, because their salaries are not necessarily at market level, or at least lag the market. So the cost advantage tends to grow the longer they are with the organization. For experienced hires, the up-front costs are much lower than for internal candidates. They arrive with the skills they need. But the compensation costs are higher. The cost advantage of outside hiring is greatest for short-term or uncertain relationships and dissipates over time.

These insights lead to the following starting points for thinking about the issue:

1. How long will you need the talent? The longer you need the talent, the easier it will be to recoup investments in internal development.

2. Is there a hierarchy of skills and jobs that can enable candidates to learn through internal development? The more this is the case—it is particularly likely within functional areas—the easier it will be to develop talent internally.

3. How important is it to maintain the organization's current culture? Especially at the senior level, outside hiring brings in individuals having different norms and values, thereby changing the culture. If it is important to change the culture, then outside hiring will do that. Although outside hiring brings change, however, it may not be easy to predict what that change will be, especially if several outside hires are brought in at the same time.

4. How accurate is your forecast of demand? How long can you be sure that you will need the talent? The less certain the forecast, the greater will be the risk and cost of internal development.

These principles suggest the direction that you should lean in the make-versus-buy decision, and they also explain something about the pattern of practices we see among employers. For example, to develop talent in a cost-effective way, you need scale. It also helps to have a reasonably predictable product market, something that makes it easier to predict talent needs and to make investments pay. That is why the companies known for talent development tend to be large, functionally oriented companies in industries like oil exploration and pharmaceuticals. They tend to have long product development cycles and reasonably predictable needs for talent as well as the scale to do development effectively.

A contemporary illustration of the trade-off is IBM, which found it had an oversupply of talent in its high-potential program—too many candidates for the available positions. Having too many internal candidates limited its ability to hire from the outside and bring in new talent with new ideas. So it decided to cut in half the number of people in its high-potential program to increase the mix of outside hires.[22]

Ideally, you should make this calculation not only for the organization as a whole but also for functional areas and jobs within each company. It may make perfect sense to develop talent in one part of a company and not in another, based on answers to the four questions. That view represents a sharp departure from earlier models, in which development practices and priorities were uniform across the organization. It was assumed that it was a good thing to offer all employees equivalent opportunities for development, just as we offered them all equal health care. Development was something like an entitlement rather than an investment.

Note also that outside hiring might include a variety of ways of securing talent. Hiring an employee from the outside is the most common example, but other options include leasing employees through temporary help or staffing agencies or outsourcing the specific work to an independent provider. Of these, outsourcing or subcontracting the work allows you to define precisely the limits of the work and to build in contingencies. For example, many companies have outsourced much of their IT work because it is difficult for them to forecast how their needs will change, and they do not have the scale or depth in that function to develop the competencies internally.

Contracting is one way to reduce uncertainty on the supply side: the contractor takes on the risk of securing the needed talent. The problem of estimating the demand remains, however, and client firms pay a price for passing that aspect of risk to contractors. Part of that price is that the contractors demand certainty in terms of demand requirements, and if they change, contracts must be renegotiated, typically with prices going up. Some clients attempt to manage the uncertainty in their demand by using shorter contracts, which in turn rely on shorter and therefore more accurate forecasts. But contractors demand premiums for shorter contracts as well. Larger contractors with an extensive portfolio of business may find it easier to absorb the uncertainty than smaller contractors, but clients still pay for the privilege. When it comes to managing the risks associated with talent management, outsourcing offers no free lunch for employers.[23]

Mind the Gap: The Mismatch Problem

In the language of operations research and supply chain management, the problems of undersupply and oversupply are collectively known as *mismatch costs*. The goal in operations research and in talent management is to deliver just the right amount of supply to meet demand, neither falling short nor going over. You should worry about and try to minimize both aspects of these mismatch costs. This is perhaps the central feature that distinguishes modern talent management from the Organization Man period, when the focus of attention was only on falling short of talent.

Mismatch costs increase when the uncertainty about demand and supply increases. The greater the uncertainty, the more likely it is that your estimate will be wrong. And, as a result, mismatch costs will increase.[24]

Estimating Mismatch Costs

It might seem reasonable to assume that the two types of mismatch costs will balance out, because you can't both undershoot and overshoot the estimate at the same time. This is what most workforce planners implicitly assume by worrying only about what we call the *point estimate* of demand, that is, the precise number our forecasts generate. If the forecast predicts that we will need one hundred computer programmers in our division next year, then we try to deliver exactly one hundred programmers and stop there. This approach assumes that the probability of overshooting the forecast is equal to the probability of undershooting it (i.e., that the probability distribution of the forecast is normal), an assumption that might be reasonable in the absence of other information. But it also assumes that the costs involved in overshooting will be the same as the costs of undershooting the forecast: if we are short ten programmers, it is as big a problem as having ten too many programmers. And that is rarely the case.

The costs of undershooting a talent forecast are much less than they were in the past, because they can more easily be offset by outside hiring. The costs of overshooting and having an inventory of talent, on the other hand, can be much greater. One reason, described earlier, is that retention problems rise when employees are sitting on a bench. Another relates to the pressure from operating managers to restructure periodically, and this means looking for "fat" that can be cut to lower short-term costs. Underused talent can look a great deal like fat to a restructuring agent, and the difference between "fat" and a "deep bench" can be in the eye of the beholder, shaped in a powerful way by how great the pressure is to cut costs. Layoffs are costly, at least for white-collar workers, because they involve severance payments, outplacement expenses, and the risk of litigation. As noted earlier, people who are parked on a deep bench waiting for opportunity are likely to leave if offered opportunities elsewhere, especially if there is a risk of restructuring.[25]

This means that a simple forecast that generates an average value of the amount of talent needed is not adequate. You need information on the likely cost associated with overshooting and with undershooting the talent forecast for the different levels of supply that you would deliver.[26] For an example of the cost of overshooting demand, see "The Mismatch Problem at Unilever India."

Mismatch costs are likely to differ not only across organizations but also by job. The mismatch costs associated with hiring too few employees can be reasonably small for lower-level jobs, where the competencies are readily available on the outside market and internal wages are close to market. In that case, the costs of undershooting talent demand are modest. For jobs requiring skills that are harder to find, unique to the organization,

The Mismatch Problem
at Unilever India

The problem of overshooting the demand for talent is illustrated at Unilever Corporation in its Indian operations after 2000.[a] Since the 1950s, Unilever had been one of the best employers in the country and a role model for efforts to develop Indian talent. Senior positions were almost always filled by promotion from within, and entry-level management jobs were filled by college dropouts after an intensive selection process.

Newly hired management trainees then went through a long period of formal training that included action learning projects in the community followed by job rotation to broaden skills. Three candidates competed for every important promotion: the winner got the job, the second choice was given an alternative assignment, and the third was allowed to drop out of the system, in some cases out of the company. About half of every new class of management trainees left in ten years, mostly leaving for competitors because their skills were sought after. The company developed an influential fast-track program, called "listers," that relied increasingly on potential.

But around 2000, things began to change. The company restructured in significant ways, flattening the organizational pyramid and reducing the need for executives. Growth in product markets slowed, as did career advancement. Because rates of pay were high relative to the national average, most executives were loath to quit. Still, by 2004, the division had fourteen hundred managers—up from eleven hundred in 2000—even though the demand for managers had declined. In short, it took a long time to turn off the pipeline for producing managers, and the company was faced with a surplus of managerial talent. Unwilling or unable to lay them off, Unilever India ended up transferring them to its international operations.

a. Ravi Madapadi, *Unilever in India: Managing Human Resources* (Hyderabad, India: ICFAI Knowledge Center, 2004).

and more valuable generally, the costs of undershooting are much higher, because it is more difficult to find qualified candidates on the outside market. Those costs include the cost of searching as well as paying a market premium for compensation and the possible costs associated with getting the new hire up to speed with the culture and the tacit knowledge needed to operate in the new organization. Finally, you need to estimate the risk that outsiders will not do as well as internal promotions—because you are less sure about their capabilities, because questions of culture and fit are more difficult to assess, and so on. These may also differ by job.[27]

Estimating Talent Demand

To generate an accurate estimate of the amount of talent you will need going forward, the trick is first to spend less time obsessing about the point estimate of demand. For reasons discussed in chapter 5, these are rarely very accurate, and it will be extremely difficult to improve on them. Second, you should spend more time worrying about what happens when your estimates are wrong, as they inevitably will be. It may be difficult to calculate the accuracy of your talent estimates with any certainty, but even a back-of-the-envelope assessment is better than nothing.

- Ask the forecasting team, "What odds would you take if you were betting that the actual demand will turn out to be, say, within 10 percent either way of your forecast?" It may be too difficult to know whether the odds of undershooting are greater than the odds of overshooting, but it is worth asking that question.

- Then ask the rest of the team, "What happens if we fall short of the actual demand by 10 percent? What would it cost us to make up the difference through outside hiring or other alternatives?" The harder but even more important question is, "What happens if we overshoot the actual demand by 10 percent? What will it cost us in idle time and retention?"

- The questions should be repeated for larger errors: "What changes if we undershoot by 50 percent? Could we still buy the talent we need with lateral hires, or will we run up against a shortage in the market?" Similarly, "What changes if we overshoot by 50 percent? For how many of those surplus candidates will we have something useful and challenging to do? How many will be vulnerable to leaving? Or is the labor market soft enough to keep them from quitting?"

Among the factors you should consider is the expected state of the labor market, which affects both outside hiring and retention. Demographics inside the organization, such as retirements and other aspects of natural turnover, affect the ability to absorb any excess supply. What scope is there in the organization for flexibility in assignments, teamwork, special projects, or other forms of development that you might use to accommodate employees who are now overqualified for their current assignment?

After two or three iterations, it is possible to develop something close to a distribution of the risks.[28] The important point is that unless the risk of overshooting is identical to undershooting, it does not make sense to plan for the point estimate of talent demand. For the risk to be identical requires the highly unlikely situation that both the probability and the costs of being wrong are identical for overshooting and undershooting.

For example, assume you estimate that you will need one hundred computer programmers. The risks are greater for overshooting demand than for undershooting: if you go over, you will lose most of them immediately to other employers; if you undershoot, you can always hire on the outside market to make up the difference. Given that, you will want to develop fewer than one hundred programmers and expect to hire others to make up the shortfall. If you think your estimate is reasonably accurate, then perhaps you should develop ninety internally and plan on hiring, on average, about ten; if you think your estimate is closer to a guess, then perhaps you should develop only sixty or so and plan on hiring the rest.

Vivek Gupta, senior vice president at Indian software company Zensar Technologies, reports that his company conducted this kind of analysis.[29] Fearing retention problems, Zensar initially undershot the estimate and filled the gap with outside hiring. As the labor market began to tighten and the ability to hire from the outside grew more difficult, the mismatch costs changed. Now it was more costly to undershoot demand because shortfalls could not be filled on the outside and the company could be stuck with too few programmers to meet business demands. So it switched its plan. It decided to increase the proportion of talent it developed internally, eventually planning to overshoot the estimate of demand to make up for attrition.

Leased or temporary employees can lower mismatch costs because the costs of adjusting to mistakes—bringing in more workers or letting some go—are lower than for hiring permanent workers. As a result, you might think of a second decision framework within the general make-versus-buy choice. You might decide to undershoot your expected demand for talent in terms of the amount of internal development you are willing to do. You might meet some proportion of the remainder of the work—the component that is most predictable—through outside hiring. The remaining component that is less certain might be met by outsourcing and using leased employees. The most flexible components cost the most per unit of work completed. You pay a premium for the more flexible components, so the more accurate the forecast, the less risk there is of mistakes and the fewer flexible arrangements you will need.

Now you have a means for beginning to manage the uncertainty in talent management. If this were a production problem and you were highly uncertain about the forecast of demand for your product, you might get out of the business, because the chances of making money go down as the uncertainty of the forecasts goes up. Unlike a production problem, however, the challenge of delivering talent cannot be avoided. But you can alter how you think about delivering talent. In the current context, in which the mismatch costs of overshooting are greater than undershooting, you should do even less internal development when the uncertainty of demand rises. The reason is that outside hiring allows you to adjust supply more easily to changes in demand, and you are likely to need more such adjustments when the variability of demand increases. This is essentially what most employers have decided to do in the face of less certainty in product markets.

Estimating these mismatch costs may sound intimidating. How do you know for sure what the odds are that someone will leave if you park her on the bench? Because virtually no employers are even aware of the mismatch costs in making talent decisions, you do not have to be very accurate with these estimates to see a huge improvement in decisions. Further, the important aspect of generating these estimates is the *relative* cost of overshooting versus undershooting, and that is much easier to estimate than an absolute assessment of the costs. In other words, all you really need to know is which is greater—the costs of falling short or overshooting. And then how much greater is one cost than the other—twice or ten times? A rough estimate is still extraordinarily useful.

Managing Talent Risk with Real Options

Another important aspect of talent management concerns a more discrete problem: knowing whether it is worth maintaining investments in given talent into the future. This problem occurs regularly in the restructuring process when you must decide whether a given group of employees truly represents fat that should be cut because there is no immediate need for them or whether they are an investment that will prove useful later. A good example is the recruiting function in a down market when the organization is not hiring: it will probably be useful again in the future, but it's not certain how far out that will be.

To address such problems, researchers have borrowed from the field of finance and the idea that options to act in the future can add value to an investor. In the financial world, *options* allow you to buy or sell something in the future at a price determined now. The value of the option is that it can reduce the uncertainty associated with future changes in prices. For example, airlines typically reduce some of the risk of a future spike in fuel prices by purchasing options to buy a quantity of fuel in the future at a guaranteed price. If the market price turns out to be higher than the guaranteed price, then the airline does well; if the price turns out to be lower, then the option is essentially worthless. You can think of these options as something like insurance against the risk of a crippling spike in fuel prices. Because that could sink the airline, the insurance is worth having.

The concept of options can also be applied to help organizations think through some business decisions. Researchers have referred to this way of thinking as *real options*—the idea of financial options applied to real decisions. The operative question is whether it is worth maintaining the option to take particular actions in the future when those actions involve costs now. Is it worth maintaining a sophisticated recruiting function, even though you are not currently using it, on the chance that you will need it in the near future?

The technical work behind real options can get complicated fast, but a simple decision-tree model can suffice. In our recruiting example, assume that it will cost $100,000 next year to retain the two key recruiters in your recruiting function. At the moment, there is nothing much for them to do. Is it worth keeping them on?

Suppose you estimate only a 10 percent chance that your business will pick up enough to make use of their skills within your planning period. If business does pick up, you will have to add staff and other expenditures for recruiting so that the total expenditure will be $1,000,000. But if you need to recruit, having the key people in place will allow you to get a big jump on the process. A back-of-the-envelope estimate is that allowing you to staff up more quickly with better-quality hires than if you started from scratch will save you $4,200,000. The net benefit from retaining the recruiters, therefore, is $4,200,000 minus $1,000,000, or $3,200,000. Because the odds of needing to exercise the recruiting option are only 1 in 10, the net benefit of retaining the recruiters is $(1/10) \times \$3,200,000$, or $320,000. That clearly beats the $100,000 cost of retaining the recruiters, so the option more than pays off.

5

The Problem of
Uncertainty in
Talent Demand

Chapter 4 explores how careful use of the make-and-buy option can go a long way toward managing the risk in talent management. This chapter focuses on the "make" side of the equation and explains how to structure internal development to reduce uncertainty and lower costs by using techniques from operations research: shortening the forecasting cycle (in part by restructuring the development process to delay the forecast decision), relying on the principle of portfolios to reduce variability, and reorganizing the delivery of development programs to improve responsiveness.

A Focus on Internal Development

Virtually every organization has begun to think about shifting to more internal development of talent. A series of reports suggests the change in attitude. In a 2002 Conference Board study on the future requirements of business leaders, companies reported a new requirement (new with respect to recent history): that the leaders also be able to develop the talent in their organizations.[1] A year later, another study of CEOs reported that talent management concerns accounted for three of their top five worries.[2]

A 2006 Society for Human Resource Management study of a representative sample of companies found 76 percent reporting that their talent management initiatives were a "top priority." Even among those with no talent management initiatives, 58 percent reported that their budgets in areas like employee development would be rising over the next five years (only 5 percent reported a decrease).[3]

Don Ruse, a consultant on talent management to companies like Corning and 3M, notes that interest—especially in technology companies—has shifted to technology and customer-facing jobs and not only leadership positions. Companies have exhausted many of the cost-cutting possibilities and are turning to both innovation and execution as sources of competitive advantage. Talent management concerns are spreading to these other areas, and funding for talent management projects is now coming from operating budgets.

Whether employers make greater investments in internal development without running into the same challenges that killed the Organization Man model depends ultimately on cost issues. And cost-effective internal development begins with new ways of thinking about forecasting talent needs.

The Forecasting Challenge

By the 1960s, forecasting for workforce planning had become remarkably sophisticated. In that period of tight labor markets, when virtually all experienced talent had to be developed from within, undershooting demand was not an option. Companies not only in the United States but also in the United Kingdom and Europe built complicated workforce forecasts that began by examining the internal supply.[4]

Companies began studying every flow, or movement, of labor—promotions, demotions, retirements, quits, and dismissals—and doing so separately for each functional area and division. Projections generally assumed that the transition rates would be stable, but exceptions were made when, for example, a particular area had an older employee population and retirement rates would increase. Some organizations adopted more-sophisticated modeling techniques, fitting statistical regression models to past changes in labor supply and then projecting them. What is impressive about these older models is that they were generated without computers, requiring reams of paper and paper-and-pencil calculations made by a staff of experts trained in statistics. Executing these models took weeks.

An examination of the accuracy of these forecasts suggested that, overall, the error rate was about 3 to 4 percent over two years. A contemporary researcher considered these error rates unacceptably high.[5] But any company now would kill for forecasts this accurate. As the SHRM study cited earlier discovered, most companies don't do *any* workforce planning, let alone planning as sophisticated as was common in the 1960s. A 2004 Conference Board study based on companies that were interested in talent management reported that even in this group, half reported that their workforce planning efforts were ad hoc (the idea of ad hoc planning is something of an oxymoron). And only 19 percent of these companies, mainly the oldest and largest corporations, had engaged in workforce planning in 1993.[6] In the 1950s, 96 percent of companies had a dedicated workforce planning *department*. The explanation, as noted earlier, is that with the glut of experienced talent in the early 1980s, most companies abandoned their planning processes and lost the know-how. And new companies never learned how.

Forecasting Talent Needs

Companies have advantages in forecasting now. A laptop computer and simple spreadsheet programs can generate more sophisticated forecasts than the teams of trained statisticians working on the same problems in the 1960s. Larger companies that have in place enterprisewide resource planning (ERP) systems have an additional advantage in that these software programs can collect accounting data, including numbers of employees by job title and pay level, from across far-flung organizations and then centralize them in a standardized way. Generating forecasts from these data is straightforward, at least conceptually.

It would be good to be able to report a great deal of progress in forecasting talent needs, but despite the potential advantages in data and tools, little progress has been made.

Models That Project from Experience

There are two basic approaches to forecasting. The first and most standard relies on statistical models to extrapolate from experience. The idea is that the future will look like the past. So to estimate the employee turnover rate, for example, you first look at what it has been in the past and try to explain why it varied over time. Suppose turnover goes up when the economy is strong and jobs are plentiful and falls when the economy declines. A model designed to estimate turnover rates would begin by using an estimate of the strength of the economy next year and then looking at turnover rates when the economy was equally strong. You factor that in, along with forecasts of business demand and human capital needs, to estimate the net demand for talent.

Building a highly accurate statistical model is extraordinarily difficult, however, because it requires capturing the many factors that might influence outcomes—in this case, the behavior of a group of individuals. Some of these factors are highly specific. In some parts of Pennsylvania, for example, quit rates and absenteeism jump at the beginning of hunting season.

An accurate model needs variables to capture each of the unique factors that influences the outcome in question. These models also require a great deal of historical data. An organization that has only two or three years' worth of data about something like turnover has a serious problem in building an accurate model. Where there is data, the beauty of statistical forecasting models is that you can estimate their accuracy by seeing how well they predict the situation in the past. If a turnover model predicts only 30 percent of the historical turnover rate, you should not be sanguine about its ability to predict any better going forward. Still, this may be a considerable improvement compared with no forecast or a wild guess.

The great drawback of these models is that only after the fact, even with an accurate model, can you know when something has changed in the basic structure of the relationships, rendering the model no longer predictive. As noted in chapter 3, forecasts of overall economic growth that were highly predictive in the 1960s were no longer very useful in the 1970s following the oil price shocks, which helped change the structure of the economy.

Models That Assess Future Factors

The other approach to forecasting, one that may be complementary, attempts to project the influence of factors that have yet to occur (or have not been in place long enough to generate data), such as a change in strategy. These models depend on assessments by experts. What will be required in new human capital, for example, if the company wants to pursue a more customer-focused strategy?

There are many ways to generate these estimates, such as scenario planning techniques. But ultimately they come down to the judgments of experts. Mary Young, of the Conference Board, describes the situation of Provident Health Systems, which operated three hospitals in Portland, Oregon, and faced a major competitor with plans to open a new hospital nearby. What would the effect be on Provident's own staffing? How many of its current employees could be expected to be hired away, and what kind of difficulty would it have in hiring new employees with an additional competitor in town? The answer was to build an assessment from the ground up, relying on the judgments of supervisors as to which individuals were likely to leave if offered positions at the new hospital.[7]

Forecasting Talent Supply and Demand

In beginning the talent management process, you need two sets of forecasts. The first looks at your current workforce and estimates what it will look like in the future: if you do nothing new, how many incumbents with relevant competencies will you have in each area in the future? This number represents the available supply of talent in the organization. This calculation is straightforward, but it requires separate estimates of promotion rates, retirements, quits, dismissals, and so on, for each relevant unit.

The more homogeneous the unit, the more accurate the estimates. Estimates conducted separately by geographic area and by occupation or labor market are more accurate than those across a company as a whole, although it is possible to generate the latter accurately by aggregating the former. Most of these estimates can be based on historical data, although you may face ad hoc events and developments like those faced by Provident Health Systems, and these must be factored in.

The more difficult of these two forecasts is the demand for talent. As noted earlier, the competitive environment is so changeable and firms adjust their own strategies and practices so often that it's tricky even to outline, let alone estimate the effects of, the relevant developments that could affect demand. As with all forecasting, the most accurate predictions are those that are closest to the action: the more decentralized (e.g., for a business line, not the firm as a whole) and the more proximate (next year, not ten years out), the better.

The gap between the forecast of supply and demand is the problem that drives the talent management process. Gerard Brossard, formerly vice president for workforce planning at Hewlett-Packard, described how he built support for a new talent management process at HP with senior executives by comparing what the businesses got in terms of talent and what they ultimately needed. In other words, what were the mismatch costs under the current system? It turned out that those costs were sizable.[8]

The Dow Chemical Company has a sophisticated forecasting model that attempts to do what the 1960s models did but with the advantages of modern computing power. Dow had a system in place based on separate estimates of talent supply and demand for each location, but they could not be aggregated up to the corporate level because of inconsistent definitions and metrics. The company moved to a system that exploited standardized data from its ERP system to produce estimates that could be aggregated for the company as a whole. Then it sought a university partner to develop an even more elaborate model, one that used the standardized data to generate estimates for each business unit. Those forecasts were then aggregated into companywide estimates.

The Dow models use the traditional statistical-based forecasting approach. They also incorporate a wide range of site-specific factors. Many of these include ad hoc developments for which there is no historical experience. For example, the forecasts include estimates of the political and business climate in each of Dow's countries of operation, changes in labor and employment legislation, and business plans for the operating unit, which include targets for operating productivity. Having a range of historical data allows the estimates to vary for the context of each facility: for example, start-ups require more labor than do established plants. And standardized systems make it possible to aggregate the individual estimates up to an overall projection for the company.[9]

The Benefits of Simulations

The advantage of modern computing power is that estimates are generated instantly, allowing you to change the assumptions and see what happens. Playing around with the assumptions turns a forecasting model into a simulation: what happens to your forecast head count if, for example, retirements rise or your rates of internal promotions change? The importance of simulation is that it allows business planners and those developing strategies to see the implications of their decisions for talent, letting them anticipate how talent constraints might affect those strategies and adjust their plans.

Arguably the most sophisticated forecasting is being done by Capital One, an innovator in the credit card business. CapitalOne had almost twenty thousand employees in 2001; through outsourcing and other decisions, its head count shrank to fourteen thousand by 2005. After a series of acquisitions, employment rose to thirty thousand by 2007. The need for talent planning became clear in 2002 with rapid changes in the employee base.

CapitalOne made its name in the product market through sophisticated analysis of customer data. Pat Cataldo, a vice president in the HR area, describes the culture of the company as one of "test and learn," in which analysis and application are encouraged.[10] Prasant Setty came into that HR group from Wharton and then McKinsey & Company with the challenge of doing something to help the company plan its workforce, at first to keep the business units within their head count constraints. Setty assembled a team—at one point as many as twenty people—with technical expertise in forecasting and planning. Most team members were from fields like marketing and operations research. The group included no traditional HR experts.

The group used data mining techniques, systems dynamics models from manufacturing, and information from the company's PeopleSoft system to generate talent planning models for each business unit. These models go beyond the usual focus on predicting the number of people re-quired in each role. They also model outcomes such as attrition rates, em-ployee morale, and rates of promotion and outside hires. Among the factors they consider are aspects of the organizational chart—span of con-trol, levels of hierarchy (which affects promotion rates), and *stretch roles* (positions that are reserved for developmental assignments).

In an effort to align the talent management practices with business goals, the HR planning team worked with the business unit leaders to develop models based on their specific business plans and goals. As with Dow, the CapitalOne forecasting models are easily turned into simulation models, and this is where the power of the analyses comes in. The models allow the line managers to see the options involved in any business plan: "If you plan to grow at 10 percent this year, here are the talent requirements. If you ac-centuate outside hiring, here's the likely effect on reducing prospects for internal promotion and the associated effects on morale and then on attri-tion. If you change the span of control, here is the effect on talent needs at the management level and also the effect on promotion rates." Most im-portant for the chief financial office, the models also allow the managers to see the total compensation implications of all their choices. The line man-agers see the talent management issues as a system and also see how their choices about any single outcome in that system affects the other aspects.

Setty, now at Google, reports that the biggest benefit of this approach is that it helps the line managers run their own businesses and under-stand the implications of their choices. The business managers have em-braced it as a useful tool. And it has raised the status of the human resource function. It shows the concrete implications of often very gen-eral statements of business goals.

Other companies, such as Citibank, have also embraced the simulation approach. Citibank's talent planning models allow it to calculate, for ex-ample, the human capital requirements and costs of opening a new branch office as opposed to expanding others in the area.

A Look at Options

The most significant developments in forecasting play on the fact that employers have many choices in closing the gap between estimates of supply and demand. An example comes from EDS, an information technology consulting and outsourcing firm. As with other professional services businesses, people are the product at EDS. Thus, forecasting is conceptually simpler: knowing how many people across job titles are required to take on a project with 100,000 hours of programming per month is much more straightforward than, say, Dow's effort to estimate the level and mix of talent required if a given chemical plant doubles its capacity.

Mary Young of the Conference Board describes EDS before 2004 as having no central planning for talent.[11] Business was growing fast enough that it hired people as fast as it could. Before then, the belief among executives (and those in many other companies) had been that the technology in information systems changed too quickly to bother attempting to forecast talent needs.

The company's new approach, put in place in 2006, has a simple forecasting aspect, which extends only twelve months. Each business leader outlines the demand he expects in terms of competencies, roles, and regions. The difference lies in understanding the current supply. Like most consultancies, the staff at EDS can work on a variety of projects and can team with others to produce a huge range of organizational competencies. The task of line managers is to match people with projects. The challenge for EDS and companies like it is to understand its own supply: "What competencies do we have, and in what ways can we deploy them to meet which customer demands?"

Answering this question demands a deeper assessment than in a typical firm, because it requires understanding the differences among individuals having similar job titles. The real asset at EDS is its *skills inventory*, which keeps track of the competencies of employees as measured by their capabilities to work with various software and programming languages, previous tasks performed, roles held in the company, and so on. To keep this inventory up-to-date in a timely manner, the company requires that employees update it after each assignment. The line managers use it to make assignments.

The skills inventory also includes salary information, which affects billing rates and charges to clients. Line managers can use that information to help make cost-effective assignments. When gaps are projected between the current supply of talent and projected demand, managers have the option of hiring to fill them (the usual approach), rearranging current employees in different ways based on the skills inventory, or using contractors.

Don Ruse of Sibson Consulting describes his work at Corning, where the talent planning process presses line managers not only to plan but also to think through the source of true value in their operations.[12] Like the EDS program, the process at Corning forces the company to take a hard look at its own supply of talent. Rather than simply extrapolate from past staffing levels, the idea here is to rethink how valuable each current role or position is for executing the new business strategy. The company must think about whether new competencies are needed for each new strategy and which ones are no longer needed, reengineering the workforce. If the process is done right, the company understands which roles should be reinforced, and which competencies—and the individuals who have them—need to be redeployed.

Matt Brush, former director of global staffing and planning for Corning, noted that the need for a new model began during the boom years when the company could not anticipate or even keep up with hiring demands. When the telecommunications bust hit in 2001, the company lost 90 percent of its market capitalization value, and the goal shifted quickly to cutting staff. "One of the things we learned was that we had to get better at anticipating demand, and to do that in staffing we had to move away from being 'order takers' to helping the business units figure out what they truly needed."[13] Again, mismatch costs were the problem.

What is perhaps most impressive about the Corning approach is that it manages to get business leaders to think seriously not only about their future human capital needs but also their current supply of talent—how many of their current staff truly have the skills they need now, how many can be expected to advance into senior roles, and so on. Cynics will notice that this is what performance appraisals are supposed to do, but they rarely work. What is different about this approach, as Brush points out, is that it avoids the difficult task of confronting employees with the assessment. Because the general discussion is about "roles needed," it is a little easier to be objective. And because some of the options include retraining and deploying individuals whose skills are no longer needed in their current roles, the business leaders are more likely to provide an accurate assessment of their workforce.

Although the results of dialogues with business unit leaders rarely lead to precise estimates of talent, at least they offer a general direction: "We need more of these competencies and fewer of these." In that way, the staffing operations can begin to identify candidates and find talent. It is easy to add or subtract the number of positions to be filled at a later date when the forecasts become clearer. In the absence of this process, Brush found that line managers consistently underestimated the talent they needed in the future.

As with all the best companies, the process at Corning does not simply build a forecast for the business. It also engages business leaders in a dialogue about the future and works with them to create simulations that can help them develop strategies. The move toward simulations is an attempt to manage uncertainty by giving organizational leaders a sense of the trade-offs involved in various strategy choices—the talent needs associated with a given approach and what would have to be done to meet them. Simulations also allow decision makers to consider the options for meeting talent needs. This approach is a paradigm shift from the Organization Man model, which took business strategy as a given and then worked backward from there.

From Forecasting to Action

In some cases, forecasts suggest reasonably clear strategies for managing talent. For example, Station Casinos has launched an expansion program that calls for opening new casinos in various locations on a predictable schedule. Because it knows precisely how many employees in which jobs are needed to run its current casinos, it can predict with great accuracy how many will be required to open a new casino.

Valerie Murzl, vice president of human resources, describes how it uses that information going forward.[14] The company knows the date when the new casino is to open, and it also knows which jobs require casino- and company-specific skills and which ones do not. For those that do not, the company can plan when to begin outside hiring and brief training and orientation programs. For jobs that require more company experience, the HR department tells current employees which jobs will be open and tells them how they can get training and experience now to move into those jobs in two or three years when the new casino opens. In effect, the company uses its current workforce and the job experience offered by its existing casinos to develop the needed talent.

The Bullwhip Problem

For most companies, though, predicting talent demand is much more difficult and uncertain. Mistakes occur largely because it's extremely tricky to forecast business demand. But there are ways in which talent management itself contributes to mistakes.

One example is analogous to what is known as the "bullwhip" problem in product markets: small moves in the handle produce wide swings up and down at the end of the whip. In the classic example, a modest increase in consumer demand over a season leads retailers to increase their orders by 10 percent. If all of them place their next-quarter orders at the same time—say, the beginning of this month—then the demand on suppliers will suddenly jump but then will fall off sharply for the rest of the quarter. The bullwhip problem is driven largely by the fact that all the retailers place their orders at the same time even though the increase in demand is reasonably gradual.[15] Research finds that the variability of demand grows when one moves back up the supply chain: changes in demand at the retail level lead to greater variation at wholesalers, greater still at the manufacturing level, and so on.

The same bullwhip problem occurs in talent management. In the IT example in chapter 4, the wild imbalances in supply and demand began when employers failed to produce the talent themselves and instead relied on students to pursue IT careers years ahead of time. The time lag meant that the supply of labor was always behind the market demand.[16] Relying on students to make those decisions individually was the other component of the problem; many decided to abandon IT simultaneously, unaware of the collective impact of their decisions. Then the next cohort made the opposite decision.

Inside companies, the most common and simplest version of the bullwhip problem appears in entry-level hiring: all the divisions in the company submit requisitions to fill entry-level jobs to a central office, which then does all the recruiting for the year on college campuses in the spring. Because such hiring happens only once a year, each division makes sure to cover all of its anticipated vacancies. The divisions don't want to fall short when business is good and then have to wait a year for more hires. Their recruiters are all over the campuses scouting for applicants.

Suppose that the next year, business softens. The divisions are concerned about committing to new hires they may not need, so they hold back on their requisitions. Recruiters sit on their hands. The following year, if business has stabilized, the requisitions come in fast and furiously to cover last year's vacancies as well as this year's. Now the recruiters are flying again: boom, bust, boom, bust. Something exactly like this happened with recruiting on MBA campuses, especially in the consulting business, from the late 1990s (boom) to 2001–2003 (bust) and then 2005–2006 (boom again).

The more serious aspect of the bullwhip problem occurs inside organizations that adopt a multistage process for developing talent. Consider, for example, what happens when a firm wins a big, long-term contract. Say that the line managers request 10 percent more senior engineers to do the work. That implies a slightly more than 10 percent increase in the number of engineers to be promoted (because of attrition), but an even larger increase in the number of engineering graduates who must be hired for entry-level engineering programs. Only some proportion will meet the performance standard for promotion to the next level, and some of those will quit. And the firm needs that increase in talent now. As a result, hiring at the entry level will jump by considerably more than 10 percent to restock the pipeline. Because entry-level hiring is done only once per year, the swing in hiring is dramatic: up sharply this year—perhaps 20 percent—to help staff the new contract, and then down sharply next year as demand returns to typical levels.

The human resource planning problem of meeting the additional demand for this straightforward contract can become quite difficult. It is not surprising that in many organizations the response is simply to hire senior engineers from the outside to avoid the problems of internal progressions and to smooth out the accompanying bullwhip problems.

Bullwhip problems can also be addressed in a straightforward fashion. The swings in supply in the IT industry came about in part because employers relied entirely on the outside labor market. Employers that had the ability to develop talent internally could have responded to the tight labor markets by doing so, protecting them from the vagaries of the outside market and in turn helping to dampen that variability.

Similarly, employers can offset the swings in demand when hiring is concentrated in time by simply spreading out the hiring process. As described later, even college graduate hiring can be spread out over time to reduce the pressure on infrastructure. Judicious use of outside hiring for senior vacancies can also reduce some of the bullwhip effects on internal promotion ladders when demand for these top jobs increases.

Designing Developmental Programs

The concept of minimizing uncertainty to reduce costs offers ideas about how to design developmental programs. For example, as noted in chapter 4, you can invest more in developmental programs when the forecasts of demand are more likely to be accurate and the risks of being wrong are lower, while relying more heavily on outside hiring when the forecasts are less certain and the risks of being wrong are greater.

Taking this straightforward advice, however, calls into question the idea that development is for everyone and leads to different opportunities depending on one's job or division. No doubt this has always been the case in practice, but for some organizations it is difficult to be explicit about this practice because it seems to violate stated norms of equity.

The Problem of Decentralized Programs

One of the biggest problems in talent management is that many organizations are decentralized. Companies like Johnson & Johnson, Textron, American Standard, and hundreds of others have always operated with a decentralized organizational structure. A great many other companies moved in this direction in the 1980s and 1990s.

From a governance perspective, the idea was to make these smaller units operate like small businesses and gain speed, adaptability, and profit orientation. But they also operate like small businesses in terms of talent management—underresourced and constrained in work-based opportunities for development. As Lou Gerstner observed, "I believe that in the 1980s and 1990s [decentralization] was carried to an extreme in many corporations, with unproductive and, in many cases, highly disruptive results."[17] Some of those disruptive results are associated with talent issues.

One of the problems of decentralized organizations is how to identify talent for corporate jobs and, more generally, how to provide corporatewide developmental opportunities. In a company like Johnson & Johnson, informal relationships at the corporate level made it possible to move candidates across its many operating companies, leading to good developmental experiences. As the company grew larger and more complex, that became more difficult. Each operating company had its own system, some more than one, and there were as many as four hundred separate developmental programs. The rise of shared service operations took certain functions out of the operating companies, and this meant that developmental experiences that were restricted to a single operating company did not include those functions.[18]

Many corporations recognized this problem and began to intervene at the operating-unit level to develop talent for the corporation as a whole. But the paths they took only exacerbated the problem. They asked managers in the smaller units to help them identify talent that could be moved into corporate developmental programs. A 2007 survey of large employers finds that 60 percent use this approach.[19]

Those managers understood the implications of this request better than the corporate staff: it meant that they were likely to lose their best and most promising employees. Yes, in the long term their unit would get other talented employees rotated in from other parts of the corporation. But this view required an assumption of trust and also a belief that the broader goals of the corporation should be placed above the more immediate goals of profit and loss in one's own division. Both assumptions were reasonable in the Organization Man era, but they are not widely accepted now. A business unit that can keep its key talent away from headquarters will be better off, an example of the classic free-rider problem, in which individual self-interest leads us to exploit the public good—in this case, corporate developmental programs—while avoiding contributions to it.

Instead of contributing talent, local managers began to hide their best employees from the corporate development staff. External consultants routinely observe subtle and not-so-subtle efforts by managers to sabotage performance appraisals to avoid identifying promising leaders. To the extent that headquarters can grab promising candidates away from the business units, the leaders in those units begin to wonder why they continued to make investments in the candidates who left. A McKinsey survey found respondents reporting that siloed practices were among the top three obstacles to more effective talent management (uncommitted senior managers and line managers were the top 1 and 2 obstacles).[20]

Many corporations have attempted to derail efforts to hide talent by declaring that certain individuals are "corporate assets" whose careers are controlled by headquarters and not by the business units in which they currently reside. Typically, a corporate organization manages the development and careers of managers and executives above the level of director, whereas business units govern those at lower levels. Such an approach is a step in the right direction, but it still must address the issue of how individuals will get into director-level jobs in the first place. And it does not solve the disincentive to develop talent at the lower level: local managers who invest in developing employees will lose them at a certain level.

Bob Allen, senior vice president at CH2M, a global construction and engineering company, notes that the careers of the two hundred top-performing managers in the company are "owned" by the corporate leaders.[21] Their career paths are laid out by the group in the company where they are based, but corporate leaders in other areas see those plans and intervene if it appears that a candidate is being hidden from experiences in other areas or is not being developed adequately.

The Portfolio Solution

An even more fundamental problem is associated with decentralized talent management practices, a problem that is caused by mismatches. Consider, for example, a company having five divisions, each running its own talent management and developmental program. For simplicity, let's assume that each division estimates it will need to develop twenty general managers in ten years, one hundred in total across the five divisions. Each division then sets about to develop its own talent for those jobs. As with any forecast of talent needs, these are subject to mismatch problems. Assuming that the operating divisions are set up to attack different markets with different circumstances, as most are, then business and talent demand will vary across divisions, as will the forecasting errors. The forecasts in some areas in a given year will, on average, overestimate demand, and those in other areas will, on average, underestimate it. As long as the programs are run separately, with separate developmental programs for each division, then the forecasting errors accumulate: the consumer products division ends up with too few candidates, and the industrial division ends up with too many. The 2007 survey noted above reports that more than a quarter of development programs are set up in this decentralized fashion.[22]

The principle of portfolios solves this problem. In the world of finance, holding a portfolio of various investments, each with a unique risk profile, is a standard way to reduce overall risk. The idea is that when some investments are down, generating low returns, others may be up, generating high returns. On balance, the pool of investments, or portfolio, is much more stable than any individual investment would be on its own.

A similar approach can even out the variability in developing talent. In our example, instead of operating five different developmental programs, each generating its own mismatch costs, the company should run, or at least coordinate, a common program. When some divisions overshoot demand and others undershoot, the company can offset the mismatch by moving candidates around. Overall, mismatch costs across the company are reduced.

Companies that have decentralized operations are making strides to better integrate their development programs. Mellon Financial is one of many companies that have created centers of excellence by function. These centers produce developmental programs that are then turned over to the individual business units, which tailor them to their own needs. These programs rely on a company's human resource business partners—senior HR managers with responsibility both to the units and to the company as a whole—to figure out which programs will work and how much they should be tailored for the business units.[23]

Johnson & Johnson has gone further. Its chairman wanted a corporatewide system for developing general management talent, and the executive committee created it, based on corporatewide competencies and tied to work experiences. To the extent that the operating companies have developmental programs of their own, they copy the corporate program. Further, the company has developed a single common database of competencies to keep track of individual managerial talent. All this makes it easier to move individuals around the corporation.

The Singapore government has a more formal arrangement.[24] The government agencies and branches have some autonomy in managing the development of their employees, and they learn and borrow from one another. Candidates who are identified as having the potential for leadership and who have an interest in administrative work are classified as "dual career officers," and their careers are governed at least in part by interests outside their current ministry.[25] Once identified, they are then posted to another agency to gain experience and also to have their potential verified by another organization. If they succeed and their potential is verified, then they become "administrative services officers"—a designation that puts them in the ranks of mobile leaders and in careers that move them from ministry to ministry. There are approximately 160,000 civil servants in Singapore, of whom only 300 are administrative services officers. They represent the heart of the government's talent management program. One can think of this program as a fast-track program, and the candidates as the equivalent of corporate assets that can be deployed across the government.

The most effective approach from the corporate perspective is to centralize talent development at the corporate level. Donna Riley, head of global talent for IBM, points out that the company never decentralized its operations in the way that became popular at other companies, and talent truly remained a corporate asset.[26] About one-third of IBM's leadership team moves every year, often changing business units. Riley serves the classic chess master model described in chapter 1. "And no," she points out, "the executives aren't given a lot of choice over where they are going."

An additional attribute of centralizing control over talent, as George Stalk of Boston Consulting Group observes, is the development of networks and social ties. These contacts, which build up when executive candidates rotate through the headquarters, help create the power that headquarters needs.[27]

Shorter Forecasts

Shorter forecasts are always more accurate than longer-term ones, and developmental programs based on long-term forecasts are much more likely to incur significant mismatch costs because they are much less accurate. A five-year forecast is now very long term, and in most industries a three-year forecast is at the outer bounds. An important goal in talent management, therefore, is to try to keep forecasts for talent demand as short as possible. There are a number of creative ways to do so.

A key point of the portfolio technique is that by allowing the organization to rearrange talent across programs after demand materializes, a program can reduce its dependence on inaccurate forecasts and thereby reduce mismatch costs. A similar logic applies when organizations structure developmental experiences in ways that allow them to use recent forecasts to adjust investments before they are made.

For example, any set of managerial and executive jobs requires a common set of competencies as well as a set specific to each subgroup. For greatest effectiveness and efficiency, the ideal approach is to treat the candidates as part of a common pool for as long as possible, first developing the common competencies and delaying those that differentiate functions and jobs. This approach imparts powerful advantages. First, it creates scale economies associated with training and developing a larger group. Programs and events that are not cost efficient for a small group become more so when the group grows. But the biggest source of efficiency is the ability to pool the candidates and redirect them according to variations in demand in functions and jobs.

Consider, for example, a company deciding how many people to put on the developmental track for general manager to achieve its forecast demand for one hundred new managers in the next ten years across five functional areas. The company first estimates how many will quit and how many will fail to advance. Then it looks at the mismatch costs, decides that overshooting demand is the bigger problem, and makes a judgment as to how close it can get to the target without running too great a risk that it will overproduce managers.

What the company should do next is develop all the common competencies, keep the group in a common pool as long as possible, and delay specialization into the functional areas for as long as possible. If, for example, it can concentrate first on common developmental experiences and delay specialized development for six years, then it can rely on updated estimates of the demand from each area in the sixth year. Rather than rely on ten-year forecasts for each function, it can update its forecasts by functional area and rely on forecasts that go out only four years. These will be dramatically more accurate.

A crucial conclusion is that the more centralized and coordinated the development programs are, the better they are in reducing mismatch costs. Delegating training and development to subunits increases sharply the possibility of mismatch errors, because the forecasts are not as accurate as if they were pooled into a common program, and there is no ability to reallocate candidates based on updated estimates of demand.

Improving Responsiveness

The longer it takes to develop talent, the more expensive it is on several dimensions. A system that responds more quickly costs less.

In the production world, the concept of the *flow rate* captures the issue of responsiveness: how long it takes for a product to be processed through the system. Longer flow rates are costly, in part because more resources are typically used in longer processes. In employee development, longer periods spent in development reduce the length of time over which the investment can be recouped. If a typical employee stays with a company only ten years, then a five-year management development program has only five years over which to pay off.

Longer development times also reduce the responsiveness of the system. With a five-year developmental program, it may take five years before you can develop candidates with different competencies to respond to changing job requirements. In the meantime, competencies continue to be produced that no longer fit the changing needs of the organization, as in the AT&T example in chapter 3. The longer it takes you to develop talent, the worse the fit is likely to be in the end because of changing job requirements.

Development time has two aspects. One is obvious: how long each specific learning or developmental engagement takes. This aspect is influenced by what needs to be learned and the type of learning systems being used, an issue considered here in more detail later. The other aspect of development time may be the more important: *waiting time*, defined as the time an employee spends waiting to receive or finish development and then the time waiting to make use of it. This type of delay is especially bad in the current environment, because it leads to the retention problems noted earlier. Good candidates can easily quit and work elsewhere while waiting to use their new skills, wasting your investment in their development. These delays are not the result of forecasting errors. Rather, they are caused by problems within the system of development and career management.

The other aspect of development time is unproductive waiting. One concerns the simple problem of a bottleneck in the training and development process. A *bottleneck* is a part of the process where capacity is especially constrained. It might be at the beginning. For example, in the security agencies of the U.S. government, it is necessary for new hires to get a security clearance before they can begin work, in some cases even before they can begin much of their training. Capacity constraints in background checks and other aspects of the clearance process cause delays of as long as two years. The rest of the developmental pipeline is then held back. In this case, the bottleneck is expensive because the candidates are already employed and must be paid while they wait to begin development.

Fixing Bottlenecks. One of the implications of a bottleneck is that the capacity of the entire pipeline is limited to the size of the bottleneck. An obvious solution is to throw more resources at the bottleneck to expand it. Sometimes substitute experiences can be provided outside the organization, such as work experience with a joint venture partner. In other cases, the bottleneck may occur only at certain points, and that suggests it may be possible to pace the flow of candidates through the bottleneck. It is a disaster, for example, if the popular training course is oversubscribed in the spring, creating a backlog, and undersubscribed in the summer. The answer is to redistribute the flow of candidates from spring to summer.

But it may not be possible to fix the bottleneck; for example, there may be only a fixed number of key developmental jobs. In that case, there is no point in having more capacity either before or after the bottleneck. Excess capacity before the bottleneck will generate a queue of candidates who are waiting to move forward and often willing to look outside for alternatives. Excess capacity after the bottleneck is wasted because there will not be enough candidates to make use of it. So it makes sense to cut back the capacity of the system to the level of the intractable bottleneck. Then you can close any gap in the ultimate demand through outside hiring.

Queuing Problems. Arguably the most frustrating and unpredictable delays are caused when developmental experiences are organized in a queue. For example, candidates at the supervisory level are waiting for rotational assignments and cannot get them because the incumbents have no place to go. Those at the end of the rotational queue should be stepping up to managerial jobs, but at the moment there are no vacancies. Until the incumbents move, no one else can move—the reverse of the bumping problem.

Queuing delays are most common when company growth slows, as in a business downturn. New positions that were planned to accompany business expansion slow, and quits that create vacancies also decline. Those at the end of the developmental pipeline have nowhere to go, and no one can move into their jobs. Although this is a problem for candidates, it is less so for the organization because the mismatch costs tend to be low: there is no unmet demand, and frustrated candidates find it difficult to leave in a down market. The bigger problem for employers comes during expansions, when some other problem in the queue holds up everyone in line, and frustrated candidates quit for opportunities elsewhere.

One cause of these holdups is that an incumbent does not want to move out of the current position. Sometimes a developmental pathway is altered, adding a new position to the pathway, but the current holder is, say, getting ready to retire and does not want to move. Ingersoll-Rand took an interesting approach to this problem. Corporate talent management gained control of all the jobs that represented important developmental assignments and of the people in them. It secured the ability to move incumbents out of positions that were holding up and effectively blocking the progress of the queue.[28]

In a more typical situation, development times are uneven. For example, suppose the first rotational assignment in a management development program is a one-year stint in finance, to follow the financial year. The next assignment, in manufacturing, follows product development cycles and lasts two years. Candidates in the first assignment must cool their heels for two years until vacancies open in the manufacturing assignments.

In an even more common situation, the length of an assignment is not completely predictable but varies over time. The length of a product development engagement, for example, may change as products are redesigned. The analogy in the world of assembly lines is an *unbalanced line*, in which inventory builds up behind the slower-moving station or, in this case, the assignment that takes longer to complete.

An obvious solution is to redesign the developmental assignments so that they are more even in length, possibly by redistributing tasks from one to the other. In practice, this can be difficult, especially when the unevenness is caused by unexpected events or delays in each assignment.

An alternative that is easier to generalize is to decouple the developmental experiences so that they do not flow directly from one to another. You might design the process so that after candidates finish a developmental assignment, they go to work and put the lessons to use. The time when they stay in "regular" work between assignments can then vary and might depend on a vacancy in the next developmental role. In other words, the process is no longer structured as a queue, and the work time provides a buffer to deal with variations in the length of developmental assignments.

Securing balance in the developmental pipeline is also hindered by having large cohorts of candidates who come through the process all at once. If a company hires new recruits once a year and puts them all through a set training experience and accompanying developmental assignment, the program requires twice as much capacity as one in which the company brings in a new cohort of recruits every six months. Smaller batches of candidates require less capacity, and more-frequent batches improve responsiveness.

If you're hiring college graduates, one solution is to allow some of them to begin employment at different times. Monitor Consulting is one of several consulting firms that now hire two classes per year, depending on project demands. Many students need to begin work in June after graduation, but others are happy to take the summer off and begin in the fall. For employers, the advantage of taking in a later cohort is that they can still lock in new hires from the graduating pool but can space their entry into any development program to make better use of its capacity.

The option of reaching an employment agreement months before employment will begin (or in some cases a year or more) appears to be popular in business schools. Many students now graduate in January or could arrange to do so if their future employment were already secured. Employers can easily bring in pools of graduates in the spring (with recent graduates), in the fall (with those who took the summer off), and in the winter (with January grads). This practice cuts the fixed costs of development by two-thirds, because it reduces the size of each cohort by the same amount. It can also increase the responsiveness of the system by graduating a new cohort every four months, rather than only one per year, thereby enabling the program to adjust faster to changing demands for talent.

More generally, having many discrete developmental assignments complicates the process because it creates queuing problems. Most problematic is a program that has many rotational assignments that must be experienced in order. If the order of the assignments is less important and if employees can experience them whenever they became available, queuing delays decline sharply. Delays also decline if the experiences can be combined. For example, rather than spend time in marketing and also in finance, a rotational candidate might be put on a team project that includes both marketing and finance challenges. This approach reduces the risk of queuing delays by more than half.

Quality Problems. A final issue associated with the structure of developmental programs is the question of quality, or what we might think of (in production terms) as the *defect* or *error rate* associated with employee development. It is common for someone to go through a developmental process and not "get it"—that is, the candidate doesn't seem to have developed the competencies to handle the jobs for which she is positioned.

The percentage of candidates who do not make it can be thought of as the *failure rate.*

In the past, it was common for organizations to simply get rid of individuals who failed to advance, and, in many cases, the definition of failure was relative. Professional service firms in fields such as law, accounting, and consulting had *up-or-out* policies effectively based on a relative failure rate—for example, promoting only the top 20 percent. A large percentage of their new hires would be pushed out as only the best of each class was promoted to partner and retained. In corporate jobs, it was less common for candidates who failed a developmental assignment to be pushed out of the organization, but it was typical for their careers to be sidelined, often permanently.

The economic logic behind the up-or-out models in professional service firms was that the associates contributed more than they cost and that the chance to make partner was an incentive that pushed all the associates along. As firms spend more resources on making the associates productive, however, it becomes more costly to push them out. In the corporate world, up-or-out policies never really made economic sense because companies were investing in candidates and lost money with every employee who left, whatever the reason. Further, even though it might have been tempting to believe that those who failed in some aspect of development were destined to be poor performers, it is an empirical question as to whether that was the case. And few employers bothered to check.[29]

Given our better understanding of the costs of investing in development, an alternative arrangement is to "rework" failing candidates and try again. The cost of rework can be far less than the cost of losing development investments. The question is how best to do it. Putting a candidate through the formal process a second time is essentially like failing a grade in elementary school and having to repeat it, with all the associated stigma. It also repeats the development costs, and, more important, it can block the developmental pathway for candidates who are waiting. Rework therefore involves alternative arrangements, such as special assignments that provide a substitute for the needed experience, and coaching, an expensive resource but one that is adjustable to the circumstances.

When you recognize that talent management is a business problem, it makes sense to apply what you know about how to structure those challenges in ways that are most cost effective. The biggest constraint in reducing costs is uncertainty, and the lessons from supply chain management offer a number of principles for reducing the uncertainty in the development of talent. Chapter 6 considers more explicitly the finances of talent development and describes how you can ensure that your investments are structured in ways to ensure a financial return, thereby ensuring that they can be sustained.

Why Traditional Succession Planning No Longer Works

Many people think of the phrase "succession planning" as representing what talent management is all about. At a minimum, they see succession planning as equivalent to promotion from within or internal development of talent. In fact, *succession planning* refers to a specific subset of the general process of talent management: planning at the level of the individual worker and the individual job.

In its simplest form, succession planning is the process for identifying which individuals should advance to the next position in a hierarchy of jobs. When all talent was developed internally, employers would first map out the hierarchy of jobs—what we might think of as a job ladder—that determines the paths that individual candidates take through the organization when advancing through a career. Succession planning then used these job ladders to develop a plan outlining which individuals from a pool of candidates at each level should advance to each step in the job ladder when vacancies occurred. The most important part of that process was assessing talent: determining who was the most ready to advance and attempting to predict who had the greatest likelihood of success in the next step up.

How does this process differ from simply making a promotion decision? The difference is that the determinations are made well in advance of the vacancy. Succession planning therefore involves predictions as to which jobs will come vacant at what time, and which individuals will be in the pipeline to take them. The discussions in this book about two things—(1) the uncertainty of long-term forecasts of demand and of supply and (2) the advantages of relying on more recent information— should make us wary of our ability to make such determinations.

The basic idea of succession planning, as well the original model, came from the military. Especially on the battlefield, the importance of the chain of command is paramount. Someone must be in a position to give orders at all times, because the need for immediate response may be crucial. If an officer goes down, it is important for someone to step in immediately, take up the authority, and start giving orders. The phrase "replacement planning" was developed in the military to solve this problem by identifying clearly who would step in if an officer in the chain of command was incapacitated. This information was widely disseminated because it was important for everyone to know whom to follow.

After World War II, businesses picked up the notion of replacement planning, largely because executives were dying in office at a remarkable rate. People asked, "What happens if the boss gets hit by a bus?" This sounded more dramatic than the real problem, which was that older executives were dying of heart attacks.

For businesses, of course, there was nowhere near the urgency of replacing leaders as there was in the military. Business leaders routinely went on vacation and stepped away from the action. Some went on extended developmental assignments or medical leave and then returned to their roles. And many, especially founders, kept their positions for years despite being incapacitated. Business continued more or less smoothly, because important decisions could be either delegated or made by someone in the next level up. Unlike battlefield situations, business leaders almost never had to be replaced instantaneously.

Some executives do get hit by buses, of course, although it is a rare event now for them to die in office. Studies of organizations whose CEOs die unexpectedly in office suggest that they do not fall apart when it happens. In fact, research has shown consistently that the stock price of such firms actually *improves,* by a nontrivial amount.[1] (Cynical readers are no doubt wondering whether financial analysts will now pressure CEOs to jaywalk.)

At lower levels of management, the need for immediate leadership transitions is even less important. Interim leaders step in while long searches take place. Any organization that is willing to take a look at external replacements—and most now do this routinely—signals that the transition does not need to be immediate. There is relatively little evidence suggesting that internal succession events are more successful than bringing in outsiders, at least at the CEO level, despite a built-in bias of organizations to promote insiders when performance is going well and go to outsiders when changes are needed.[2] Of course, that result may also speak volumes about how poor the internal development of talent is in most organizations and not that internal succession per se lacks merit.

Today, the risk is much greater that an executive will be fired or quit than be hit by a bus, but it is easier to rally support from leaders for a program designed to guard against their untimely demise than to plan around their being fired. However it is framed, there is still little evidence to support the common argument that it is important to maintain a bench of talent in case bosses leave unexpectedly.

In the Organization Man period, when succession planning was in full flower, the motivation had little to do with a concern for uncertain turnover. Rather, it was driven by the highly predictable transitions associated with retirement. Individual executives rarely quit and were even less often dismissed, so turnover almost always came with retirement at age sixty-five. Because all such vacancies were filled from within, it was important to plan for those transitions, and because they were predictable, doing so was straightforward. In other words, traditional succession planning was premised on the notion that talent management decisions were highly predictable.

A typical succession plan in that period showed the designated successors for each key position. More elaborate plans attempted to ascertain which individuals at each level had the right stuff to become candidates for promotion to senior positions later in their careers. This approach was based on the idea, first, that it was possible to make that determination years in advance and, second (and more reasonably), that the number of good developmental roles was reasonably limited. So it was necessary to begin to sort out candidates for senior positions early to allocate them across the scarce developmental roles.

It was never clear how effective these succession plans were, whether they really identified talent early on, and what the effects were of those decisions on the chosen and those passed over. But today, this approach is highly suspect because of the basic assumption of certainty in talent demand and supply. The mismatch between the assumption of certainty and the reality of uncertainty explains one of the most common contemporary outcomes of the succession planning process: an executive vacancy occurs, the leadership looks at the succession plan and the designated candidate, and they then consider what they want in that position and decide to appoint someone from outside the organization. There may have been nothing wrong with the internal candidate except that the requirements for the position changed much faster than the succession and development process was able to track.

The Chartered Institute for Personnel Development, of London, described the change in practice in the United Kingdom: "With growing uncertainty, increasing speed of change in the business environment, and flatter structures, succession planning of this [traditional] sort declined in the 1990s. How could one plan ahead, it was argued, for jobs that might not exist next year? One apparent result was that more and more people came to be appointed to top jobs from outside organisations."[3]

Proponents of traditional succession plans may argue that an incomplete plan is still better than no plan at all. But that is not likely to be the case. The reason is that all plans come with costs. Those costs include the out-of-pocket costs in time and resources of developing the succession plan in the first place and other, more important costs, which are manifestations of the mismatch costs. The fact that business changes are likely to alter the requirements of these senior jobs means that there is a high likelihood that the appointed candidates may not fit the jobs when they come open, a mismatch risk that increases the further out in time the succession plan extends. A recent McKinsey study of talent management quotes a human resource manager in Europe describing a widespread problem: "We do succession planning to an unbelievable degree. But once we do it, we don't use it. Never have we reviewed a senior vacancy and looked at the succession plan. It's almost done as just another tick in the HR box."[4]

One reason succession plans do not work, at least for executive jobs, is that the events that trigger them—usually dismissal—signal that the organization wants to move in a different direction with the next hire: "We don't want someone like that last guy." And succession planning is designed to produce candidates who look more or less exactly like that last guy. It is almost impossible to predict when the organization will want to look in a different direction for replacements, and the desired new direction, as well as the needed new competencies, is almost impossible to predict.

There are other problems with succession planning as well. If candidates are kept ready to step into senior roles at any time, they are sitting on the bench. The risk that they will take a more advanced role at another organization, rather than wait for a vacancy, grows the further out in time the succession plan goes.

The other complication is that succession planning creates expectations among employees that often cannot be met. It may sound great to tell an employee that we think so much of her that she is next in line to fill the vice president job, but what happens when the leadership changes, strategies and priorities change, and the new team wants to bring in an outsider? Or when the organization restructures, consolidating roles, and the position goes away? The employee feels entitled to the position, perceives the developments as unfair, and responds either by leaving or by withdrawing effort. One option is to not tell employees when they are in high-potential categories, and most employers, 57 percent, do not, at least officially.[5] Employees still find these things out, of course, and then the damage is done.

A possible solution to these planning challenges, as with the forecasting issues, might be to reduce the time involved in the plans and thereby make them more accurate. Most companies already do an annual update to their succession plans. A downside of more-frequent updating is that each plan and each update takes time, energy, and money. And it is outdated whenever there is an important change in direction, such as the appointment of an outsider with new ideas at a senior level in the organization.

What about doing just-in-time succession plans? That is effectively what many companies do. When there is an opening, they define what the job requires and then figure out who internally is the best match for it, and they sometimes benchmark that choice against external candidates. This approach is basically "succession" without the "planning." These programs are essentially replacement plans: "Who among our current

candidates do we believe should step in if a vacancy occurs, given the current requirements of that vacancy?" In that case, it is difficult to see what
the advantage is to having a succession plan as compared with waiting
until a vacancy actually occurs and then deciding who can fill it.

Replacement plans can make sense as a way to force the organization
to assess the talent it has. A related planning process that makes sense for
virtually every organization is talent reviews, the process of reviewing the
competencies and capabilities of the most important employees and considering how they could be reviewed. Talent reviews began in the 1950s,
and diaries of how CEOs spent their time in the 1970s suggested that
more time was spent on talent reviews than any other activity! What follows from that assessment depends on the circumstances, but it typically
involves suggesting assignments and processes that can be used to develop competencies further.

Both of these are just-in-time practices, and neither involves the type
of long-term planning that was at the heart of traditional succession planning. First Horizon National Bank in Memphis has an interesting, just-in-
time succession practice. Executives in the organization cannot accept a
promotion until they have identified a successor for their position.[6]

Finally, there may very well be situations in which the chance that a
particular executive will leave truly puts the organization at risk in an immediate way. This is especially likely in smaller organizations, where the
performance of an individual can have a huge effect and where systems
and procedures are not sufficient to offset many of the distinctive competencies of individuals. I remember an account in 2000 from an executive
in a London-based company whose board of directors was panicked at the
risk that its chief financial officer might leave the company and pressed
the organization as to how it would handle such an event. The company
did not have internal candidates in place and did not have the scale and
functional depth in finance to be expected to produce internal successors,
although the directors seemed to expect a solution along the lines of a traditional succession plan.

Instead, the company did something very different. It asked a search
firm to generate a list of five candidates having the competencies and experience to step into the CFO role immediately if the current executive

left. The company took this list of five to the board, whose response was, "Yes, but you don't employ any of these people." The counter was, "All we need to do is hire one of them. Nor could we be sure that internal successors will remain in place until needed." The board was satisfied. Now, it is a common practice for smaller companies in particular to retain search firms to develop such replacement plans for their key executive jobs.

To summarize the problem with traditional succession planning, it is that by trying to plan down to the level of individual employee and job, it assumes much greater predictability than the process possesses. Succession plans cannot deliver what they promise given this uncertainty, and yet they create a false sense of security in the organization while at the same time costing time and resources. A study of leadership development in the United States in the late 1990s reports companies shifting away from the individualized approaches to planning, not only succession planning but also high-potential designations, and toward talent pools, which represent a broader approach of developing groups of candidates for a group of generally similar jobs along the lines of the portfolio approach. The move was in response to the rapid pace of change and uncertainty at the job level.[7]

Not doing detailed succession plans is not the same thing as doing no planning, of course, nor is it the same as doing no development.

- It clearly makes sense to try to predict talent demand.

- To allow for flexibility in eventual assignments, it makes sense to try to develop candidates broadly for a broad set of jobs.

- It makes sense to conduct talent reviews, assessing individuals' skills and the experiences they need next to keep advancing.

- It makes sense to do replacement planning to identify the pool of available talent as a means of updating development plans.

What does not make sense is to try to estimate which individual will move into what job years in advance. The process is so uncertain that it causes more problems than it solves. For an object lesson in uncertainty, see "Unintended Consequences."

Unintended Consequences

In the U.S. Navy, the talent pipeline used to fill the difficult but important officer roles in the submarine fleet was always reasonably stable and predictable:
although the most popular roles for cadets at the Naval Academy were in aviation, many of those interested in flight school could not pass the eye exams
required for pilot positions, so the group gravitated to the submarine service.
The introduction of laser eye surgery, however, now makes it possible for a
great many of those cadets who otherwise would have failed the eye exams
to qualify for flight school. The Navy reports that almost one-third of all the
cadets now have corrective eye surgery. As a result, the applicant pool for the
submarine service has plummeted.[a]

a. See David S. Cloud, "Perfect Vision Is Helping and Hurting the Navy," *New York Times,* June 17,
2006.

6

The Return on Talent Management Investments

The previous chapters describe the costs associated with uncertainty as the factor that undermines the ability to make internal development pay. If you can find different and better ways to recoup your investments in development, you can dramatically improve your talent management options as well as expand your investments in employees. Such investments are crucial not only for their careers but also for the economy as a whole.

Despite the significant shift away from internal development over the past generation, it is almost impossible to imagine a company that does no internal development. Internal development appears to offer a great many advantages. Reams have been written about the competencies companies should develop, especially in leaders, and the best methods for teaching them. What has not been explored is what comes before that: the underlying economic factors that make internal development possible.

Economist Gary Becker won the Nobel Prize in economics in part for explaining the simple economics of training and employee development. The key to understanding these arguments is to remember that individuals, especially now, have an attachment not only to their employers but also to the outside labor market.

Employee skills and competencies can be sorted for the purposes of economics into two categories. The first are those that are useful only inside a given firm—a set of skills with only one potential user. Employees are wary of making investments in such skills because it is not obvious that they can benefit from them: "We want you to spend a year learning our system, and then you'll really have the opportunity to advance" is the kind of offer that is easy to refuse. Employers may pay you more after you acquire those skills, but then again, they may not because there is nothing else you can do with them.[1]

Skills that are useful elsewhere, on the other hand, will make the employees who possess them attractive to other employers, raising their market wage and the wage that the employer must pay to retain them. Employers are reluctant to foot the bill to develop such general skills because they can easily end up paying for them twice: the first time paying the direct costs of training and development, and the second time paying higher wages to prevent the employee from taking these valuable and marketable skills elsewhere.

In the days of the Organization Man, the conceptual problem of general training was not much of an issue for employers, because there was essentially no hiring of experienced employees and therefore no real market for their skills. Companies provided management development, because growing your own talent was the only way to get managers and executives having the necessary competencies. Managers and executives didn't leave by choice; there were no job offers, and this meant that there was no market to bid up their wages. In other words, all skills functioned for practical purposes as if they were unique to the employer.

Now, almost all employers actively seek to hire talent from their competitors. There is a clear market for virtually all skills, employees can and do leave, and wages are much more likely to adjust to something like the market level. In these open labor markets, it is hard to identify many competencies and experiences that are not useful elsewhere. In fact, empirical evidence shows that almost all training is general in the sense that it is useful to some other employer.[2] Managerial development, the focus of attention here, is clearly useful elsewhere, and such development is exactly what the highest-performing employees want if they are to remain with the organization.

It is easy to see how the finances of internal development worked for employers. Given that they had considerable control over compensation—and even more so for jobs that were removed from entry-level positions—they could generate substantial returns on early investments in training and development (as shown earlier in the shaded area of figure 4-1) by retaining employees and holding pay below the level of performance.

For higher-level managers, the net contributions from their work could be considerable. For example, suppose a typical midlevel manager produced value for the firm net of the cost of employing her of about $100,000 per year over the course of a twenty-year career, for a total of $2,201,900. Such a stream of benefits justifies an initial development investment up to a whopping $330,000 at the beginning of the executive's career and still falls within a typical constraint of earning a 10 percent cost of capital. That much money translates into a decade of development time at the beginning of one's career, given that compensation costs are relatively low then.

The situation between employers and employees with respect to training was described earlier as an incomplete contract: the employer makes an investment in the employee but does not require anything in return because, historically, the employee has had little opportunity to leave. Employment law in the United States—especially the Fair Labor Standards Act, which requires employers to pay all costs associated with required training for covered employees—assumes this context. Now, with outside hiring, an employee's competencies are useful elsewhere and have a market value. In fact, employees may actually be more valuable to a competitor than to their current employers, because they bring with them not only their own performance but also knowledge and insight about how their old employers operated. The competitors can pay such employees more than the current employers do and still make money on the deal because they have no early investment costs to recoup. The market value of the employees moves closer to the line representing their true value to an employer. Employers then face what seems an impossible choice: either stay with their development practices and watch their newly developed employees leave for better-paying opportunities elsewhere, losing their investment in them, or raise wages to the new market level, losing the ability to recoup the investments they have just made.

These developments explain why every employer seems to be advertising for candidates having at least three to five years of experience—close to the point when intensive development stops and performance begins to rise. They also explain why employers have pulled back from making those investments and why it has become difficult for entry-level candidates to get hired for jobs that offer good opportunities for development. Attempts to address talent development must deal with the challenges associated with recouping development investments.

The Costs of Internal Development

The place to begin considering that problem is on the cost side. If the costs of development could be reduced, then those investments would be easier to recoup and more development could be funded. Some design factors affecting those costs are outlined in chapter 5. A more thorough list includes the obvious direct costs: expenses associated with training facilities, the wages of instructors, and the costs of administering the programs. The biggest direct costs, however, are the wages and compensation that support employees while they are being developed. This is especially so for managerial employees, whose compensation costs can be considerable.

These costs are offset by any contributions that employees make to the organization during development through the work they do. Arguably the most important factor in determining the costs of various developmental programs, then, is the extent to which they take employees away from their usual work. Programs in which candidates contribute nothing, either because they are learning in a classroom setting or because they are overwhelmed by learning in the workplace, are extremely expensive.

It is important to be realistic about some of these cost relationships. A training program that pulls hourly workers off an assembly line or away from a call center for a day results in the loss of a day's productivity, but that tends to be less the case for white-collar and managerial employees, who have greater control over how they get their work done. A manager who attends a day-long workshop is likely to complete the tasks that should have been done that day by working longer the rest of the week. My experience watching several thousand executives in Wharton's executive education program over the years is that most of them try to keep up with their work obligations even when they are engaged in programs of a week or so and then make up missed work when they get home. In this case, the "cost" of that workshop is not so much the loss of performance for that day but its contribution to longer-term employee burnout. Also, the focus on their work back home keeps them from learning much from the program.

The more significant losses of productivity are likely to be in longer programs and experiences, the most costly of which are developmental assignments. For example, programs in which candidates shadow senior managers and executives whose jobs they might someday hold—perhaps with job titles like "deputy director"—are expensive, because the compensation costs are high and the contributions low. Perhaps the most common example are rotational assignments, in which the goal is to broaden an employee, who is rotated out just at the point when he begins to figure out what he is doing. One good reason that developmental assignments are concentrated at the entry level is that the value of lost productivity is lower for employees whose contributions and compensation costs are modest.

Comparing Other Uses for Development Funds

As you would expect, the greater the initial investments in employees, the higher must be the rates of return to pay them off. Historically, recouping these large investments required that compensation be held below the value of performance, something that was easy to do before labor markets opened up.

To benchmark these developmental investments, you also need to consider the cost of money: breaking even on an investment in development means at least equaling the alternative uses of funds. The cost of money is determined by the return on the other forms of investment that you could be making. An additional complication during the past generation is that the other opportunities for investments have been tremendous, as illustrated by the U.S. stock market, whose value rose by ten times from 1980 through 2000. If, for example, a company's business investments earn 10 percent per year—a representative figure in this period—then, just to break even, an investment must equal that rate, producing a return equal to twice the cost of the original investment in seven years. The longer it takes for an investment to begin earning a return, the more expensive the investment becomes and the higher the return must be to justify it.[3]

The Cost of Uncertainty

An additional aspect of the costs associated with internal development, and one that is particularly important now, is the economic cost of uncertainty. With financial investments, we know that uncertainty about returns, or risk, represents a cost to the investor. Other things being equal, an investment with greater risk needs to generate a higher level of return on average to be equal in overall value to a more certain investment with a lower rate of return.

With investments in talent development, risk also matters. Here, the uncertainty comes from two sources: demand and supply. Will the demand for the skills being developed continue, and will the supply of talent being developed stay with the employer? It is impossible to drive the risk of being wrong to zero, and you need to account for the costs of that uncertainty.

Suppose, for example, that your cost of capital—the rate of return the company could earn in its business operations—is 10 percent per year. Suppose also that the investments in training and development are estimated to earn, on average, about the same rate of return as the cost of capital and that the risk of these investments paying off is exactly the same as the risk in the business operations. Development would then be as good an investment as the average opportunities facing the business.

For the purposes of illustration, suppose that the uncertainty of training investments paying off as expected (because job demands may change or employees may leave) is now twice as great as the risk associated with the company's other business investments. To be equal in value to less-risky business investments earning a return of 10 percent, training and development investments must earn about 15 percent.[4] Greater risk means that fewer investments in development will now pay off, and therefore fewer should be undertaken, at least from the perspective of organizations interested in making money.

All this helps explain why programs of employee development, and especially management development, have been decimated in recent years. Things seem bleak for the future of internal development unless we think very differently about developing employees to make the financing work for employers. The good news is that it is possible to do that.

Lowering the Cost of Development

The search to lower costs focused attention on the out-of-pocket costs of training and development, turning initially to online and Web-based instruction as an alternative. Although the fixed costs of developing a curriculum for this kind of instruction can be enormous, the costs per employee served can easily be driven down to next to nothing. Even small employers that do not have the resources to develop their own content can easily buy what they need.

The other great advantage of online or distributed learning is that it can be delivered exactly when needed. A classroom-based program must have sufficient numbers of students to be cost effective and therefore can be offered in most contexts only sporadically. But an online system is always ready, always available when an individual needs it. And there are few things as motivating for learning as having a pressing need for the content.

The unexpected drawback of online learning for most organizations, however, turns out to be the question of motivation. The social context of learning—having a class at a scheduled time with an instructor and a roomful of peers—creates pressure not only to show up but also to come prepared and pay attention, if nothing else to avoid looking foolish. Content that is offered online creates no such demand. The convenience gives way to other demands on one's time. Even though online presentations of content are typically much more effective than in the typical classroom, the lack of social pressure to pay attention and absorb the content sharply reduces its effectiveness.

These delivery mechanisms turn out to be effective when other arrangements create the incentive to use them and take the content seriously—for example, when mastery of the content, as assessed by a test or exam, is required for a license, a certification, or advancement. For management development, in which skills are less quantifiable, more interpersonal, and strongly work-based, online learning has not made much impact.

The most important cost is the time spent away from productive work and not the direct costs of training and development. The most significant way to reduce development costs, therefore, is to reduce the amount of time it takes from work. Online and other forms of distributed learning provide greater flexibility for employees to arrange learning when it fits their schedule, but it still requires time.

The best way to reduce time off the job is to combine work with learning. The strategies in this approach date back to the earliest models of work-based learning, such as craft work, in which apprentices learn by watching, helping, and then doing the tasks along with the experienced workers. The importance of experiential learning has been clear for decades, especially for managerial jobs. The Center for Creative Leadership's surveys of executives consistently found that the most important sources of learning were work experiences, especially working with peers and superiors and being involved in assignments that stretch the learner's capabilities.[5] According to the most recent survey by the Chartered Institute for Personnel Development, human resource executives believe that on-the-job training is the most important source of learning, followed by simply performing new tasks. Deloitte's survey of development research finds that the most important sources of learning are from working with a team.[6]

Action learning takes experience a step further, integrating workplace tasks into the learning model. For example, a real task or project is assigned that will help a participant apply the conceptual lessons for developing a new competency, such as leading a team on a project in order to practice the lessons of teamwork management.

For the purposes of pedagogy, the action learning project is often designed around the conceptual material to be taught, such as teamwork or project management: "Here's the concept we want you to learn; now go create or find a project where you can try it out." For cost effectiveness, however, it would be better to do it the other way around, starting with an existing useful project and seeing what could be learned from it. A project that takes time and teaches but does not contribute to the organization is a very expensive project.

Further, organizations have many informal ways of devaluing projects that are strictly developmental, and few things are as demotivating as working on something that the organization does not value. Individuals no doubt learn a lot by doing these projects, but making sure that they learn the right things requires support along the way and systematic debriefing. Arguably the most important use of coaching in organizations now is to help employees learn from work-related experiences.

A useful and cost-effective approach comes from The Boeing Company. Boeing asked its top executives to identify the work experiences from which they had learned the most and then looked for patterns in the responses. The company put together a short list to help teach the essential competencies needed to be an effective leader in the company. One of the most interesting of these was "taking over a failing operation." The list became the basis for a talent review process that assigned leadership candidates to positions, with the goal of moving them through all the assignments on the list. This approach should not be confused with job rotation; the experiences are not consistently identified with specific job titles. The skill of the Boeing talent management process is to identify appropriate opportunities to learn these experiences and then make appropriate matches—a just-in-time process rather than one that can be planned.[7]

Of course, on-the-job learning is not always the cheapest nor even the most effective way to develop employees. Supervisors and managers should not spend their time teaching the fine points of using Excel spreadsheets. And supervisors and peers do not always pass along the approved methods for getting things done, such as how to handle business expenses. The variations in what they tell subordinates can be amusing as well as destructive. Nor are they trained to be teachers.

Even when supervisors and peers are effective teachers, their time is not free. Consider a common situation. An entry-level manager—let's call him Max—is working on a problem that requires knowledge of the organization's internal accounting system. Max's supervisor, "Maria," takes time to explain the system to him. An hour of Maria's time may seem free, but at some point there are no additional free hours in Maria's day, especially if she has many subordinates to supervise and other tasks to perform. Many companies have cut back sharply on formal training and development and have effectively pushed the problem of learning to supervisors. These efforts only appear to lower costs, because few internal accounting systems are sophisticated enough to capture the lost opportunities for performance, the contributions to burnout on the part of employee-teachers, and the ineffective lessons learned.

The other problem is that such ad hoc training may not happen. Supervisors and peers may not have the time or the inclination to train people, especially when their own performance assessments focus only on their own tasks. As organizational charts flatten and spans of control increase, the time available for supervisors to train employees has diminished.

Whether informal training takes place can depend on a range of interpersonal factors, such as whether the current employees like the new workers. And that may depend on similarity of backgrounds and interests, leaving plenty of room for discriminatory outcomes.

Learning from Peers

An alternative approach is a structured arrangement for learning from other employees. Such a model was developed at Intel. Although it is called a mentoring program, it is really closer to a file-sharing program like Napster, in which employees teach each other workplace skills.

The program begins with a database where employees self-identify skills that are important in the company—not only technical skills but also skills like networking, understanding company culture, or leading teams. When participants enter a skill they would like to learn, the database produces a list of people from whom they can learn it. The volunteer "teacher" and student participate in a required session. Details of their arrangement are set up in the form of a contract: "Here's what I want to learn, here's what I'm willing to do to help you." After that, the parties are on their own to figure out how to pass along the knowledge and skills.

These programs typically are short term, lasting about six months. The teacher is not necessarily a superior, and the arrangement is focused on learning well-defined skills.[8]

Programs like these help define a series of tangible skills that can be taught in a self-contained manner. This is in contrast to traditional developmental programs, which organized development around job titles and

positions. The advantage of a task-based approach is that you can organize experiences without requiring employees to change jobs or positions.

Separating the work from the job title is one of the keys to developing
talent cost-effectively. *Stretch* assignments, in which employees take on a
variety of functional tasks as well as leadership roles whenever the opportunities arise, do not require waiting for a rotational assignment. State
Farm Insurance has been moving its managers in this direction. Managers
identify themselves by their level in the managerial hierarchy and then
by the work they are doing: "I am a director working in underwriting"
rather than "I am director of underwriting." The difference is subtle, but
it represents a lesser attachment to a job function and a more general connection to the organization. Pfizer and Interbrew are other companies
seeking ways to separate assignments and work from specific job titles.[9]

Opportunities Outside the Organization

Even large organizations may not have enough interesting developmental opportunities to go around, and smaller organizations are especially
constrained in this regard. One interesting solution is to find work-related
experiences outside the organization.

The classic example is for local divisions of major companies to "lend"
promising executives to run projects for charitable organizations. Managing the annual campaign for the United Way is among the most visible of
these, a model that was used extensively by local phone companies under
the old Bell system. These efforts are valuable for the local charities, and
they are useful for the company because it can observe how well its junior
executives function in what is often a first attempt to manage something
of significance. These efforts are designed so that failure, if it happens, is
cheap and quick: these volunteer projects are typically short in length
and small in scale, and if the executive fails, the costs are small. The company can bail out the project at little cost.

Mercer Consulting allowed its consultants to leave the firm to work for
a client for as long as two years—on the client's payroll—and then return
to Mercer. The benefits to Mercer? Tighter relations with the client and a
deeper understanding of its issues, along with a broadening experience for
the consultant.[10] International law firm ReedSmith has a program wherein

young associates are lent to work in the district attorney's office, remaining on the ReedSmith payroll, for six months. In that period, the associates gain much more exposure to trials than they could ever get in the firm.

Tim Gardner, of Brigham Young University, examined alliances that firms have made for the purposes of sharing and developing talent. A small study, for example, found that about 14 percent of firms in the high-tech world have ways to share or borrow talent from each other. Among the most important of these arrangements are training consortia in which several firms put together training experiences for their employees, sharing the developmental costs.[11] Robert Wegman of Wegmans Food Markets donated $5 million to start a new pharmacy school, in part to alleviate the shortage of pharmacists the company faced in trying to staff its stores in upstate New York. Wegman chose a location for the school near the largest cluster of Wegmans stores in hopes that the graduating pharmacists will stay in the area.[12]

Getting Employees to Share the Costs

In the current context, employees, and not employers, are the main beneficiaries of most training and development investments. Virtually all such investments increase the marketability of employees and raise their wages even if they stay put. As a result, it might seem reasonable to expect employees to share in the costs of training, especially because employers otherwise might not be able to offer it.

Here we see some interesting conflicts with the principles of U.S. employment law, which are rooted in the older, Organization Man model of employment relationships. The assumption under that model was that employers were the beneficiaries of training and development and should therefore pay for it. Blue-collar workers, in particular, needed protection from their employers, but white-collar workers did not because employers naturally looked after these workers' best interests. After all, they *were* the organization.

The main employment law governing training—the Fair Labor Standards Act—covers hourly paid workers (salaried workers are known as "exempt" employees because they are exempt from the act). The act requires that employers pay all the costs of any training that is required of hourly employees, including wages for their time spent in training. The employees cannot share in any of the costs. Although this requirement does not apply to exempt employees, almost all employers have followed its principles in dealing with white-collar employees as well.

This U.S. legal requirement may explain why employees in other countries are more likely to seek out and pay for training on their own. Whereas employees initiated only 31 percent of all training experiences in the United States, the equivalent figure for employees in Switzerland is almost 60 percent. In Canada, a country quite similar to the United States, it was 45 percent. Workers paid for less than 10 percent of all the training engagements in the United States but almost 23 percent of similar experiences in Switzerland.[13]

U.S. employers, however, are free to ask employees to contribute to the costs of training and development that is not mandatory for their current jobs. This includes training for competencies or experiences that may be required for other jobs in the organization, including ones that would be logical promotions. A typical approach for employers is to offer optional training programs after hours, when employees are not being paid, and to let those interested in taking the programs do so on their own time—in effect, advancing their own prospects for promotion in the process. An interesting example is the extensive training programs made available by temporary help agencies for their workers in areas related to their work, such as the use of desktop software. Some of these programs even lead to recognized credentials. The employees take these classes on their own time and are then eligible for better jobs at higher pay. The employees benefit, as does the agency.[14]

Another way to get employees to share the costs is through *training wages*, a wage or compensation level that is held down during training. A training wage reverses the logic of the figure 4-1 model because the employees pay for their training up front by receiving less than they are worth. This pay-as-you-go model has the advantage of eliminating the incentive for either the employee or the employer to break its side of the contract. The best-known example of training wages is in craft work, in which apprentices make substantially less than journeymen but soon become worth much more. Wages go up as soon as workers advance to the journeyman level. This practice compensates the firm for its training costs.

The economic model of professional services firms in law, accounting, or consulting is essentially based on the idea of training wages. The work of associates is billed to clients at a substantially higher rate than the associates themselves are paid, a rate that more than compensates for the administrative costs of employing them. That practice stops when they are promoted to partner, because partners receive profits from the relationship with associates. The lure of making partner keeps associates in the game, along with the fact that the period of suppressed wages is relatively short.[15]

In the corporate world, similar arrangements sometimes apply. For example, it's widely thought that Procter & Gamble can pay lower salaries than its competitors because it offers much better developmental opportunities for new entrants.

E.J. Gallo Wineries has long been known for having one of the best training and developmental programs for sales jobs. Drew Logan, a former Gallo sales associate, notes that there were twenty-five applicants for every position in the Gallo sales class of twelve in which he was hired.[16] The program is rigorous, demanding a great deal from the trainees. It is also known as a program in which employees are not paid particularly well, and many wash out. Those who make it to seven years are given equity in the company and rarely leave.

But participants are highly sought after by other employers, bidding up their wages considerably after they have been in the program. Logan went on to a sales job at Boston Scientific and helped form what became a pipeline from the Gallo sales program into the Boston Scientific sales organization. Even though Gallo was a wine program and Boston Scientific was a medical device company, Gallo became the number 1 company from which Boston Scientific hired—all through the sales function. Thus the hard work and relatively low pay of the Gallo program led to a payoff for the employees later, sometimes at other companies.

Tuition Assistance

A clever way to share the costs of skill development with employees is through tuition assistance programs. In most of these programs, the employer pays part or most of the tuition costs of a postsecondary education program, and the employees typically do the work on their own time. Classes are scheduled after working hours, and students do their course work and studying after working hours. The Bureau of the Census estimates that the average level of employer-provided assistance was equal to about one-third of the total costs of tuition and fees paid by postsecondary students.[17]

The American Council of Education calculates that roughly 20 percent of graduate students receive financial assistance from their employers to attend school, and roughly 6 percent of the much bigger pool of all undergraduates receive such aid.[18] Considering only adult students—who are more likely to be employed when they are in school and therefore have the possibility of receiving aid from employers—the Adult Education Survey of the National Center on Educational Statistics found that 24 percent of adults in postsecondary education programs of the kind that offered credentials (degrees or certificates) were receiving tuition assistance from an employer.[19]

The extent to which employers provide assistance can be measured more directly from surveys of employers, and those results suggest that employer-provided support is ubiquitous. My own work with the Census finds that about 85 percent of employers provide some tuition assistance for course work that they have approved. A Hewitt Associates survey found that about 6.5 percent of all employees in those firms take them up at any point in time.[20] There is some evidence that support for tuition assistance may be declining; a 2002 survey by the Society for Human Resource Management found only 79 percent of larger employers offering some kind of support for education.[21] Still, most employers help pay for their employees to receive postsecondary education.

Because the most important aspect of development costs is the cost of the time candidates spend in training, tuition assistance provides an attractive option for employers. Still, it is surprising that so many employers offer tuition assistance; it represents the type of investment that we would not expect employers to make, because the skills and knowledge it produces are useful to other employers. Postsecondary education is about as transparent a credential to other employers of one's ability as could exist.[22]

Ultimately, employers must recoup the investment in tuition, and they must do that by getting value from employees that exceeds their wages.

My research found that tuition assistance programs seemed to attract higher-quality applicants. It's easy to see how this happens. Any employee who is willing to go to school in the evenings and weekends while working full time is a hard worker, and those individuals are the ones attracted to employers that offer tuition assistance. How much more productive or effective would a worker have to be to pay off the costs of using tuition assistance? About 10 percent better for the average worker *in just one year* is enough to recoup the employer's costs for the typical worker who uses the program, less for higher-value employees. If performance is even trivially above average for more than one year, the employer makes money on the investment. In other words, a small increment in productivity advantage over the several years an employee is likely to be with the organization makes it worthwhile.

But do education and its credentials make employees more likely to quit for jobs elsewhere? After all, the education makes them more valuable to a range of employers, raising their market wage. If they leave, tuition assistance programs would be a nightmare for employers in that all the investment would be lost. But in fact, these programs are associated with lower rates of turnover.[23] A possibly cynical explanation is that employees who use these programs stay around just to take advantage of them. It takes a long time for someone going to school in the evenings to secure a degree or other marketable credential. Even if the tuition benefits were seen simply as a retention bonus, they would be more than worthwhile.[24]

Harleysville Insurance is a Pennsylvania-based company that has taken the use of tuition assistance programs to a new height. The company has a generous program, and its leadership pushes employees to use the program as a way to keep learning and developing themselves. At any given time, about one-third of the company's employees—including the executives—are taking college-level course work. Many of the advanced jobs in the company, especially in the technical aspects of insurance, have requirements that can be met through outside course work and credentials offered by insurance industry association classes. Engaging in these classes is an important part of the formal advancement process. Employees share in the costs by doing a large part of the learning on their own time.[25]

Education and Development Contracts

An increasingly common method of securing a return on an investment in employees is to use legal contracts to exchange education and other expensive developmental programs for continued service. These arrangements are ubiquitous for programs such as executive MBAs, in which employers provide tuition assistance and time off from work. In return, employees agree to stay with the employer for a specified period.

These contracts often require that if employees leave before the contract is up, they must pay back the employer's investment in their education. At a minimum, they ensure that the employer does not lose money on the deal. About 20 percent of U.S. employers have such requirements, and the average required length of stay—six months—is remarkably small.[26]

Perhaps the most extensive use of development contracts takes place in Singapore's Public Service Division. The first step in formation of the government's talent management programs, and arguably one of the first policies when the country was formed, was to create a set of high-potential programs to fill the most important government jobs. The Singapore government seeks out talent early—in high schools—by identifying the best students and selecting them for future employment. Selection is based in large part on high school examination results, the British "A" level exams. Approximately two hundred of these high-flying students are identified each year, and they are offered an interesting proposition: they are sent abroad at government expense to the best foreign universities, typically in the United States and the United Kingdom. This is a substantial investment that even upper-middle-class families would otherwise find difficult; it is impossible for those with less income. The students have an obligation when they return—and they are required to return— to work for the Singapore government for six years to pay off their "bond," or debt, to the government.[27]

The back-and-forth experience of U.S. employers in sponsoring MBA students suggests how the incentives behind these contracts operate. Before the mid-1990s, employers typically paid for executive MBA programs. In some schools, such as Wharton, it was a requirement for entry.

After 1995, employers grew so concerned that the students would take their degrees and go elsewhere that a great many began to withdraw their support, and many of the programs were at risk of going under. Education contracts turned things around, and within a year or so, virtually every student in these programs had a legal obligation to their employers of the kind I've outlined.

After 2001, employers began to reduce the proportion of program costs they would pay, in part recognizing that the employees would ultimately be the beneficiaries. Now, students in these programs have begun to say that the employers' limited financial contributions no longer justify the legal obligation to stay with them after finishing the program. Many are turning down employer support and paying for their own expenses.

Training Before Hiring

Arguably the most straightforward way to have employees share the costs is to ask them to take a training or developmental program before they are hired. This sounds like a sneaky idea, but it happens all the time. Most jobs have requirements that candidates are expected to meet: skill credentials such as being Cisco certified in certain IT systems, licenses in the brokerage industry, MBA degrees in some business jobs. But it is unusual for employers to require candidates to pay for and receive training programs that are quite specific and unique to the employers. In 1985, United Airlines surprised many observers by bringing five hundred pilots into its flight training program but not actually employing them. The candidates were taking the training on their own time without pay, but with the implicit promise that completing the program would lead to a job.[28]

Other interesting examples are in technical skills and involve community colleges, which in the United States have become one of the most important sources for employee training. In North Carolina, for example, community colleges help employers design new-hire training programs that provide general skills, targeted now at the biotech industry. The colleges deliver them to potential candidates, who pay the tuition themselves at relatively low cost. Successful candidates are offered jobs by the employers. Relationships like these have become particularly strong with equipment vendors, especially foreign companies trying to get a foothold in the United States, which use the community colleges to teach employees and customers how to use their products.[29]

To see how extensive the move toward requiring credentials in advance has become, look at the changes over time in the choice of college majors. In 1971, for example, students with business-related degrees accounted for one-fifth of all undergraduates. By 2004, they accounted for one-third.[30] It is also clear that people are making greater use of community colleges as a means of improving work-related skills: some 28 percent of community college students taking nondegree courses have bachelor's or higher degrees, and the courses they take tend to be job related.[31]

Of particular interest is the MBA degree, which accounted for only about one in eight master's degrees in the 1970s but rose to about one in three by 2004.[32] The increase was driven by hiring practices. Before 1980, it was common among large employers to hire graduates right out of undergraduate programs and then put them through an extensive classroom program that gave them some of the experience of an MBA degree. Now, they are much more likely to hire recent MBA graduates for similar jobs.

What's the difference? In the former, employers hired cheaper employees but made an investment in them; in the latter, they hire more-expensive employees who pay for that business education themselves. From the perspective of the employer, the difference is all about risk—the risk of losing the investment if the employee leaves or of overestimating the need for talent. Hiring MBAs is a way of reducing that risk by pushing it off to employees.

Promote and Then Develop

A novel model in management development is the practice of providing developmental support and experiences for individuals after they have been promoted into new positions. This approach makes sense now because it eliminates the risks associated with mismatch problems: by investing only in candidates who you know for certain will be doing the job, you eliminate the uncertainty and the potential costs of wasting or losing that investment. Once in the new role, employees receive extensive support—coaching, on-demand training programs, assistance from centers of excellence, and so on. One can think of this as just-in-time development.

The cost of this approach is that you must deliver developmental experiences irregularly, as needed, and you lose advantages of scale. Employers often use outside contractors—in particular, executive coaches—to provide this kind of development and reduce some scale costs. Union Carbide adopted the interesting practice of using retired executives or those about to retire as part of a pool of mentors and advisers—essentially coaches—for executives in training.

Part of the explanation for the promote-and-coach approach may be that traditional developmental efforts no longer exist and that inexperienced candidates are promoted by default because there are no experienced candidates. Libby Sartain, former head of human resources for Southwest Airlines, reports that Southwest routinely promoted line workers to supervisory jobs and then developed them, in large part because the company was growing so fast that it could not meet the demand otherwise.[33] And in contrast to more typical models, the individuals in these new roles are highly motivated to learn. They have a clear need to know the material, they see why the content matters, and the combination of instruction and practice leads to immediate benefits.

Extending the Benefits of Development Through Retention

You can make your investments in training and development much more cost effective through better employee retention. Retention keeps developed employees on the job longer, giving you a longer period to recoup your investment. Retention programs can also make employee tenure more predictable even if it does not necessarily keep employees longer. In that case, the return on your investment becomes more certain and does not require as large a payoff to compensate for the uncertainty and to be competitive with other investments.

An enormous practitioner literature discusses how to retain employees, but the basic principles are straightforward. The first is based on the fact that virtually all employees who leave jobs move immediately into other positions elsewhere. This implies that the important issue is how your job stacks up against the alternatives.

The *employer of choice* approach, which began in the tight labor market of the late 1990s, was based on the realization that good employees were in a competitive labor market and that it was essential to provide better terms and conditions than competitors offered. This spawned the concierge services, gourmet lunches, and pet-sitter programs that were popular at the time. Although there is a competitive market for employees and they will leave jobs that fall below the standards offered elsewhere, there are more-strategic approaches for managing retention than simply chasing each new employee perk.[34]

One of the most fundamental tools for managing retention is employee development, a powerful tool given the earlier findings about its importance to employees. For example, the Sun Healthcare Group was concerned about employee turnover and surveyed employees on what would make their jobs better. The leading response was opportunities to advance in their careers. So the company launched a training and development initiative designed to expand internal promotions, and turnover fell by 20 percent.[35] This option can be a sustainable source of competitive advantage in the talent market if you can find ways to deliver development in a cost-effective manner.

Better Matches. The first approach is based on the fact that employees who feel that they truly fit the organization are much less likely to quit.[36] The implications for employers are to be clearer about the distinctive aspects of their organizations when recruiting so that employees who do not fit do not bother to apply. They should also be careful in selecting employees to ensure that they truly fit.

You make better matches by allowing employees to craft arrangements that suit their needs. Flex-time work schedules, cafeteria-style benefit programs, and other policies help. Denise Rousseau, of Carnegie-Mellon University, says that a remarkable number of employees have special arrangements on issues like work schedules with their immediate supervisors that go beyond the official arrangements.[37]

Social Relationships. Individuals are committed to people as well as to organizations, and the ties that bind people to one another can easily be more powerful than those that bind them to an abstract entity such as a corporation. As a result, social relationships can provide a means for retaining talent. Programs that foster personal relationships at work—social clubs and community-based activities—are one way to build those relationships. But workplace arrangements also can build them.

Teamwork is a special means for building social relationships and making individuals feel collectively obligated to their work. Team members can be motivated to work hard at their jobs because they do not want to let down the rest of the team. And the more accountable a team is for its performance, the greater the peer pressure on members to make sacrifices for the good of the team. Team-based compensation, in particular, helps create the sense that the fate of the community relies on the performance of its individual members. Even in industries long characterized by hostile relations between employees and employers, such as the U.S. auto industry, the redesign of production work around teams has contributed to sharp improvements in quality and overall performance, at least in part by engendering greater worker commitment.

Even with these techniques, however, it is not realistic, nor is it necessarily desirable, to expect to keep all employees forever or to reduce voluntary turnover to zero. Making turnover more predictable, however, is a reasonable and useful goal. Here the techniques are also straightforward.

Compensation. Techniques like stock options and retention bonuses clearly work, in that they hold employees until the options can be exercised and the bonuses received. Employees are then much more likely to move, but that in no way suggests that the techniques do not work. Their goal is to retain employees for a fixed period, influencing when they leave.

Project Work. Organizing work in projects is another way to shape retention. Studies have shown that when employees have control over a distinct piece of work, they have greater commitment to seeing it done well because they "own" it. If the project goes well, they get the credit, and that increases their prestige (and helps build their resume). They stay to complete the project because they are committed to it psychologically and also materially.

Poaching. One way to improve retention is by making it less attractive for competitors to poach your employees. Training and developmental programs can convey signals to the outside market about the value of an individual. As noted earlier, the clearest of these signals are skills credentials or educational credentials. Some organizations have become careful about granting these credentials.

For example, when the Monterey language institute (at the U.S. Naval Postgraduate Institute at Monterey) was designing a master's degree experience for its candidates, the program it had in place was one course short of completion of an MBA degree. The institute decided not to offer that course, in part because it would make the graduates much more marketable.[38]

Companies seem much more reluctant now to send their employees to executive developmental programs that offer a general credential, such as a certificate program in finance. Instead, they have shifted to offering programs that teach the same content but do not offer the same credential. At Wharton, for example, the percentage of executive education students has shifted over time from 60 percent taking these general certificate programs to less than 30 percent. An offsetting increase has occurred in customized programs, wherein a company sends a group of its employees to a program that is similar in content but is focused on the company's issues and comes with a company credential, such as the Acme executive program.

More generally, signals about investments in development are less clear to the market if they are broken into discrete pieces and combined over time with work experience. Consider, for example, the Organization Man approach, in which candidates were put through a regimented and intensive program that came with a clear completion date and something like a credential—the Acme leadership program. Contrast that with a model in which candidates are placed in short developmental courses, sent back to work to use the content, later taken back out for development, brought back to work, and so on. The development in the latter case is spread over time, reducing the risk of losing the bulk of the investment if an employee quits. It also eliminates the bright light focusing the attention of recruiters on candidates just at the point when the investment in them is completed.

Larger businesses have another good mechanism for managing retention: their ability to choose geographic locations for their operations. By assigning different groups of employees to different locations, they can influence the turnover rates of the people in the groups. A high-tech company, for example, might find it useful to have a research and development operation in Silicon Valley and tap in to cutting-edge thinking. The turnover rate will be high, but that's an advantage. By constantly bringing in new people, the company will be able to expose itself to the broadest array of ideas.

When the company wants to set up an R&D project with a long lead time, however, it might want to shield the project members from Silicon Valley's hyperactive talent market. A high level of turnover could doom the effort. The company would be wise to house the project in a location where the skills of the project members are not in high demand—perhaps a bucolic rural community. People will still leave from time to time, but overall turnover will be much lower.

SAS Institute's software operations have famously low employee turnover—about 4 percent in an industry that averages around 20 percent per year. SAS relies on a host of employer choice perks as well as workplace flexibility policies that allow employees to craft special working arrangements. But it is also located away from other competitors—North Carolina, not Silicon Valley—and this means that employees who want to leave the company will have to pack up their families and move them.[39]

Making Turnover Predictable. Even if you cannot reduce the rate of turnover or increase average tenure, it is still possible to improve the returns on employee development by making turnover predictable. Wall Street investment firms were once plagued by erratic, unplanned turnover among junior analysts. The companies addressed the problem by requiring the analysts to leave after three years.

Forcing people to quit may seem like an odd way to solve a turnover problem, but it made a lot of sense. The real issue, after all, was not that the junior analysts were leaving—it was expected that many would go on to business school—but that the firms could not precisely predict who would leave and when. As a result, project teams were often left understaffed, leading to delays and quality problems. Now that they know junior analysts will depart at the end of their third year, the firms can design projects to coincide with analysts' tenures.

Having clear termination dates also creates large, well-defined employee cohorts, easing training and development. And the fact that the three-year tenure is now an industry standard helps ensure that employees stay for the full period. It looks bad on a resume to have been in a junior analyst job for less than three years.

Leaving Without Letting Go. In an earlier period, perhaps extending through the mid-1990s, leaving a corporation voluntarily was seen as the ultimate act of disloyalty. Those who left were cut dead, at least officially, by those who remained. There were, of course, exceptions. McKinsey & Company retained a famously loyal group of alumni, as did The Chase Manhattan Corporation.

But groups like these were largely self-organized until the tight labor market of the 1990s caused many employers to think differently about those who had left. Employers developed an interest in using them as another source of talent, one that was essentially prescreened. Selectminds .com helps client companies develop and stay in touch with their employee alumni. The hook for the alumni is to get in touch with the people they used to work with. The benefit for the company is the opportunity to find out what the alumni are doing now—essentially to look over their resumes—and perhaps to bring the most attractive candidates back into the fold.[40]

Active approaches involve getting and keeping hooks into employees before they leave. During the IT downturn after 2001, Cisco offered a voluntary sabbatical to its employees: the company would pay one-third of their salaries for a period if they went to work for nonprofit organizations. Although this practice certainly helped the nonprofit world and may have helped the Cisco brand, it was also a clever way to keep employees in the Cisco orbit. A nonprofit was by definition not a competitor, and few people could live on one-third of their salaries. So there was a good chance that the employees on sabbatical would not want to stay in their new roles and would be ready and willing to come back to full-time employment when business picked up and the need for them at Cisco returned.[41]

Deloitte has a wide-ranging program that keeps former U.S. employees of Deloitte and Touche plugged in to the company for as long as five years after they leave. The Personal Pursuits program is offered for those better employees who leave the company for reasons other than a new job. (Family issues are the target motivation.) The program pays to keep the certifications and skills of the participants up-to-date (a policy that can be expensive for accountants), offers access to company career and work–life programs, and requires regular checkups with company human resource staff to keep the participants up-to-date about career opportunities and company developments. The company's motivation is to make sure that when these highly skilled, high performers are personally ready to come back to work, they are also professionally ready, and that the easiest place by far for them to work would be Deloitte.[42]

Maximizing the Value of Internal Development

The examples illustrate that reducing the costs and risks of internal development can expand its use. Another approach to creating value is to find ways to increase the benefits from development.

Compensation does not necessarily reflect the value of one's contribution to the current employer but instead signals to the market one's value to employers elsewhere. Developmental programs and experiences may signal value to the market, but the most important signals come from the jobs employees hold and the tasks they perform. It is difficult, for example, to have someone hold the title of systems analyst in an IT department without signaling that this person can do the work of a systems analyst.

In the late 1990s, there was a move afoot to change job titles to conform more closely to the types of tasks individuals performed. Business cards began sporting job titles like "Project Leader for XYZ Initiative." Such titles conveyed little to outsiders about what the person actually did. Companies like Cigna made efforts to disguise the e-mail addresses of key employees, in part to keep recruiters from pestering them. Now company-specific job titles have disappeared, in large measure, I believe, because the individuals wanted people outside their own company—in the market—to have a clearer sense of how the jobs they performed mapped to jobs elsewhere.

The key to earning a return on investments in employees, therefore, is to find those practices that improve value without necessarily raising wages. The one advantage that you have in this regard—and it is considerable—is to exploit your superior knowledge about the abilities of your employees. Because you can observe behavior on the job and measure performance, you are in an ideal position to know what individual employees are capable of and to place capable workers into jobs where they can contribute the most. Knowledge of the value of those individuals will ultimately get to the market. Search consultants are in the business of sniffing out high performers. But it will take awhile to get there.

Consider two candidates for promotion. "Linda," who has an MBA from a prominent business school, worked her way up the hierarchy of the company's corporate financial staff to the director level before being appointed CFO of that division. The second candidate, "Bob," has no graduate degree and was pulled up from managing the finances of one of the business units to be CFO of the division because of excellent performance in that small operation.

The market understands Linda's value because of the prior signals—the graduate degree, the previous positions. Assuming no stumbles in her performance, competitors will soon be willing to hire her away at the market wage. Thus, her employer will have to pay that amount. Bob, in contrast, gives no such signals to the market. If anything, other employers would see his promotion as a puzzle, premature at best. It will take considerable seasoning and some visible successes in his new role before competitors will see Bob as a viable candidate for their vacancies. From the perspective of the employee, the promotion is worth much more to Bob, who is likely to be more grateful. It is also possible to pay him much less because no outside employer is willing to offer him the same job. Given equivalent levels of performance from the two, the employer makes much more money from Bob than from Linda.

Some companies try to delay the market signal of a promotion by having employees take on the tasks associated with a promotion but giving them the new title (and associated compensation) only after they have proven themselves in the new role.

The best returns from talent management come from giving capable employees good opportunities before they can get them on the outside. Two actions are crucial. The first is spotting talent. Can you identify who is ready to take a role that adds more value to the organization? The sooner you can do that, the more value you create. The second is keeping track of opportunities and being able to place capable individuals in them when openings occur. The sooner you can make a match between capable candidates and openings that maximize their value, the more value you can create.

Most companies do not think this way. A survey of large U.S. employers about their staffing practices indicates that only one in four currently requires that hiring managers look inside before going to the outside labor market to fill vacancies. Less than half even delay the posting of jobs on the outside market to give internal candidates the opportunity to apply first.[43]

Spotting Talent Through High-Potential Programs

One approach to spotting talent is through high-potential programs. These arrangements identify individuals early in their careers who appear to have the talent and ability to hold executive positions and then mold them for those positions. Developmental experiences are concentrated on these people, and they are targeted for faster promotions and feature prominently in long-term succession plans.

Are these programs good ideas, and if so, how should they be executed? Recall from chapter 2 that after World War II, companies created fast-track promotion paths to get a new generation of leaders into the leadership ranks quickly. High-potential programs were created to identify and then develop the candidates to fill those fast-track paths.

There is no equivalent problem now. Even if new generations with new skills are needed in certain industries and companies, lateral hiring makes it easy to bring them aboard. As described in detail later, promotion paths are now so open that promising leaders do not need to wait around before they see real action. Special fast-track arrangements are rarely needed. But companies do not have unlimited resources for development, and they must somehow decide which individuals get the most important developmental assignments.

The usual approach has been to attempt to predict early in people's careers who has the right stuff to become executives. Historically, these efforts relied heavily on assessment tests. The problem is that these efforts were virtually leaps of faith based on assumptions that the criteria being measured were the important factors in leadership. These tests within companies were almost never validated or examined. They were difficult to validate because only high-scoring candidates were promoted; without systematic experimentation it was impossible to tell how much better the high scorers ultimately fared in their careers compared with those who scored lower. It is like trying to see whether grades in school predict business success but looking only at straight-A students.[44]

Yet many companies still rely on tests and assessments of various kinds of potential. A study of companies with high-potential programs in the mid-1980s found that about one in five selected candidates when they were hired, before they were even employed. Virtually all the companies made that determination in the first few years on the job.[45]

Randall Redd describes his experience as a new hire at DuPont in the early 1980s.[46] DuPont conducted a "corporate promotability" ranking, a separate review that was done for new hires after roughly two years of service and every year or so after that. As Redd describes it, "The goal was to identify potential future senior executives and get them onto the corporate radar screen early enough that they could wind their way up the ladder fast enough to be useful. An engineer or chemist had to be promoted an average of every twelve to eighteen months if they were to make CEO before retirement age because there are so many levels."

Candidates were assessed against a list of criteria for their promotability score. "But it was obvious when I met the mid- and upper-level managers that there was something else they valued. At six feet tall, I am normally one of the taller people in the room, but these guys were all six feet two to six feet five. So, being very conscious about promotional opportunities, I asked my boss at the time if there was a height requirement for senior management. He said yes, they considered being more than six feet tall to be a key element in creating an 'executive presence.'" Most corporate executives were tall then, and if one relied strictly on predictions that mapped to the attributes of successful executives, height would be on the list. If managers acted on that information in making promotability judgments, executives would continue to be tall because short ones would never get the opportunity to advance.[47]

Royal Dutch/Shell Group of Companies is perhaps the best-known example of relying on paper-and-pencil tests and other measures of potential as the most important factor in determining access to management track positions, having done so for more than a generation. Many other companies use assessments of potential provided by vendors. The better ones include in-box-style simulations of work tasks. The evidence suggests that these assessments are predictive at least of job performance, but why they work is not entirely clear—that is, what key factors they identify that drive performance. They do not seem to add much value beyond what is already known about candidates based on current job performance and attributes such as education and experience.[48]

I see nothing but problems with traditional high-potential programs in the current environment. First, as noted, the problem these programs were designed to address no longer exists. Second, they represent the most extreme example of long-term career planning, which, for the reasons noted earlier, is not likely to be functional. Third, these arrangements generate a range of equity problems inside organizations. For example, to the extent that high-potential programs are seen as special recognition and a reward of sorts, the reward is not for performance, which is the usual goal in organizations. It is for potential, something that is hard to see and can easily appear arbitrary.

Telling someone that he is not being recognized or promoted because of a lack of potential is devastating, because it is saying that he has a flaw he may not be able to do anything about, especially if the assessments rely on factors like cognitive ability and personality. It essentially says that he has no future career here. If he is interested in advancing, he should probably leave. That might be the appropriate action if you are absolutely sure that criteria like cognitive ability and personality are necessary conditions to being successful in senior jobs. But factors that cannot be observed in the current job performance are so trivial in predicting future performance that relying on them is not worth the costs.

Another issue with high-potential programs is how individuals will move in and out of them: how do you determine whether someone no longer has "potential"? If it is difficult to fall out of the high-potential program, then it is easy to perceive the whole effort as something like a caste system, driven largely by accidents of birth and experiences that have nothing to do with job performance.

There are also important legal issues associated with efforts to assess potential. Various court rulings in civil rights cases, most prominently the landmark *Griggs* v. *Duke Power* case, established the principle that the criteria used to hire should be limited to predicting the ability to perform in the job that is being filled, and not future jobs in the organization. If it is possible to be taken out of these programs and placed into them later, as most observers would think is reasonable, then the most relevant criterion for doing so would be job performance. In practice, talent pools have the key attribute that candidates are moved into and out of the pools based on factors like performance.[49]

As with succession planning, high-potential programs create expectations for advancement and also foster divisions in the workplace. Libby Sartain, now senior vice president of human resources at Yahoo!, says that the company does not label anyone a "high potential." She says, "You've found out that a colleague has been labeled high-potential: Think of how you'd feel. You're going, 'If he's a high-po, and I don't know I'm a high-po, does that mean I'm a low-po?'"[50]

These problems argue strongly for using performance rather than potential as the main criterion in assessing candidates for developmental experiences. Yet it is possible to be a star contributor as an individual and not have the capabilities to be a leader. One reason is that some measures ignore or downplay some aspects of behavior and performance, such as relations with coworkers, which are important for leaders. But we can measure interpersonal skills in current jobs and at least some of the aspects that are relevant for advancement if we are so inclined. If the problem is that the requirements of current jobs do not allow us to observe the important attributes and competencies that senior positions require, then we are more constrained. But there are still alternatives to tests or other indirect measures for assessing potential, and these rely on the straightforward approach of creating opportunities to observe actual behavior.

Spotting Talent Through Opportunities

The ultimate prediction mechanism—and the only one that is truly reliable—is to give the candidates a chance to perform. The downside of this approach is that such opportunities can be costly. When candidates fail in their jobs, part of the organization also fails. Procter & Gamble has a motto about new product development, which is equally applicable in this context of employee development: "Learn how to fail quickly and cheaply." For employee development, this means we must identify or even create situations in which candidates can take on leadership roles but the associated consequences are small. If the candidate fails, the organization finds out about it quickly and can intervene before there are big problems. Or, if the consequences are not immediate, the downside risk is small.

If scale matters—for example, when you need to evaluate many candidates—it may make sense to create systems for trying them out. Assessment centers are an effort to simulate some of the important tasks involved with senior jobs and then examine how well candidates handle them. Federal Express designed a sophisticated simulation of the front-line supervisor's job in an effort to let candidates try it out for a day. A benefit of the program was to persuade many of the candidates—perhaps even most—that they did not want that job and therefore should not clamor to be promoted. Clothing retailer Lands' End allows employees to request two-week assignments in another department. If that assignment works out for both parties and there is an opening, they can then transfer to that department; if not, they go back to their old area.[51]

General Electric is known for its use of these try-out positions. The company maintained many so-called popcorn stands—small businesses with separate profit-and-loss responsibilities that otherwise could have been consolidated—precisely to support these low-risk opportunities. Many organizations have similar opportunities that they fail to exploit. For example, many retail banks complain about the lack of developmental opportunities. Yet they also have large numbers of retail branches, which can be operated like small businesses with their own profit-and-loss requirements. These jobs could give local managers the opportunity to fail quickly and cheaply in that they tap the same competencies needed to run larger operations with smaller potential costs of failure.

In part as an effort to jump-start new business development but also as part of a management development process, IBM has begun pulling its star senior executives from executive jobs and moving them into start-ups or emerging business opportunities. They are sent—on their own or with a colleague—to figure out how to turn a new idea into a business opportunity. In the process, the executives are shaken out of their old behavior and assumptions and get a low-cost opportunity to run a business from the ground up.[52]

Self-Selection as an Alternative

An even simpler model for identifying people to receive scarce developmental resources relies on self-selection. Rather than try to estimate who is worthy of support, these arrangements let individuals nominate themselves. The idea is that individuals know things about themselves that their employers cannot easily discover, in part because the employees may have no incentive to be truthful. For example, few people will give an honest answer to that favorite interview question, "What is your worst characteristic?" The key is to design the self-selection process so that it creates incentives to be honest. Among the important information that you might want to know is how hard the candidate is willing to work if given a leadership role. Most ambitious people might be willing to answer, "Very," but will they put their money where their mouths are? The clever self-selection arrangements offer developmental experiences that supplement volunteers' usual workloads.

A good illustration of self-selection comes from PNC Bank of Pittsburgh, where the development team meets with the bank's senior executives to develop a list of projects the executives would like to have done in their areas. Then the development staff contacts a group of potential candidates, typically at the director level, to see whether they are interested. Because the projects are designed to be broadening experiences, the candidates cannot apply for projects in their current functional areas. The projects must be done along with their current jobs, although the development staff meets with the candidate's current bosses to negotiate some leeway. In return for the extra work, candidates get exposure to a new functional area and to the senior executive team.

Not everyone finds this deal attractive. Only some apply to work on a project—those who truly value development and are willing to pay a price to self-select into the program. The program sorts out those who are truly interested.

Nugget Markets also allows individuals to self-select into development roles. In addition, it addresses the concern that their managers and organization might not support their interest: the corporate office subsidizes the compensation budget of those who undertake these experiences.

Commonwealth Edison, the New York public utility, goes a step further. Self-nomination is the first step in a person's becoming something like a high-potential candidate, necessary for promotion in the management ranks. The process is similar to tenure review for academic professors: a potential candidate submits a list of five peers and three superior managers to her supervisor, who then selects one peer and one superior to complete a competency assessment. If she surpasses the target score, her name is added to a succession pool. If not, she remains in her current circumstance. In either case, she receives feedback on her assessment, learning about her strengths and weaknesses.

The company maintains different succession pools for different types of promotions, and the successful candidates are sorted into those pools based on the patterns of their competency assessments. Once in the succession pool, they receive additional developmental experiences, including a 360 degree feedback assessment. When a vacancy appears, the candidates in the appropriate pool can again apply for it. The hiring managers then choose among the applicants, going outside only under limited circumstances.

The idea of this arrangement is to make promotion and advancement more transparent, open, and fair—something it surely does—and to get away from the "tap on the shoulder" model, wherein ambitious employees had to simply wait around until someone picked them for advancement.[53] It empowers the employees, eases anxiety, and reduces the likelihood that ambitious workers will get antsy waiting for opportunities and leave for positions elsewhere. It can also be cheaper than a system of tracking management performance across the workforce and picking candidates.

As in the PNC example, an ideal nomination system requires that individuals sort themselves out in ways that reveal useful information. This requires that there be some costs or aspects of applying that are not desirable for those who lack the appropriate attributes. Self-nomination attracts ambitious candidates, and ambition is an important component for advancement. The risk of being turned down and the social cost of asking peers and supervisors to evaluate one's potential and performance may be enough to keep those who lack the appropriate attributes from applying. However, those who are ambitious but who lack enough self-awareness to gauge their own capabilities are probably not put off by this arrangement.

Satish Pradhan, executive vice president of the Tata group of companies in India, describes its process. Candidates for development bid for openings in the TAS division, which is known for establishing leadership credentials. Candidates must demonstrate how the desired job will help them build their own competencies. Candidates who secure these positions are then slotted into leadership positions in the other Tata companies after they finish these developmental assignments.

Tatweer, one of the development companies under the Dubai Holdings umbrella, goes further. It asks potential candidates to apply for its high potential program, but the application process, which includes panel interviews with company outsiders, is difficult enough that those who are not truly motivated shy away. As described earlier, the company also expects the participants to help pay for the program by taking it on in addition to their current position—a requirement for continuing in the program is to maintain above average performance reviews in their current job.

Creating a Market for Opportunities

The Goodrich Company has developed an interesting innovation for matching candidates with assignments at the entry level of the engineering function. Andrew Chrostowski, a vice president in manufacturing, describes how the company developed a series of job rotational assignments for new engineers coming into the program. The first challenge was to identify interesting and useful tasks that offered real learning opportunities. The company did not want to create "make work" jobs that add no value to the businesses. The second challenge was to find a good way to match the development needs of candidates with the opportunities available.

Goodrich's Manufacturing Leadership Program begins with an incentive for the business units to use the new engineering candidates in developmental assignments. The company covers half the salary costs, and the business units pay the other half. To get candidates, the business units essentially bid for them by submitting an application describing the job, the tasks to be performed, and the learning candidates will gain. Because of the labor cost subsidies, these candidates are desirable for the operating units; there are roughly twice as many positions as there are candidates, so the program's managing committee can be choosy. The business units know that their proposals must deliver learning for participants. A bad experience damages their ability to get a candidate next time.

For its part, the program's managing committee tries to match the needs and interests of the candidates to the proposed projects. Because each candidate goes through three developmental assignments, one criterion is how the next assignment will fit with previous ones.

This kind of developmental program has an additional benefit in that it provides a faster path for the most able candidates, arguably faster—and clearly easier—than they could get by shopping for opportunities in the outside market. The self-service aspect of some of these arrangements offers employees an element of control over their circumstances that helps reduce stress and may be of particular value to the most ambitious employees. Faster promotion paths and the opportunity to control one's destiny are perhaps the ultimate factors in building retention, an issue we take up in chapter 7.

Chapter 6 Appendix

Development Models
from Abroad

The Singapore government takes a systematic approach to talent development, beginning with something like an open market where the sponsored scholars list their preferences for work. (Recall that these students have received postsecondary scholarships in return for a commitment to serve in the government.) At about age thirty, a subset of these administrative services officers is selected into the ranks of the Senior Management Program based on an assessment of their managerial potential.

The Senior Management Program offers a two-month training course on management and administrative principles, further job rotation, and exposure through various projects to the thinking and decision making of the most senior government officials. From this point forward, candidates are in the hunt to become the next generation of senior officials. For positions above the level of director—what one would think of as entry-level executive ranks—selections are made by the permanent secretary of each ministry. The secretary is aided by a committee of insiders that assesses potential and also keeps in mind the managerial pipeline: how positions will affect the development of candidates, which vacancies are likely to occur in the future, and so on.

For the most senior positions—referred to as public service leadership posts and including permanent secretaries and agency heads—appointments are made by the Public Service Commission, which oversees virtually all aspects of the government. There is an understanding that appointees do not stay in these most senior jobs for more than ten years. In this way, turnover creates opportunities for mobility further down the ranks.

In 2003, the government faced another challenge with respect to the opening of labor markets, this time a demand by some scholars that they be released from their government obligations and be allowed to pay off their debts and go immediately to the private sector. In this case, the government held its ground, threatening, among other things, to shame any scholars who failed to complete their bond by publishing their names and stories in the media.

Development in India

Infosys is one of the most important companies in the world, a key player in the Indian economy and in the global world of information technology. The demand for talent at Infosys has grown so rapidly—with a few hundred employees in 1999, by 2005 it had more than forty thousand—that it could not meet its needs by hiring college graduates with IT training or with other outside hiring. So it turned to internal development. Its new training and development center in Meysore, India, is spread over 287 acres, with its own sports complex, multiplex cinemas, and dormitory complexes. The campus is so big that it appears to spell out I-N-F-O-S-Y-S when seen from the air.

When I visited the campus, Infosys was preparing to accept four thousand trainees at one time. The company now hires bright college graduates from a range of fields and puts them into a fourteen-week on-site training program to turn them into IT professionals. About twelve days of annual training are expected thereafter. Its human capital planning process builds out twenty months in advance and includes special leadership development programs to pull front-line workers into the management ranks.

Meanwhile, WiPro, its cross-town competitor in Bangalore, has similar arrangements, including highly detailed competency models outlining the exact skills that new hires need to become proficient in their jobs, along with the training and work experience steps needed to achieve that proficiency.

The most sophisticated and largest-scale employee development programs in the world now take place at companies like these in India. The reason has to do with the talent crunch they face. Just like U.S. firms after World War II, these companies find that there is not enough talent coming out of the universities to meet their needs, nor can they hire enough from their competitors. So their only alternative is to do it themselves.

7

Managing an Internal Market to Match Talent to Jobs

Previous chapters describe the challenge of uncertainty in talent management, an important consequence of which is that employers no longer can plan long-term careers for individuals. The notion of a career plan (from the perspective of the individual) or a succession plan (from the perspective of the employer) that identifies certain employees to move to certain jobs at certain times is a thing of the past. Even identifying a particular career pathway is hard.

What is taking the place of these outmoded practices? How do you determine which employees get which jobs, and more broadly, how will employees move and advance in their careers?

Given that few employers are able or willing to provide developmental experiences or even to guide career advancement in their organizations, it is probably no surprise that their lack of availability now makes these practices desirable for employees. When you factor in the benefits of internal development for recruiting and employee retention, it might well make sense for you to provide more developmental experiences and more internal career advancement opportunities than would be justified strictly from the perspective of meeting anticipated demand in recruiting and retaining talent. Career development appears to be one of the most desirable attributes for employees, and yet from the perspective of the employer, career development is at best highly uncertain and costly. What can you offer that is realistic, does not risk disappointing employees, and still addresses their interest in development?

A further complication is that employees do not want to be "developed" along the lines of the older model, in which the employer shaped careers to serve its own goals and the individuals had no choice in the matter. In the American version of these arrangements, employees' status, tasks, and prospects were entirely defined by their positions in the bureaucracy, by their job titles.[1] Career advancement meant changing jobs and climbing a well-defined hierarchy of promotions.

The candidates had the ability to turn down new positions, although often such choices were seen as career-ending moves because the new position was a stepping stone to further advancement, one that could not be skipped. Cyril Sofer's account of career advancement in large British corporations during the 1960s notes that taking the decision-making power from employees was precisely the point of these arrangements: "Rather than leave this process [of career development] to chance and to the inclination of the individual to determine for himself the moves that appear to him to be in his own best interests, many senior managements have in recent years embarked on formal schemes for management development."[2] And as Rosabeth Kanter later observed, the fact that employees did not control their career advancement meant that those who did not advance to the positions they wanted or at the pace they expected felt frustrated; the fact that they did not know where or when they would move made them feel helpless.[3]

Employees want as much control over the development process as possible. Research on stress shows that one of the most effective practices to reduce anxiety is to give individuals control: patients on pain medication need less of it when they control the delivery, employees report fewer work–family conflicts when they control their schedules, and we would expect less stress associated with career issues when employees have greater control over the process.

The solutions look a great deal like an open market for talent inside the organization, wherein the employer cedes much of the decision making to employees. If the metaphor for the earlier arrangements was planning, then the one for the new model is search. Candidates as well as employers now actively seek information and opportunities to make good short-term matches inside the firm and to assemble them in ways that meet talent needs and lead to meaningful careers.

The Rise of a Market Model

The most important new idea in the management of careers is the effort to turn over control for at least some aspects of the process to employees. In the early 1990s, when the economy was still reeling from round after round of corporate layoffs, many employers began to tell their employees to manage their own careers. But they did not tell them how to do it nor give them tools for doing so. The charge was more appropriately described as, "Don't expect any help from us." Employees got the message that they needed to be more involved in advancing their own careers.[4]

Opening the internal labor market has largely been a white-collar phenomenon, but its roots are in unionized production work. In the early days of factories, managers had unilateral authority to pick who got which jobs. As one might imagine, the workers were not happy with this model and saw favoritism as the driving factor. Change came with the rise of industrial unions; the criterion determining who should get which job was seniority.

An encyclopedic study of collective bargaining by Harvard professors Sumner Slichter, James Healy, and Richard Livernash outlined how the application of seniority to career advancement led to the job-posting system.[5] The idea was to take discretion and control of the process from individual managers, whose judgment and fairness could not always be trusted, and turn it over to bureaucratic principles embodied in written contracts. The job-posting system was the result. Employers listed (or posted) vacancies, typically on a bulletin board, and employees could then bid (or apply) for the job based on seniority. Management selected the best candidate from those who had bid. As with many unionized arrangements, job posting soon spilled over to nonunion facilities (in an effort to essentially buy out the interest in unionizing) and, on equity grounds, to the white-collar workforce, which was not covered by union contracts.

The constraints on job-posting systems in the white-collar world, however, were considerable. No management jobs were posted, nor typically were the positions that represented the important steps on promotion ladders. Restrictions were placed on which employees could apply for which positions. Most organizations had strict requirements as to how many years potential candidates had to have been in their current positions before they could apply for any internal posting. The idea seemed to be that workers had to pay their dues in a job, basically pay off the investment in training for their current jobs, before they could be allowed to choose something different.

To further limit the costs of individual moves, a worker's current boss typically had to sign off on letting the candidate go if he was selected for the new position. That is, a worker's boss could effectively block the move if the boss thought it would disrupt operations. As a result, often the better a worker's performance, the less likely it was that he would be allowed to move on his own: "You're too important to us to let you go." But if a worker was a poor performer, it was unlikely that anyone would accept him if he were to bid for a position. It was the catch-22 principle operating in the world of career advancement. In practice, this meant that even with a job-posting system, "voluntary" movement was difficult.

It was never clear just how open the posting process was in the white-collar world, because management could manipulate the system informally to select the favored candidate. The "wrong" people could be discouraged from bidding, or the job could be designed so that only a certain candidate fit the criteria. A Society for Human Resource Management publication, for example, recommended to managers that "even if you have an internal process for posting available jobs, there may be times when you decide not to follow this process."[6] For example, you might want to advance the development of particular candidates.

For most organizations and especially for management and white-collar workers, the job-posting systems were a footnote to their career advancement arrangements. But in the economic context of the 1990s, these systems evolved into something much more important.

The Internal Job Board

When many talented employees began leaving for jobs elsewhere in the 1990s, employers could no longer overlook the problem of employee retention. It was galling when it was easier and faster for employees to find new jobs at other organizations than with their current employers—and not necessarily even promotions, only different jobs.

One reason it was easier to find outside jobs was that many companies turned to outside hiring. But it also had to do with the decline of centralized talent management and the decentralization of business operations, a practice that gave operating units profit-and-loss responsibility and autonomy over their operating decisions. Identifying internal opportunities and getting permission from one's current supervisor to apply for them turned out to be big roadblocks. Employers had little information about the knowledge, skills, and abilities of potential workers other than those in their immediate area of responsibility.

A famous anecdote about an important Silicon Valley company told the story of its struggle to find two hundred computer programmers having Java programming skills to fill standing vacancies. The company authorized lucrative signing bonuses to attract outside candidates. At the same time, it took an exit survey of employees who had left the company and found that at least two hundred Java programmers had left, in part, to make better use of their Java skills. Similar developments played out at many other companies.

Beyond the problem of lack of information, divisions that had talented employees saw no reason to share them, especially in tight labor markets. Managers hoarded talent. Examples in consulting firms include partners who strung out projects for star associates until a new project came along, preventing those associates from being released into the pool for other assignments; in the corporate world, outplacement consultants reported that some local managers appeared to have deliberately held down the performance appraisals of their best employees to prevent them from coming to the attention of corporate staff, who otherwise would have pulled them away into corporate jobs.[7]

This problem resembled a game of hide-and-seek between the local and corporate managers. This was in contrast to the preceding generation, when talent management was centralized and the opportunity for advancement extended across an entire enterprise. The employees may not have had any choice about where they were going, but the high performers would definitely move up.

The other development that employers could not fail to miss in the 1990s was the rise of job boards like Monster.com. Employees whose career advancement was blocked could now easily use job boards to look for opportunities elsewhere. They were able to benchmark their internal prospects against those in the outside market and leave if the outside opportunities were better. And when they found those opportunities, they were gone in a shot. The old job hunting model—typing up a resume, identifying companies to contact, sending them letters and hoping they were hiring, and then waiting for interviews, a process that could take weeks—was now condensed to a matter of hours.

The Empowerment of Employees

Some companies developed innovative arrangements to address employees' interest in controlling job changes and, in the process, to retain them. Duke Power offers an example of the entry-level approach to empowering employees. Duke Power employees can, with their supervisor's permission, post their job to see whether someone in the company at an equivalent job level and pay grade would be interested in swapping. Coca-Cola has long had a job fair for its junior auditors; after three years they can look for other jobs inside the company. Clothing retailer Gap created an internal headhunting office where workers with at least two years' experience can look for other positions in the company.[8]

The most important response, however, was the radical expansion of the traditional job-posting system, an expansion that has the potential to transform the entire experience of career progression. The metaphor and language used to describe these new arrangements are very different from the job-posting system and suggest the different purposes behind these new arrangements.[9] The term *internal job board* borrows the idea of the Web-based job board pioneered by Monster.com, an explicit attempt to convey the idea of employee empowerment in career management.

The first electronic internal job board appears to have been created at Household International in 1992 in response to difficulty filling jobs during a period of rapid expansion.[10] The program began with a "skills bank," something like a resume file, where employees entered information about their preferences for new positions as well as detailed facts about their skills and experience. Managers with vacancies accessed the skills bank to find internal candidates. The company then created a software program called Inside Trak that listed the job openings throughout the company. Employees could access this information and apply for the positions, whether or not they had submitted their information to the skills bank.

The system was not completely open, however, in that only employees with satisfactory performance appraisals could apply for new positions. There were also requirements for minimum service, and not all openings in the company were posted on Inside Trak. But the effect on career advancement was profound. First, the system effectively broke down the decentralized and fragmented system of regional management that had operated with respect to careers. Employees from across the country now had access to information about jobs everywhere in the company, and local managers now had access to the company's national employment pool. More important, the company reported that employees began to use the Inside Trak data to plan their own careers, finding vacant jobs, identifying their requirements, and matching them with their current and planned resume.

At about the same time, Federal Express developed its own internal job board, coming at the issue from a different direction: cost and efficiency. It established an elaborate information technology system designed to automate much of the transactional aspects of human resources to help meet the company's anticipated expansion. One of the functions it automated was the existing job-posting and bidding system. Hiring managers posted job descriptions and pay rates online, and they were instantly available to all employees anywhere in the world. The system analyzed information about an employee's qualifications and determined whether the employee met a job's requirements. The increase in information available was huge. The system also alerted the candidate's immediate supervisor about the employee's application, however, and required that the supervisor approve it before the candidate's name could go onto a list of approved applicants for the hiring manager. Information increased, but employee control over the process still had some distance to go.

As labor markets tightened in the 1990s, more companies embraced internal job boards as a means of addressing retention problems. Nortel was one of the first. It contracted with Monster.com to set up an internal job board that would have the look and feel of Monster.com's own Web site and with Monster.com managing the site. Nortel posted all except executive openings and allowed all employees to apply for any job, eliminating tenure requirements. The rationale was that in the competitive fiber optic product market, any employee who left for a job elsewhere would likely go to a direct competitor. In that sense, losing a good employee hurt twice as much. Even if internal moves disrupted line management, it was better to have good workers go elsewhere in Nortel than to a competitor. The corporate interest in keeping talent in the company overcame the line's interest in keeping individuals in their current jobs.

In 2003, Bell Canada came to the same conclusion about using internal mobility to reduce the churning costs associated with layoffs and outside hiring. "[Employees] felt it was easier to get a job at another company than here," an HR manager noted, and the sense was that hiring managers were using their own networks to fill positions and not necessarily looking within the company. With the new policy, hiring managers must search internally for ten days before asking their business unit president for permission to search outside. The company also offers hiring managers $5,000 in training to retool any internal candidate hired who is otherwise at risk of layoff.[11]

The company also addressed the important managerial constraint to internal mobility. As an HR manager noted, "Many departments succeeded at developing talent, but some were not readily willing to transfer or release their talent to other departments." The new policy allows employees with satisfactory performance evaluations to move without the permission of their managers after spending eighteen months on the job, and the managers must release them to a new job within forty-five days.[12]

Boston's Fleet Bank discovered that the most important factor driving turnover was concerns about internal advancement. The single most important factor explaining individual turnover decisions was whether a worker had previously been promoted: more promotions meant less turnover. To reduce what had been a 25 percent turnover rate, the bank worked on opening its internal labor market to ease internal moves and promotions from within.[13]

Among the interesting innovations was at Hewlett-Packard, which has had a system of job postings for most positions for at least twenty years. The company allowed applicants to test themselves online to see how they might stack up with respect to the requirements of openings. The system helped change the culture of the organization by putting the onus on employees to assess their own attributes.[14]

The Dow Chemical Company posts all its jobs, even international positions, on the corporate internal job board. Approximately 10 percent of Dow employees change jobs within the company every year. Despite the concern that internal job hunting would cause employees also to look outside and hurt retention, overall turnover in the company fell by half after the system was introduced. However, internal job changes doubled.[15]

A recent survey of *Fortune* 500 companies by Taleo Research reports that the vast majority of these companies—80 percent—now have a formal internal mobility policy in place, with the stated goals of improving retention rates (76%), lowering staffing costs (56%) and filling positions faster (53%) (see figure 7-1). Ninety-six percent post openings on an internet site to alert employees and 62 percent turn to internal sources first to fill a position. In terms of restrictions on employee movement, 89 percent say that employees with a less than satisfactory performance review rating cannot bid for new jobs; the goal is to prevent poor performers from avoiding detection by moving around before corrective actions can occur. Only half the companies now require that employees have permission from their

FIGURE 7-1

Internal hiring practices of large companies

Among large companies . . .

- Internal mobility programs
  - 80% have a formal internal mobility policy in place
  - 62% turn to internal sources first to fill an open job position, at least three-quarters of the time
  - 96% post jobs on an intranet site to alert employees to internal opportunities

- Criteria for moving
  - 51% say internal mobility linked to performance management
  - 60% say internal mobility linked to succession planning

- Goal of internal mobility initiative
  - 76% say "improve retention rates"
  - 56% say "lower staffing costs"
  - 53% say "fill positions faster"

Source: Internal Mobility, Taleo Research, 2005.

supervisors. It is also clear that employers are keeping their own options open. One-third post openings internally and externally at the same time. This ability is a pushback from line managers who want their hiring needs to trump the corporate interests in retention.[16]

Balancing the Interests of Line Managers

The interests of line managers in not having their work disrupted by employees who move within the company are important, of course, and it's essential to find a way to balance that interest against the goal of retaining employees in the company by empowering internal movement. Two interesting approaches suggest the range of options.

Bear Sterns operates in the wide-open labor market of investment banking, where hopping from company to company is routine. The bank has a simple arrangement for addressing the internal conflicts associated with internal moves: a mediation office steps in to negotiate a solution. Typical solutions might be to work out delaying the move or getting the employee to help train a new hire. But the process is informal and tailored to each setting. If the office cannot work things out, the problem is kicked up to the executive committee, which essentially acts as an arbitrator, ruling on the dispute. In most organizations, it is not a career move to be involved in a dispute that must be resolved at the top of the company, and this creates an incentive for these disputes to be worked out informally.[17]

Chubb has a different approach to solving these internal conflicts. It was one of the first companies to open up its internal labor market by eliminating both job tenure and supervisor approval as requirements. The potential disruptions of employees hopping from job to job never materialized. One reason is that the company continues to have a strong corporate culture and an orientation to the core underwriting business. Hiring managers are reluctant to poach talent if employees have not been in jobs long enough to pay back the investment in them, because it violates the cultural norm. Employees are reminded of issues like these on Chubb Net, the internal job board. A worker's reputation in the company is important both as a hiring manager and as a candidate. Employees are motivated to pay attention to their reputations as good citizens, in part because the prospects for internal development are good.

Chubb also helps to offset the costs to managers and their business units of losing employees through use of its "farm system," an internal temp agency that provides interim replacements in contexts like these. The company covered (it's not clear whether they still do this—the exec I spoke to last week couldn't confirm) the costs of using replacements so that they are almost free to the business unit that loses them. This helps reduce some of the incentives to hold on to talent.[18]

The Significance of the Internal Job Board Model

The most important attribute of the internal job board model is that it transfers to employees the power and responsibility of managing their careers. It is still possible for management to shape informally how employees move by leaning on some employees not to bid on jobs, manipulating job requirements to favor certain candidates, and so on. But the concern about employee retention—that frustrated employees will simply leave the organization—keeps much of this in check.

The internal job board also has replaced bureaucratic rules as the mechanism for advancing careers with something closer to a market. The interaction of applicant interests and the preferences of hiring managers determine which individuals go where. From the perspective of employees, this situation clearly represents an advance because they now have at least some influence over their careers. There are no longer any "career-ending moves." If employees want to stay put, they simply do not bid on new jobs. If they want to move, they can avoid the jobs they don't like and at least try for those they find attractive.

Internal job boards, however, are not exactly like an open market. In a market, there is a mechanism—prices—that adjusts to bring supply and demand into balance. In most internal job boards, there is no such mechanism. Jobs are posted, each with a set of attributes, and employees react to them. One would suspect that a queue forms for the more desirable jobs and few or no applicants vie for those less so. From the perspective of employers, such a situation would be highly undesirable. Not only would they lose control over who will take which position, but also they cannot even be sure of having an adequate supply of candidates across positions.

If this were a real market, the employer could adjust the wages to make the undesirable jobs more so and even cut wages in the attractive positions to reduce supply. This response does not appear to feature prominently in any systems. Most companies have at least an implicit norm that it is not appropriate for hiring managers to try to bid employees away from their current managers. However, the market mechanism does have a back door into the process. When hiring managers cannot find suitable candidates internally, they can turn to the outside labor market. At that point, they must adjust wages and conditions, presumably upward, to get an adequate pool of candidates. The next time a vacancy occurs in that job, the terms and conditions presented to the internal market are presumably at a more desirable level.

It is also possible to manage the market in ways that help equate supply and demand. Quaker Oats, for example, finds jobs that are not being filled through internal processes and intervenes with some career planning for those positions—identifying which competencies are required, which other jobs in the company develop those skills and which individuals have them, and drumming up interest in possible candidates for the open positions.[19]

Improving the Efficiency of the Internal Market for Talent

IBM has for generations been a leader in talent management, and its reversal of field on issues like career planning in the past two decades suggests a great deal about broader changes in the economy. The Organization Man model was arguably most entrenched at IBM through the early 1980s, and its dismantling, signaled first by managerial layoffs, was one of the most important signals of a new employment relationship in society.

As part of another reorganization beginning in the late 1990s, IBM recognized that it had to become more responsive to the changing demands of customers. The best way to do so was by redeploying its current workforce faster and more effectively, retraining current employees and filling vacancies internally. Interestingly, this was exactly the argument that IBM had made for its Organization Man model two decades earlier: that lifetime employment and corporatewide careers made it easier to redeploy employees and, in turn, restructure operations quickly, because employees would be less likely to resist such moves.[20] It is not that it was wrong then and right now. It is that the restructuring required now is so much greater than before that it could not be accommodated in the earlier model.

The goal for IBM was to find ways to match supply with demand at a micro level: to match workers having just the right competencies to individual task needs around the globe. Mark Henderson, manager of IBM's Workforce Management Initiative, notes, "We needed a comprehensive ecosystem for tracking skills and job opportunities and matching those skills to current and future job opportunities."[21] IBM created a common taxonomy to describe the requirements of all positions across the organization; it was based on job descriptions from five hundred core jobs. Each job was described in a common language, outlining what was required from workers, including temporary help and contractor positions. Each worker was also described using the same taxonomy. Then matches were made quickly and efficiently.

The company also uses this software to generate a "hot skills index," which shows the particular competencies that are in greatest demand—for example, Spanish-speaking Java programmers. All IBM employees have access to the hot skills index and can use it to see where the career opportunities are and, in turn, how they need to reinvent themselves to secure one. The company estimates that the new system improved employee utilization by as much as 7 percent, saving $1 billion per year through reduced outside hiring, reduced layoffs, and reduced training.[22]

One of the most interesting developments in talent management in recent years has been the recognition that a "job" may not be the most appropriate unit for thinking about how work actually gets done or how employees learn. As job requirements become more flexible and teamwork becomes more common, the range of tasks that could be performed within a given job title is so broad that it may not be very meaningful. The more useful unit of analysis may be the specific project on which an employee is working, or even the specific tasks to be performed.

In the preceding generation, when jobs were narrowly defined, employees had to change positions, sometimes relocating, to be exposed to new environments and learn new skills. With flexible job structures, matrixed organizations, and project-based work teams, it is possible now to get the same experiences without changing jobs. Nowhere is this more obvious than in professional service firms in which the specific client engagement is a project. In these firms, it has become common practice to allocate projects to associates through something like a bidding system.

Michelle Horn, a partner in McKinsey and Company's Atlanta office, describes how the company's bidding and posting process allocates associates, the junior employees below the partner level, across the company's projects.[23] All the projects that use associates are listed on a worldwide system, along with descriptive information about each project: the industry, the client, and the type of work being done, the lead partner, and so on. Associates rank their preferences, which are entered into the system along with information about each associate, including assessments of prior performance. The partners running each project then see who wants to work with them, and they can rank those associates they most want to take on.

So far, this sounds like a market-type system. There are incentives for the partners to develop a good reputation for working with associates and get their pick of the best associates. This is much like the Goodrich model described in chapter 6, in which manufacturing units bid for low-cost interns. Here, there are also incentives for the associates to do a good job in their assignments in order to get their pick of the best projects.

There are numerous sophisticated algorithms that could be used to match these preferences. Perhaps the best example is the mathematical model used to match the preferences of medical school graduates (who rank hospitals) with the hospitals (which rank the applicants) to allocate internships in a way that maximizes the preferences of both sides. The problem with those algorithms, and indeed with market-based solutions of any kind, is that they see the goal as being simply to satisfy the immediate preferences of the players. Indeed, market solutions generally declare victory when the market clears—when all buyers and sellers are somehow matched up. Organizations, however, can have more important goals—in this case, to develop talent for the future—that go beyond the immediate preferences of the participants.

What is different about the McKinsey model is that it finds a way to consider the preferences of employees and still focus on longer-term development while avoiding complicated market-like algorithms. It uses a small group of professional development staff, often senior partners, who make matches by focusing on the goal of matching assignments to the developmental needs of the associates. They factor in the preferences of the players, but they are thinking mainly about the associates' prior experiences and what they can learn from assignments.

The system is complemented by elaborate arrangements for feedback: in written form after each assignment, in formal assessments twice a year that are based against a set of thirteen skills, and in advice as to which skills they need to develop and what type of assignments would help. Various e-learning modules provide just-in-time help in developing those skills.

The McKinsey development staff who make the matches look remarkably like the old chess masters who allocated managers and executives across corporate jobs in the 1950s, albeit in this case shaped powerfully by the preferences of the parties. Norm Tonina spent thirteen years working at Digital Equipment Corporation before its collapse and reports that it had an arrangement in 1990 wherein candidates ranked their preferences for assignments, an arrangement that was similar to the McKinsey approach.[24] And General Electric, as early as the 1920s, allowed its candidates to express their preferences for assignments following their developmental, rotation assignments. What is unique about the McKinsey approach is that these preferences are expressed at the project level and that they are given so much weight in the process.

For the ultimate in formal systems, see "Sailor's Continuum."

Traditional companies have also experimented with an open-market assignment of projects. Oticon A/S, a Danish electronics company, established an electronic exchange for matching employees to projects. It was much like the McKinsey model except that the engagement manager had discretion over which bidders to assign to the project. It later abandoned the electronic version when informal and personal contacts were found to be more effective, perhaps not surprising in a small, centralized company.[25]

When we look back on the history of corporate development, models like the informal networking at Oticon A/S worked reasonably well in many companies as a way to both allocate and develop talent across organizations, albeit without giving employees much say in the process. But

Sailor's Continuum

At the end of the spectrum in terms of formal systems for career management is the new Sailor's Continuum developed for the U.S. Navy, which creates a career road map for every individual in the Navy. It is based on five competency areas, each with articulated "advancement criteria," which determine whether an individual is promoted to the next level along clear promotion hierarchies. An individual's performance on each criterion is assessed relative to that of peers, and the scoring system is transparent so that the participants can see where they stand with respect to advancement prospects, which are based on those relative performance scores.[a] Candidates have little choice in their careers, but they always know where they stand.

a. Jerry W. Hedge, Walter C. Borman, and Mark J. Bourne, "Designing a System for Career Development and Advancement in the U.S. Navy," *Human Resource Management Review* 16 (2006): 340–355.

that was before companies decentralized, when all managers saw their allegiance as being to the corporation as a whole, and before their financial interests were oriented to the performance of their own units.

Will Talent Be a Local or Corporate Asset?

An interesting side benefit of these new arrangements is that they have helped headquarters and corporate offices deal with one of the fundamental problems of talent management: getting access to talent in decentralized operations. It can be argued that a business that turns over promising managers for development will, in turn, get access to developed managers from elsewhere. But that argument requires trust that the corporation will follow through on its end of the deal, and it also must confront the skepticism that an unknown future manager will be as good as the one we have now: a manager in the hand is worth two in the pipeline.

Many companies try to fight these practices at the corporate level. IBM, for example, sanctions managers who do not seem to cooperate with the corporate goals for talent development, either by hiding talent or by bypassing formal arrangements for moving candidates. Internal job boards and other employee-initiated arrangements, such as the self-nomination processes described in chapter 6, provide another solution.

Career Management Problems

The most important limitation of the job board and open-market models is that they do little to help with the longer-term issue of development and career planning. Internal job boards and bidding and posting processes help eviscerate the old job ladder system. The notion that career advancement will take place along predictable steps of a job ladder and at a predetermined pace is blown up by a market model in which the employee initiates the moves.

The problem for employees is that they have no road map for advancement when thinking about bidding for jobs. A particular job and the experience it offers will open some doors for future advancement but will likely close others, if for no other reason than the time they consume. But employees have no way of knowing which jobs open what doors. In part, that's because the old job ladders are largely gone. Within functional areas, it is still possible to say, for example, that the manager job leads to the director job, which leads to the vice president job. But there are few of these job ladders left, and even here, individuals can get to the advanced jobs through many paths. Few employers can say how that initial manager job might feed into other jobs across the company or, Heaven forbid, outside the company. What other doors does it open or close?

Doug LaPasta recalls in the late 1970s seeing a Bank of America human resources display that allowed the company's employees to enter their current job, age, and seniority and then see which jobs they could expect to advance to in the company at a given point in time.[26] Remember, this was before modern computing power. Employees would like something similar now, and the phrase *career pathing* is used to describe such efforts. The drawback is that without rigid job ladders, the possible routes for advancement seem almost infinite. Career pathing is typically only a snapshot taken of the speeding train of the organization. Efforts to suggest likely paths for advancement are basically guesses about the moves that seem to build on each other, based on the "look" of the current organizational chart. And these are only as good as the most recent merger, acquisition, or restructuring.

Nevertheless, some companies still do something like this. Exxon, for example, posted descriptions on the company intranet that described what people do in different jobs, how long they typically stay in each position, and the next job they typically move to in the company. These statements were reasonably accurate, based on average experience, because Exxon has been a highly stable operation. But the company also worried about even these statements generating expectations that it might not be able to deliver if the business environment no longer remained stable because of, for example, the merger with Mobil.[27]

A different approach is to abandon the effort to construct logical paths for advancement and instead use something like data mining to see how employees actually move. American Express is one of many companies that attempted to find patterns in the paths that their executives actually had taken. The problem it found, as did virtually everyone else, is that no obvious patterns emerged. A small company called Naviquest took on the task of finding these patterns by building models from the much larger population of all the managerial-level employees in midsized to large companies. With many more careers to look at, patterns emerged, although it is fair to say that they are fuzzy at best. Only a small percentage of incumbent executives in a company are likely to have taken even roughly similar paths, but those paths do emerge when you look at big enough samples. The information that could be generated through this approach provided something like a rough guide employees could use in thinking about their careers.[28]

Fidelity Investments Limited constructed something similar for its employees. Whereas most banks and other financial institutions in the past found much of their entry-level talent through positions like tellers, Fidelity's entry-level positions were in call centers. As with other call center employees in technical businesses, the company made considerable investments in training these employees, only to see many of them leave in the first fifteen months or so when they did not advance. Often, those who left were the most ambitious and promising candidates. In an effort to develop a career path to retain more of these employees longer, the company interviewed five hundred of its employees to establish how they had advanced and to identify the typical paths. Then it identified the competencies that were required for each job in the company.

As a final step, Fidelity created software that allows employees to enter their current jobs and then pick a job to which they aspire. The software calculates the difference in competencies between the two jobs, providing a guide to what the employee needs to learn. Its My Job Connection feature also gives employees information on how the previous incumbents in the chosen job got to that position.

Fidelity also took steps to encourage internal advancement by making supervisors more responsible for the careers of their subordinates. If a subordinate leaves the company, the supervisor is penalized; if a subordinate advances to another job in the company, the supervisor is rewarded. A bonus kitty was created to offset any losses in an area that can be attributed to the loss of a star employee. Employees who apply for an internal position and are not accepted for it receive detailed feedback about why they were not hired and what is missing from their current experience and competencies.[29]

It is probably not a surprise that the company with the most sophisticated use of information for career management is Microsoft. Norm Tonina, an executive in Microsoft's "people and organizations" group, observes that in its earlier years, "the company had been very unintentional about how people moved in the company and about how leadership developed."[30] More recently, CEO Steve Ballmer asserted that Microsoft had to develop a different kind of talent if it was to succeed in the future. Although it had a lot of functional talent, like most newer companies it was short on general management talent that is best developed internally. It had to become much more intentional about developing that talent.[31]

Career Compass is the company's tool for doing that. It begins with an annual self-assessment of executives' experiences, including their aspirations for the future. Supervisors assess those responses and also inform the candidates about a separate set of eleven "career derailers," such as failing to attract talent to work with them, changing positions too quickly to learn from them, lacking credibility with their associates, and so on. This information is catalogued and reduced to a one-page score card known as a "prep card."

Employees, in turn, have access to something like blueprints that identify the competencies that are required and the results expected for each job in the executive ranks, down to the level of subdisciplines within each functional area (for example, the business valuation side of the finance function) as well as for general management jobs. Employees are asked to create a personal development plan based on their aspirations, their current experiences, and the blueprints. The plan identifies, first, the higher positions that interest them; second, the gaps in their current competencies and the experiences they need to get those jobs; and, third, a schedule of activities based on work experience, learning from others, and formal training that will help them close the gap. They negotiate how to implement the plan with their immediate supervisor.

Although many organizations ask employees to develop career plans, what is different about the Microsoft model is the depth of information that is available to develop these plans: online information about the competencies required for each position, the current capabilities of each employee and the gap with any specified position, and the menu of developmental activities that can close competency gaps.

At the midyear point, employees have a performance review with their supervisors in which they are asked to identify jointly two career moves that they could conceivably make with their current competencies but that would represent a stretch. These assignments should be central to an effort to close their competency gap. That information, along with the one-page prep card, is used in a talent review process conducted for the top one thousand executives by the business leaders and the CEO. Microsoft has also identified a series of jobs that are crucial to the development experience of executives, and those positions are kept open to be filled by the talent review process. In other words, the leadership team directs promising candidates to those relevant jobs, just as the old chess masters used to do.

For the other jobs and other employees (the system rolled out to the entire workforce in 2007), the internal job board plays an important role in career planning. All vacancies at Microsoft up to the most senior positions are posted, and employees who have been in their current positions more than eighteen months do not need permission from their supervisors to bid for a new job. In addition, employees can create a "job agent" that searches openings and alerts them if a position that interests them comes open. Microsoft encourages hiring managers to give interested employees informational interviews to let them learn whether they are suited for a position before they formally apply for it; the idea, in part, is to avoid rejecting internal candidates. There are about ten thousand internal job changes per year in the company.

As with most other new approaches to talent management, the arrangements at Microsoft are driven by the employees themselves. Two things make its process distinct. The first is the rigor and depth of the planning process. The drawback to the rigor, however, is that plans like these are ultimately only as good as the ability to predict where the business is going and where the future jobs will be. Employees can prepare themselves for advanced jobs, but those jobs still must be there when the preparation is completed if the process is to work. There also must be vacancies in those jobs. The fact that the individual career planning process at Microsoft extends only two moves increases the likelihood that the positions will be there, especially for lower-level employees. In that sense, Microsoft offers reasonably reliable career planning, but the plans are short term. Shorter plans offer less in the way of direction, but the odds of mismatch problems rise with longer plans.

The second distinctive aspect of this process, at least among modern arrangements, is that it engages supervisors directly in the development of their subordinates. This approach points back in the direction of the earlier, Organization Man period, when the supervisor was the chief mentor, developer of talent, and gatekeeper to advancement. The approach at Microsoft and at other companies does not go nearly that far. The employee remains the responsible party, but at least the supervisor is pushing the process along.[32]

Overall, these new internal market mechanisms shift the focus of employees' career planning away from the organization chart as the guide to their futures and toward the more immediate target of a specific job that exists now. This is a sensible move that reflects the uncertainty about career hierarchies and business operations. The shortfall is that employees are likely to want, and perhaps to have, a planning horizon that extends well beyond that of their employer. A typical employee should be thinking about where she wants to be in ten or more years and has commitments—home mortgages, college tuition for kids, retirement—that are predictable and extend for decades. How do you reconcile the long-term career planning needs of individual employees with the short-term necessity of business planning?

One answer in some companies is to offer employees explicit help with planning their long-term careers. In contrast to the Organization Man period, the advice now tends to be built on employees and their interests. Toronto-based TD Bank, with thirty-five thousand employees, moved toward offering career guidance for its employees because it discovered through internal surveys that internal advancement and skill development were the number 1 factors driving employee engagement. The bank concluded that the training investments in recent years had been directed at and had achieved improvements in organizational performance but had not done much for the individual employees. Its response was to create the Career Advisor Web site to provide help for employees to manage their own careers and get ahead. The site begins with interactive diagnostic instruments that lead to individualized reports about employees' interests and abilities along with guidance about how to develop their capabilities. This is a self-service approach, but the demand from employees for it has been remarkably strong.[33]

The most advanced career management guidance anywhere may be delivered at Deloitte's U.S. operations through the Deloitte Career Connections (DCC) program, established in 2002. The idea is to help Deloitte employees manage their careers—helping them advance in the organization but more generally helping them figure out where they want to go. The ultimate goal for the company is to improve retention by helping meet the career needs of employees and, in particular, making it easier for them to address those needs by staying at Deloitte. The DCC Web site offers a range of self-assessment and feedback tools as well as information on building career plans and improving advancement-related skills (such as networking and interviewing). It also offers detailed information on job openings around Deloitte, what is required to secure those jobs, how each position might contribute to career growth, and so on.

What is most remarkable about the DCC program is its use of coaches. The coaches are dedicated to the DCC program and include Deloitte employees, but the relationship between the coaches and the Deloitte employees who contact them is strictly confidential. The coaches advise employees on all manner of career-related issues, including when it might be time to leave the company. More employees have used the DCC services than are currently employed at Deloitte (turnover accounts for the difference), and more than four thousand (from an employee base of thirty-five thousand) have received some form of coaching. Deloitte calculates that it costs an average of $150,000 for each employee who leaves the company prematurely, and it estimates that at least five hundred fifty employees have stayed with the company because of a DCC intervention. That translates into a savings of about $83 million on turnover reduction alone.[34]

The fact that employers are now willing to help employees think about their careers from the employee's own perspective is a remarkable change. The shift from the Organization Man model, in which career plans were rigid and oriented entirely to the interests of the employer, to a situation of no planning and help, in which employees were on their own, and now to an emerging model in which employers help employees figure out their own interests and plans is a significant development. All this has been driven by employers, of course, so the obvious question is, What's in it for them?

It may seem odd that a company would spend money on career advice that could help employees figure out that they might want to leave and take up other kind of work. The reason it now makes sense is that the glut of talent in the 1980s through the early 1990s is gone. The explanation has to do with the fundamental talent management challenge of reducing uncertainty. Career advice helps individuals figure out where they are going and plan their future. When employees have a clearer sense about what they want to do, it makes it easier for the company to plan around them. Matt Brush of Corning cites a simple example that has considerably increased the company's ability to plan: "We ask if they are willing to move. If not, we take them off the candidate list." As a global company, Corning finds that its ability to move talent around is crucial not only to development but also to running the company. Without knowing the candidate's interests and intentions, Brush notes, "it's easy to persuade yourself that your bench is deeper than it is."[35]

The most obvious win for the company comes when good and ambitious employees find an opportunity that suits their needs inside the company as opposed to elsewhere. When employees have a plan for their careers, they are less likely to jump at opportunities that may come along, including outside offers. And for the employer, the biggest problem with retention is not necessarily that people leave. After all, everyone eventually left in the Organization Man period. The difference is that they did so at the predictable point of retirement. Having a career plan reduces uncertainty, and that saves employers money.

Further, it may be necessary to offer objective advice that reflects employees' interests in order to get them to trust the process. If employees do not believe that the coaches and company representatives are truly interested in their concerns, they may not believe the information and advice they get about opportunities within the company, and then the process becomes worthless. And finally, we know from the information in chapter 4 that uncertainty about career prospects can cause employees to jump at outside opportunities.

The self-knowledge that comes from career planning also helps with engagement. Prospects for advancement are a key factor driving employee engagement. Employee frustration with career issues peaks when employees feel no control over it. Career planning may help simply by increasing the sense of control. It may also help employees figure out when they are in jobs that are mismatched with their true interests and move on—perhaps inside the company—before they cause trouble.

It might also be fair, however, to expect that the enthusiasm and resources that employers invest in career management for employees, as with many other employer-centered efforts, will vary directly with the state of the labor market: as it gets tighter, you can expect these efforts to increase in an effort to stem retention concerns; as it softens, expect commitment to these policies to weaken. The interests of line managers will reassert themselves, as they have in every downturn since WWI, pushing the corporate headquarters to give the line more control over the employees who work for them.

8

Promises and Challenges of the Talent on Demand Model

Students of scientific endeavors note the constraints on progress that are created by established paradigms.[1] Existing frameworks and paradigms create the language that describes the challenges as well as the solutions. Even though few employers still pursue the Organization Man model, for example, it remains for most observers the framework for thinking about talent issues because there has been no alternative. The language of the Organization Man paradigm comes from engineering and is rooted in the idea that we can achieve certainty through planning: workforce "plans" that determine the number of employees needed at a future point, "pipelines" of talent that candidates enter and exit at a predictable point and rate, succession "plans" that map individuals to jobs, and so on.

The effect of the Organization Man paradigm has been to discourage efforts to think differently about talent management, because new approaches do not fit the established paradigm. In particular, addressing the challenge of uncertainty has been difficult because the model does not acknowledge it as a challenge; the assumption is that forecasts and planning eliminate uncertainty. Even though the effectiveness of the old model has been destroyed by uncertainty, it has been difficult to acknowledge the problem because the language of the paradigm does not recognize uncertainty as an issue.

Paradigms come undone when they encounter problems that they cannot address. But before the old paradigm is overthrown, there must be an alternative, one that describes new developments better than the old one does. An important motivation for developing the talent on demand framework, therefore, is to create a language that allows us to consider broader goals for talent management that go beyond internal development for its own sake.

Those goals include cost and financial effectiveness, and especially the new challenge of managing risk—a challenge that did not exist when the old paradigm was created. This new paradigm also allows us to consider alternative approaches, especially outside hiring, to meet talent demands. If the language of the old paradigm was dominated by engineering and planning as the mechanism for meeting demand, the language of the talent on demand framework is driven by markets and operations-based tools to meet the new challenge of uncertainty.

Thinking Differently About Talent

The new paradigm includes the following assumptions. First, we must recognize the limits of our ability to forecast the future. It is clearly useful to invest in the best possible forecasts of future talent needs, but we must recognize that even the best forecasts are inaccurate over the long term. We cannot expect to forecast and plan our way to certainty.

Arguably the first and most important break with the old paradigm is to develop an objective assessment of the likelihood that forecasts will be wrong and—this is crucial—of the consequences if they are wrong. Historical records of previous forecasts are usually a sobering reminder of their inaccuracy. Techniques like scenario planning can present planners with concrete alternatives to their current forecasts to see how accurate they are. The consequences of being wrong are perhaps easier to assess than the chances of being wrong, because they are based on calculations of mismatch costs: what happens when actual demand turns out to be different from our forecasts and we have either overshot or undershot the real level of demand.

Business strategy has moved away from the assumption that we can plan our way around uncertainty, heading instead toward a model wherein the key competency is the ability to react and respond quickly to new opportunities. Talent management must move in the same direction if it is to support this new orientation in strategy.

The second break from the older paradigm is that we need to consider explicitly both "make" and "buy" choices. Outside hiring is not going away, and we need to include it in our decisions. The estimates of uncertainty and mismatch costs allow us to calculate how much talent we should be developing internally and how much we should be hiring from the outside. The mix of the two allows us to minimize uncertainty and reduce our overall talent costs.

Third, we need to think differently about how to develop talent internally to reduce uncertainty and to minimize risk and costs. The practices we use for development must go beyond identifying competency requirements and developing the best systems for teaching them. They must be organized in ways that help us minimize costs, including elements of risk. Such practices include using portfolio principles to allow errors to cancel out, organizing the process to reduce the length of required forecasts, and structuring the flow of individuals through development experiences to reduce the uncertainty of the process. We need to choose specific development techniques with an eye toward recouping the investment. The most effective of these approaches involve work-based learning and opportunities in which employees can share the costs of development.

The fourth break with the old paradigm is to think differently about how to match individual candidates with development opportunities and, ultimately, with jobs. The chess master model is gone, and as long as employees can leave for employers elsewhere, it is not likely to resurface. We've also seen the decline of traditional succession planning approaches. Although many companies still generate them, they are as often ignored as actually used, making it difficult to see what their purpose really is.

An important consideration in creating new matching approaches is how decentralized talent management should be. Decentralized processes defeat the natural advantages of talent development that are created by having more jobs and more candidates, and therefore better opportunities for matches. If properly organized and executed, a strategy of internal development can offer employers considerable cost advantages. Internal development that relies on matching candidates with work experiences is cost effective. It quickly moves candidates up the learning curve, increases their value to the organization, and improves retention, and it can lead to a considerable payoff.

The problem, however, is that most companies, especially the larger ones, have been driven since the 1980s by the notion that smaller and more autonomous operations are better. No doubt there are considerable advantages from decentralization in making local managers feel accountable. But decentralized operations undercut the natural advantage that larger organizations should have in talent management: having more candidates and more opportunities allows for better internal matches. At least for the purposes of talent management, employers need to find a way to break down the silos and open up the internal marketplace of candidates and opportunities, or else they risk losing their best opportunity for adding value. Centralizing talent management, or at least the ability to match candidates with assignments, is an important and manageable goal.

Employers also must balance the trade-off between the interests of local managers in holding individual candidates longer—something that increases the risk of their leaving the employer altogether—against the broader interests of developing talent.

The talent on demand approach is clearly different from other methods as described in the contemporary literature on talent management. These approaches focus on organizational development issues associated with the psychology of developing individual capabilities, such as identifying the competencies that leaders need and the particular interventions and experiences that help individuals develop those experiences. The issues of leadership development are a crucial component of talent management, but they are only a component of that process. They sit within the broader framework outlined in these chapters, which determines the economic context for talent.

The reason is that talent management is not an end in itself but a means to an end. No employers have as their primary goal the development of their employees. The goal is to make money or to advance broader organizational objectives, and the purpose of talent management is to help achieve those goals. Talent management matters to the extent that it facilitates these goals.

The talent management framework outlined here is a general way to think about almost all talent problems, but employers still must make choices about the strategies they pursue. We would probably conclude that it is a mistake for an organization not to develop any of its own talent internally, but exactly how much it should do itself is a question that requires careful analysis. For a handful of organizations that still have great predictability and little possibility for lateral hiring—the military comes to mind—a framework close to the Organization Man model may still be best. For a different handful of organizations, a more open-market approach might still make sense. These are organizations in which human capital needs are almost completely unpredictable and a supply of talent is readily available on the outside market; examples are small law or accounting firms in rapidly changing markets, or Silicon Valley–type IT firms in which product changes cause constant restructuring. Virtually all employers fall somewhere between these two extremes.

Once you have determined which category your organization falls into, then you must consider how talent development should be structured to maximize value. There is no trick to developing talent if you do not care what it costs. Traditional leadership development topics—including which competencies to develop, how to do it, and whom to develop—matter only after you decide the extent to which internal development of talent is appropriate. All organizational goals benefit from a cost-effective approach to meeting talent demands. If there is an overriding priority in the talent management process, it is to deliver talent in as efficient a manner as possible.

Challenges for Talent Management

A range of issues confronts executives who are interested in taking a talent on demand approach. Let's look at each of them in some detail.

The Limits of Management Attention

If uncertainty is the main challenge, then management impatience is the biggest roadblock to success in managing talent more effectively. Executives have short attention spans, and their ability to focus attention and effort on initiatives is limited, especially if they do not see a clear connection between those initiatives and the overall goals they are pursuing.

In talent management, the nature of the crisis is highly dependent on the state of the outside labor market. In the late 1990s when the labor market was red-hot, recruiting and retention were crisis-level issues and were at the top of the agenda for most CEOs. When the economy fell into recession after 2001, recruiting became easier and retention was a lesser concern. Many organizations abandoned the initiatives for addressing recruiting, retention, and talent management challenges. At a superficial level, the perks such as free meals, concierge services, and other efforts to pamper employees disappeared along with substantive internal development programs. In 2007, with labor markets tightening, at least for some key skills, the interest in recruiting, retention, and talent management in general is making a strong comeback. A 2007 survey finds, for example, that 41 percent of firms have completely or significantly redesigned their internal development programs in the last 18 months.[2] In less than a decade, then, we have seen these efforts come and go and come back again. To put it more bluntly, companies abandoned efforts that they then had to resuscitate about two years later.

The use of outside hiring at the senior level helps create a culture that works against talent management and perpetuates outside hiring: "I came from the outside, and I worked out fine. What's wrong with just-in-time hiring?" Although we now have an overall framework for employers to use in making talent management decisions, the question is whether they will have the patience to do so. To the extent that executive attention and support are provided only on a crisis management basis, then the answer is likely to be no.

The ability to sustain a focus on talent management is driving an important division internationally in the use of, and the sophistication of, talent management practices. The vast new industry of talent management vendors in the United States is producing the most-sophisticated tools for specific talent management tasks. But U.S. employers are no longer the leaders overall, and in large part the reason appears to be that they are not paying attention to it.

The most extensive—and increasingly, the most sophisticated—users of something like the old Organization Man approach are now in Europe. The reason is that these corporations take a long-term perspective on talent decisions. Companies like Allianz, Deutsche Post, and Royal Dutch/ Shell Group of Companies rely on extensive selection, assessment, and internal development practices based on long-term planning and traditional succession plans. One reason is that protective legislation makes it much more difficult for companies operating in Europe to dismiss employees. Without the ability to dismiss talent, companies have few vacancies to fill from the outside. As a result, talent management is by definition a much more internally oriented function.

Whether the long-term planning arrangements work for these companies, even in a context where outside hiring is constrained, is not obvious, however, because business demands are not predictable. With the absence of outside hiring, internal development must be even more responsive in order to meet changing business requirements, and it is not obvious that a long-term planning orientation can be more responsive. European companies pursue the Organization Man approach at least in part because of inertia and an absence of alternative models.

The most sophisticated of corporations in their thinking about talent management appear to be Indian companies such as WiPro, Tata, HCL, and Infosys. First, the talent needs of these companies are growing so quickly, far outstripping their ability to simply hire talent laterally, that talent management is likely to remain a huge issue for the foreseeable future. Second, these new companies had no legacy systems to provide resistance to new ways of thinking. The individuals designing their systems were just as likely to be industrial engineers as human resource specialists. Companies like LG of Korea and most of the corporations centered in Singapore also realize that their needs for talent are so large compared with the amount and mix of skills being produced by the education system and by other employers that they simply cannot rely on outside hiring. And so they have also developed sophisticated talent management practices.

Getting and keeping the attention of senior managers require more than simply pointing out the crises that may happen if they do not take talent management seriously. They require a compelling explanation about how to do it better and how doing so will help the organization meet its goals.

The Policy Perspective

It is sometimes tempting to look back on the period of the Organization Man as a golden age. It had many pluses, especially the stability it gave employees, but that stability created rigidities with clear drawbacks. Employees were effectively serfs to a feudal employer, tied to its prospects and culture. For those who did not fit or whose orientations changed, they were essentially stuck, because the prospects of finding equivalent employment elsewhere were limited. For the economy, the ability of companies to restructure and change direction and for new companies to start up was limited severely by the virtual impossibility of hiring experienced talent from the outside.

The one aspect of this period that we can envy, however, was its ability to develop talent, to give promising managers the skills and the experience to run large and complex organizations. Clearly, the lack of employee development in the United States is creating problems. The vicious cycle—outside hiring leading to retention problems elsewhere, leading to an erosion in development—is difficult to stop.

One of the important problems facing market economies is that perfectly sensible decisions made by individual employers considering their own interests may turn out to be detrimental to the broader community, and that appears to be the case with talent management. The interest of individual employers in making investments in their own employees is limited because of the difficulties they have in recouping those investments. Individual employers that have made such investments have been punished, because other employers hire their workers away. As fewer employers make investments in developing talent, those who do are increasingly targeted for poaching as those investments become more valuable.

Meanwhile, in the broader community, employers complain of a "shortage" of talent. Individual employers and their associations have gone to great lengths to argue that there is not enough talent available in the U.S. labor force and, by implication, that this situation is not their fault, nor something they can be expected to solve. A real shortage in economic terms means that one cannot acquire goods or services at the market price: there is no shortage of diamonds even though they are expensive, because we can purchase all the diamonds we desire at the right price. Although employers routinely use the term *shortage*, they typically mean something different: that they cannot afford to pay the market wage required to get the talent they need.

The more serious complaints, however, come when employers report that they simply cannot find employees having the needed skills. Despite the never-ending attempts to blame this situation on demographics, that argument is a red herring. The labor force continues to expand every year, and the problem has nothing to do with a shortage of people. In the 1960s, when labor markets were far tighter and wages were rising much faster than now, there were nothing like the complaints we hear now about shortages of skills. An important difference was that companies hired un-skilled front-line workers and generally educated college graduates and developed them into the skilled employees they needed, increasing the supply when demand increased

As late as the mid-1980s when labor markets were soft, employers were still saying that they would develop their own talent, but we began to hear a new demand: candidates needed to have better levels of basic skills and also a stronger work ethic before employers would invest in them. The mid-1990s brought a different approach along with the information technology boom. Employers wanted to hire the latest, fast-changing technology skills, many of which could be learned in college. Employers were willing to pay quite a bit for these skills, and they did not expect to train these new hires. They expected to put them directly to work. The old approach of hiring raw talent and developing it into the needed skills now seems quaint.

By relying extensively on outside hiring, employers have placed them-selves at the mercy of the labor market. The complaints we now hear from competitors about a labor shortage are therefore driven by this move to a market-driven workforce, relying on the outside labor market to provide all the skills they need. This approach pushes the problem of develop-ment onto employees. As noted earlier, individuals are investing in their own development in record numbers, not only in formal education but also in work-based training, such as certificate and credential programs that acknowledge mastery of specific workplace skills.

There are limits, however, to how much of this problem can be solved by individual investments. The skills in shortest supply are those that can be learned only in the context of real work, such as the skills of general management or of leadership of a specific part of an organization. Even for those skills that can be learned in classroom settings, there are limits to how much money individuals can afford to spend on their own development, especially when they are young. Banks and financial institutions do not and cannot treat human capital like physical capital for the purposes of making loans and investments. Laws against indentured servitude and bankruptcy protections rightly prevent creditors from "collecting" on defaulted human capital loans in the same way that they recover a mortgage loss through foreclosure and sale.

For these reasons, potential employees may not respond to market signals in the way that employers hope. High-tech employers and Silicon Valley firms, in particular, complain that they cannot find enough graduates with the science and engineering degrees they say they need, despite high starting salaries. One explanation is simply that these jobs are not attractive enough, despite the high starting pay, because they do not last very long. A student who must spend $150,000 on a college degree should be thinking about the long-term value of that degree. Even if IT and science jobs pay a substantial premium over alternative careers, the problem is that these skills can become obsolete in about five years. And in most firms, the possibilities for careers thereafter are limited. The lack of talent management in the form of career prospects for IT candidates means that the number of individuals interested in such short-term careers is limited, almost no matter what the starting wages are.

Employers have responded to these problems by trying to engage public policy as a solution, opening immigration to allow them to hire more graduates from other countries. As long as high-tech wages in the United States are higher than in the countries from which we are recruiting, we can pull their science and engineering students into the United States. For other potential immigrants, the ability to enter the United States through work-related visas provides the equivalent of a wage premium. Even if the current job does not last very long, the opportunity to get into the country and then find a way to stay may offer sufficient compensation.

Another solution, and a much better one, is for employers to get better at their own talent management processes and not rely entirely on the outside labor market—or, in this case, colleges and universities—to produce their talent for them. The solutions outlined in chapter 6 to help employers recoup investments in employee development can go a long way toward making that possible. In the process, the entire economy benefits by having higher levels of skill, particularly managerial skills.

The Way Forward

The talent problems of employers, employees, and the broader society are intertwined. Employers want the skills they need when they need them, delivered in a manner they can afford. Employees want career advancement prospects, and they also want control over their careers. The economy as a whole and the societies in which it operates need higher levels of skills, particularly deeper competencies in management.

The ability to meet these challenges turns on whether employers can find a way to manage the uncertainty that has led to the downward spiral in talent development. Talent on demand provides a way out—a way for employers to manage their talent needs and recoup investments in development, a way to balance the interests of employees and employers, and a way to increase the level of skills in society.

Notes

Chapter 1

1. Esther Rudis, *The CEO Challenge*, Research Report 1337 (New York: The Conference Board, 2003).

2. Lynn Morton, *Integrated and Integrative Talent Management: A Strategic HR Framework*, Research Report 1345-04-RR (New York: The Conference Board, 2004).

3. Matthew Guthridge, Asmus B. Komm, and Emily Lawson, "The People Problem in Talent Management," *McKinsey Quarterly*, no. 2, 2006. The responses were in the form of rankings of issues, so they do not imply, for example, that those who did not report concerns about talent management thought that it was fine.

4. Center for Corporate Futures, www.zoomerang.com/web/reports/printresults page/.aspx.

5. *Leadership 2021*, Research Report, Corporate University Xchange, Harrisburg, PA, 2007, p. 4.

6. The distinction between events that are truly uncertain and those for which we can assign some rough probability is an important one. Most of the principles described here, however, apply even for events that are truly unpredictable. See Frank H. Knight, *Risk, Uncertainty, and Profit* (Boston: Houghton Mifflin Company, 1921), for the seminal discussion of this topic.

7. Gilbert L. Johnson and Judith Brown, "Workforce Planning Not a Common Practice, IPMA HR Study Finds," *Public Personnel Management*, 33(4); 379–389.

8. Some industries still have stability in their markets. For example, in oil companies the development and exploitation of oil fields can take generations; in pharmaceuticals, product cycles can be equally long. Not surprisingly, these companies are much more likely to use the longer-term, Organization Man approach.

9. I am not persuaded that work–life issues are truly new, although as the demands from work rise along with single-parent and two-career couples, they clearly can be more intense. What is new is the employer's need to address those concerns, at least when labor is scarce. It is less clear that employers pay much attention beyond lip service to work–life issues when recruiting and retaining employees are easy.

Chapter 2

1. Alfred D. Chandler Jr., *The Visible Hand: The Managerial Revolution in American Business* (Cambridge, MA: Belknap Press, 1977), 3.

2. Ibid.

3. Oliver Zunz, *Making America Corporate* (Chicago: University of Chicago Press, 1990), 81.

4. See ibid., 17. A description of agents having multiple clients, including

DuPont, is provided in JoAnne Yates, *Control Through Communication* (Baltimore: Johns Hopkins University Press, 1989), 205.

5. Yates, ibid.

6. Robert H. Wiebe, *The Search for Order, 1877–1920* (New York: Hill and Wang, 1967).

7. Daniel Clawson, *Bureaucracy and the Labor Process: The Transformation of U.S. Industry, 1860–1920* (New York: Monthly Review Press, 1980).

8. Zunz, *Making America Corporate,* 41.

9. Thomas C. Cochran, *The American Business System: A Historical Perspective, 1900–1955* (Boston: Harvard University Press, 1960), 74.

10. Zunz, *Making America Corporate,* 48.

11. Sanford M. Jacoby, *Employing Bureaucracy: Managers, Unions, and the Transformation of Work in American Industry* (New York: Columbia University Press, 1985), 279. You will note that throughout the quoted matter in this discussion, managers and executives are referred to exclusively as men. This is not strictly a matter of the former practice of using the male pronoun to refer to people in general. In this period, it was assumed that virtually all executives and managers were men, and indeed that was most often the case.

12. Chandler, *The Visible Hand,* 358.

13. Ibid., 424.

14. For a biography of Carnegie and a discussion of his business practices, see David Nasaw, *Carnegie* (New York: Penguin Press, 2006).

15. Ibid.

16. Samuel Crowther, "What Carnegie Looked For," *System* 42 (July 1922): 41–43.

17. Ibid.

18. Nasaw, *Carnegie,* 100.

19. "The Talent Search to Beat Executive Shortage," *BusinessWeek,* December 10, 1949, 30.

20. Alfred P. Sloan, *My Years with General Motors* (New York: Doubleday, 1963), 8–9.

21. Alfred D. Chandler Jr. and Stephen Salsbury, *Pierre S DuPont and the Making of the Modern Corporation* (New York: Harper and Row, 1971).

22. Sloan, *My Years with General Motors,* 53.

23. Chandler and Salsbury, *Pierre S DuPont,* 499; Sloan, *My Years with General Motors, 54–56.*

24. Sloan, ibid., 56.

25. Cochran, *The American Business System,* 70.

26. Herbert J. Hapgood, "The Managers of Tomorrow," *System* 8 (December 1905): 565–569.

27. William H. Whyte, *The Organization Man* (New York: Simon and Schuster, 1956), 112.

28. Edward Plaut, "Train Men as All-Around Executives, Rather than Specialists," *Printer's Ink,* March 18, 1926, 49–52.

29. Augustus D. Curtis, "We Stopped Taking Chances on Our Future Executives," *Sales Management* 11 (October 30, 1926): 701.

30. "This Plan Uncovers Executive Talent," interview with Britton I. Budd, *Printer's Ink,* March 4, 1926, 78.

31. See David Loth, *Swope of GE* (New York: Simon Schuster, 1958).

32. Whyte, *The Organization Man,* 121.

33. Lloyd Warner, Darab B. Unwalla, and John H. Trimm, *The Emergent American Society: Large Scale Organizations* (New Haven, CT: Yale University Press, 1967), 217.

34. "Why All the Fuss about Executive Development?" *Chemical Engineering,* February 1953, 24–28.

35. G. L. Bach, "Where Do Executives Come From?" *Personnel* 29 (July 1952): 50–56.

36. J. Elliott Janney, "Company Presidents Look at Their Successors," *Harvard Business Review,* May–June 1953, 59–70.

37. G. L. Bach, "Management Development: The Care and Feeding of the Junior Executive," *Steel,* February 11, 1957, 93–100.

38. *BusinessWeek,* October 16, 1948, 19.

39. Eugene Whitmore, "The Executive Manpower Shortage—and What Can Be Done About It," *American Business,* March 1952, p. 9.

40. Corinne J. Carden, "Executive Training," *Journal of Retailing* 22, no. 1 (February 1946): 1–4.

41. Ibid., 21.

42. "Can Job Agencies Find Your Man?" *BusinessWeek,* January 1, 1949, 21.

43. Ibid.

44. Eugene Whitmore, "The Executive Manpower Shortage," 8.

45. "Shorts and Faces: Ivory Hunting on the Charles," *Fortune,* January 1948, 116.

46. Austin S. Ingleheart, "Training the Executive: The Forgotten Man in Industry," *Food Industries,* January 1947, 32–34.

47. "Can Job Agencies Find Your Man?" 22.

48. E. P. Hollender, "Buddy Ratings: Military Research and Industrial Implications," *Personnel Psychology* 7, no. 3 (Autumn 1964): 385–394.

49. J. C. Rupe, "When Workers Rate the Boss," *Personnel Psychology* 4, no. 3 (Autumn 1951): 271–290.

50. E. Donald Sisson, "Forced Choice: The New Army Ratings," *Personnel Psychology* 1, no. 3 (Autumn 1948): 365–382.

51. See, for example, Reign Bittner, "Developing an Industrial Merit Rating Procedure," *Personnel Psychology* 1, no. 4 (Winter 1948): 403–432.

52. James R. Berkshire and Richard W. Highland, "Forced Choice Performance Rating: A Methodological Study," *Personnel Psychology* 6, no. 3 (Autumn 1953): 355.

53. McNamara's observations appear in the documentary *The Fog Of War,* Sony Pictures Classics, Inc., 2004.

54. X "Selection Program Cuts Executive Turnover," *American Business,* August 1949, 12–13.

55. "Multiple Management: Top Executive Seedbed," *BusinessWeek,* June 11, 1949, 82–83.

56. Bernard J. Muller-Thym and Melvin E. Salveson, "Developing Executives for Business Leadership," *Personnel* 25 (January 1949): 250–260.

57. A. V. Feigenbaum and H. W. Tulloch, "Management Apprenticeships: An Executive Development Program," *Personnel* 26 (September 1949): 77–85.

58. Whitmore, "The Executive Manpower Shortage," 8.

59. Warner et al., *The Emergent American Society,* 199.

60. Ibid., 215.

61. Ralph J. Cordiner, "Industry's New Challenge: Developing Tomorrow's Leadership," *Edison Electric Bulletin* 18 (1950): 233–236.

62. This incident is described in "Management Development: Grooming Middle Managers," *Steel*, March 18, 1957, 93–100.

63. Whyte, *The Organization Man,* 121.

64. Evelyn Dawn Fraser, "Executive Trainees Earn While They Learn," *Journal of Retailing* 29 (Summer 1953): 71–84.

65. "Bringing Up Tomorrow's Brass Hats," *BusinessWeek,* November 3, 1951, 86.

66. Whitmore, "The Executive Manpower Shortage," 8.

67. Janney, "Company Presidents Look at Their Successors."

68. Milton M. Mandell, "How to Gage Executive Potential," *Dun's Review & Modern Industry* 69, March 1957, 43–45.

69. Janney, "Company Presidents Look at Their Successors."

70. J. Dennis O'Brien, "Finding Future Executives," *American Business*, September 1955, 22–23.

71. "Personnel Staff Increase," *American Business*, 23.

72. Whitmore, "The Executive Manpower Shortage," 8.

73. Harry Rubey, "The Engineer Becomes a Professional Manager," *Journal of Engineering Education* 43 (January 1953): 338–341.

74. Edwin C. Nevis, "The Personal Side of Engineering," *Machine Design*, July 25, 1957, 103–104.

75. H. E. Linsley, "Lockheed Trains from the Top," *American Machinist* 95, October 15, 1951, 123–126.

76. Eugene Whitmore, "Monsanto's Plan for Executive Development," *American Business*, April 1952, 10–11.

77. H. L. Samuelson, "Tools and Techniques of Executive Development," *Personnel* 28 (May 1952): 446–456.

78. "Shirt-Sleeve Training for P&G Bosses," *BusinessWeek,* November 4, 1950, 31–32.

79. M. S. Kellogg, "Appraising the Performance of Management Personnel: A Case Study," *Personnel* 31 (March 1955): 442–455.

80. Ernest Dale and Alice Smith, "Now Report Cards for Bosses," *New York Times,* March 31, 1957, 221.

81. Whyte, *The Organization Man,* 173.

82. Alvin Gouldner, *Patterns of Industrial Bureaucracy* (Glencoe, IL: Free Press, 1954).

83. Warner et al., *The Emergent American Society.*

84. Clifford E. Jurgensen, "What Job Applicants Look for in a Company," *Personnel Psychology* 1 (Autumn 1948): 423.

85. "Landing the Top Executive," *Steel*, May 27, 1957, 57.

86. Mabel Newcomer, *The Big Business Executive: The Factors That Made Him, 1900–1950* (New York: Columbia University Press, 1955).

87. Eugene E. Jennings, *The Mobile Manager: A Study of the New Generation of Top Executives* (Ann Arbor, MI: University of Michigan, 1967), 97.

88. Ibid.

89. Norman H. Martin and Anselm L. Strauss, "Patterns of Mobility Within Industrial Organizations," *Journal of Business* 29, no. 2 (April 1956): 101–110.

90. For evidence, see Oscar Grusky, "Corporate Size, Bureaucratization, and Managerial Succession," American Journal of Sociology 67, no. 3 (November 1961): 216–269.

91. Newcomer, *The Big Business Executive: The Factors That Made Him, 1900–1950*, 20.

92. Albert S. Glickman, Clifford P. Hahn, Edwin A. Fleishman, and Brent Baxter, *Top Management Development and Succession: An Exploratory Study* (Washington, DC: American Institutes for Research, 1968).

Chapter 3

1. A description of the AT&T assessment centers is provided in Michael Beer and Ellen Stein, "Assessing Managerial Talent at AT&T," Case 9-482-035 (Boston: Harvard Business School, 1982).

2. See Phyllis A. Wallace, ed., *Equal Employment Opportunity and the AT&T Case* (Cambridge, MA: MIT Press, 1976).

3. This account and details of the AT&T story from interviews with Hal Burlingame, 2004.

4. Doug LaPasta, interviews with the author, 2005 and 2006.

5. Walt Burdick, interview with the author, 2005.

6. Louis V. Gerstner Jr., *Who Says Elephants Can't Dance?* (New York: Harper Business, 2002), 30.

7. Donna Riley, interview with the author, 2005.

8. John Kotter, *The Leadership Factor* (New York: The Free Press, 1987), 112.

9. See, for example, Monica Langley, *Tearing Down the Walls: How Sandy Weill Fought His Way to the Top of the Financial World . . . and Then Nearly Lost It All* (New York: Simon and Schuster, 2003).

10. Cited in Kotter, *The Leadership Factor*, 67.

11. Anit Dennis, "Succession Planning Do's and Don't's," *Journal of Accountancy* 199, no. 2 (2005): 47–50.

12. Jeffrey Cohn, Rakesh Khurana, and Laura Reeves, "Growing Talent As If Your Business Depended On It," *Harvard Business Review* 83, no. 10 (2005): 62–70.

13. For evidence, see David Fairis, "Internal Labor Markets and Worker Quits," *Industrial Relations* 43, no. 3 (2004): 573–594.

14. Darren Grant, "The Effect of Implicit Contracts on the Movement of Wages Over the Business Cycle: Evidence from the National Longitudinal Surveys," *Industrial and Labor Relations Review* 56, no. 3 (2003): 393–409.

15. The list includes transportation (railroads, trucking and warehousing, water and air transport); communications and public utilities; electric, gas, and sanitary services; finance; and insurance.

16. This case is argued persuasively in D. Quinn Mills, *The IBM Lesson: The Profitable Art of Full Employment* (New York: Times Books, 1988).

17. Larry Lapide, "Evolution of the Forecasting Function," *Journal of Business Forecasting* 25, no. 1 (Spring 2006): 22–25.

18. Janger R. Allen, *Personnel Administration: Changing Scope and Organization* (New York: National Industrial Conference Board, No. 203), 1966.

19. See James W. Walker, "Models in Manpower Planning," *Business Horizons*, April 1971, 87–95.

20. James W. Walker, "Manpower Planning: An Integrative Approach," *Management of Personnel Quarterly* 9, no. 1 (1970): 38–47.

21. See, for example, Kendrith M. Rowland and Michael G. Sovereign, "Markov-Chain Analysis of Internal Manpower Supply," *Industrial Relations* 9 (1969): 88–89.

22. For examples, see Walker, "Models in Manpower Planning."

23. See, for example, W. R. Dill, W. P. Gaver, and W. L. Weber, "Models and Modeling for Manpower Planning," *Management Science* 13, no. 4 (1966), B142–B167.

24. James W. Walker, "Models in Manpower Planning."

25. Data on gross national product over time is available from the Department of Commerce, Bureau of Economic Analysis, http://www.bea.gov/bea/dn/gdpchg.xls.

26. Sandra F. Beldt and Donald O. Jewell, "Where Have the Promotions Gone?" *Business* 30, no. 2 (April/May 1980): 24.

27. Among the more influential arguments that the U.S. economy had undergone fundamental and painful change in this period was Michael L. Dertouzos et al., *Made in America: Regaining the Productive Edge* (Cambridge, MA: MIT Press, 1989); Peter Cappelli et al., *Change at Work* (New York: Oxford University Press, 1997), suggest that the economic restructuring of the 1980s had a range of negative consequences for employees.

28. Jim Williams, interview with the author, 2006.

29. Howard S. Gospel, "The Long-Run Dynamics of Big Firms: The 100 Largest Employers, from US, UK, Germany, France, and Japan, 1907–2002," *Oxford Economic Papers,* forthcoming.

30. County Business Patterns, http://www.census.gov/epcd/susb/introusb.htm and http://www.census.gov/csd/susb/defterm.html.

31. See *World Development Indicators, Economy* (Washington, DC: World Bank, 2006), table 4.5.

32. Lapide, "Evolution of the Forecasting Function," 23.

33. "Evolution in Business Forecasting: Experts Share Their Journey," *Journal of Business Forecasting* 25, no. 1 (Spring 2006): 6.

34. Chaman L. Jain, "Business Forecasting Errors," *Journal of Business Forecasting Methods & Systems* 21, no. 3 (Fall 2002): 21.

35. See Andrei Shleifer and Lawrence H. Summers, "Breach of Trust in Hostile Takeovers," in *Corporate Takeovers: Causes and Consequences,* ed. Alan J. Auerbach (Chicago: The University of Chicago Press, 1988), 33–67.

36. Deborah Seidman, interview with the author, 2006.

37. Jan Rivkin, "An Options-led Approach to Making Strategic Choices," Case 9-702-433 (Boston: Harvard Business School Publishing, 2006).

38. Kathleen M. Eisenhardt, "Speed and Strategic Choice: How Managers Accelerate Decision Making," *California Management Review* 32 (1990): 39–54.

39. Clint Chadwick, Larry W. Hunter, and Stephen L. Walston, "Effects of Downsizing Practices on the Performance of Hospitals," *Strategic Management Journal* 25, no. 5 (2004): 405–427.

40. These surveys are discussed in Richard S. Belous, *The Contingent Economy* (Washington, DC: National Planning Association, 1989).

41. HR Executive Review, *Implementing the New Employment Contract* (New York: The Conference Board, 1997).

42. Steven Hipple, "Contingent Work," *Monthly Labor Review* (March 2001): 3.

43. See American Management Association, *Survey on Downsizing, Job Elimi-*

nation, and Job Creation (New York: American Management Association, 1996).

44. Henry S. Farber, "Has the Rate of Job Loss Increased in the Nineties?" Industrial Relations Section Working Paper 394, Princeton University, Princeton, NJ, January 1998.

45. For an explicit comparison, see Peter Cappelli, "Examining Managerial Displacement," *Academy of Management Journal* 35, no. 1 (March 1992): 203–217.

46. Raghuram Rajan and Julie Wulf, "The Flattening Firm: Evidence on the Changing Nature of Firm Hierarchies from Panel Data," *Review of Economics and Statistics* (2006).

47. The rise of these pressures from investors is perhaps the most important development in the world of business in a generation. See Michael Useem, *Investor Capitalism* (New York: Basic Books, 1996).

48. Economist Intelligence Unit, *The CEO's Role in Talent Management: How Top Executives from Ten Countries Are Nurturing the Leaders of Tomorrow* (London: Development Dimensions International, 2006), 21.

49. This estimate is from Bruce C. Fallick and Charles A. Fleishman, "Employer-to-Employer Flows in the US Labor Market," Federal Reserve Board Working Paper, Washington, DC, 2002.

50. Sara L. Rynes, Marc O. Orlitzky, and Robert Bretz Jr., "Experienced Hiring Versus College Recruiting: Practices and Emerging Trends," *Personnel Psychology* 50, no. 2 (Summer 1997): 309–339.

51. Peter Cappelli, *The New Deal at Work* (Boston: Harvard Business School Press, 1999), chapter 6.

52. Clifford Adelman, "A Parallel Universe: Trend Toward Replacing Academic Degrees with Information Technology Certificates," *Change*, May 1, 2000.

53. Deloitte Development LLC, "It's 2008: Do You Know Where Your Talent Is? Why Acquisition and Retention Strategies Don't Work," 2006.

54. See Cappelli, *The New Deal at Work,* 215.

55. C. Benner provides a good typology of labor market intermediaries. He distinguishes between private-sector, membership-based, and public intermediaries. Private-sector intermediaries are of four types: temporary help firms; consultant brokerage firms (which recruit professional contractors for temporary positions); and Web-based job sites and professional employer organizations (which provide administrative HR services to firms and are the legal employers of record for employees working for the client firms). Membership-based intermediaries such as guildlike and professional associations place the employees who constitute their membership. Public-sector intermediaries include the range of institutions that make up the workforce development system and aim to connect disadvantaged workers with jobs; education-based institutions that provide adult education and job-related training to employees and have increasingly become market intermediaries; and community and nonprofit organizations that engage in job training and placement services. See C. Benner, "Labor Flexibility and Regional Development: The Role of Labor Market Intermediaries," *Regional Studies* 36 (2003): 621–633.

56. Staffing industry report, 2004, Staffing Industry Analysts, www.staffing industry.com/issues/sireport.

57. See Association of Executive Search Consultants, http://www.bluesteps.com/help/generalfaqs.aspx#executiveprofile.

58. International Association of Corporate and Professional Recruiters, 2003 survey (New York: IACPR) 2004.

59. William Ocasio, "Institutionalized Action and Corporate Governance: The Reliance on Rules of CEO Succession," *Administrative Science Quarterly* 44, no. 2 (June 99): 384–416.

60. Kevin J. Murphy and Ján Zábojník, "CEO Pay and Appointments: A Market-Based Explanation for Recent Trends," *American Economic Review* 94, no. 2 (May 2004): 192–196.

61. See Chuck Lucier, Paul Kocourek, and Rolf Habbel, "CEO Succession 2005: The Crest of the Wave," *Strategy and Business* (Summer 2006), online edition.

62. A description of the search and staffing industry is provided in Peter Cappelli and Monika Hamori, "The Institutions of Outside Hiring," in *The Handbook of Career Studies*, ed. Hugh Gunz and Maury Pieperl (New York: Sage 2007).

63. Steve Pogerzelsky, president of Monster, interview with the author, 2005.

64. See www.bluesteps.com/information/presidentsletter.aspx.

65. A good survey of the results, at least through the 1990s, is in David Neumark, ed., *On the Job* (New York: Russell Sage Foundation, 2000).

66. See Christopher J. Ruhm, "Secular Changes in the Work and Retirement Patterns of Older Men," *Journal of Human Resources* 30, no. 2 (Spring 1995): 362–385.

67. H. S. Farber, *The Changing Face of Job Loss in the United States, 1981–1995* (Princeton, NJ: Princeton University, 1997).

68. See Daniel Polsky, "Changing Consequences of Job Separations in the United States," *Industrial and Labor Relations Review* 52, no. 4 (July 1999): 565–580. The other two studies are Annette D. Bernhardt, Martina Morris, Mark S. Handcock, and Marc A. Scott, "Trends in Job Instability and Wages for Young Adult Men," *Journal of Labor Economics* 17, no. 4, part 2 (October 1999): S65–S126, and Robert G. Valetta, "Has Job Security in the U.S. Declined?" *Federal Reserve Bank of San Francisco Weekly Letter*, February 16, 1996.

69. David Neumark, Daniel Polsky, and Daniel Hansen, "Has Job Stability Declined Yet? New Evidence for the 1990s," *Journal of Labor Economics* 17, no. 4, part 2 (October 1999): S29–S64.

70. Allison J. Wellington, "Changes in the Male/Female Wage Gap 1976–85," *Journal of Human Resources* 28, no. 2 (Spring 1993): 383–411.

71. "Number of Jobs Held, Labor Market Activity, and Earnings Growth Among Younger Baby Boomers: Recent Results from a Longitudinal Survey Summary," U.S. Department of Labor 04-1678, August 25, 2004, http://www.bls.gov/nls/. This study and the others in this section rely on the National Longitudinal Surveys.

72. Ibid.

73. Annette Bernhardt, Martina Morris, Mark S. Handcock, and Marc A. Scott, *Divergent Paths: Economic Mobility in the New American Labor Market* (New York: Russell Sage Foundation, 2001).

74. See Matissa Hollister, "Occupational Stability in a Changing Economy," paper presented at the annual meeting of the American Sociological Association, Montreal Convention Center, Montreal, Quebec, Canada, August 11, 2006.

75. Gueorgui Kambourov and Iourii Manovskii, "Rising Occupational and Industry Mobility in the U.S.: 1968–1993," working paper 04-012, Penn Institute for Economic Research, Department of Economics, University of Pennsylvania, Phila-

delphia, 2004. This paper uses a different longitudinal survey: the Panel Study of Income Dynamics.

76. Steffanie L. Wilk and Elizabeth A. Craig, "Should I Stay or Should I Go? Occupational Matching and Internal and External Mobility," working paper Wharton School, Department of Management, Philadelphia, 1998.

77. Claire Brown, ed., *The Competitive Semiconductor Manufacturing Human Resources Project* (Berkeley: University of California, 1997).

78. Keith W. Chauvin, "Firm-Specific Wage Growth and Changes in the Labor Market for Managers," *Managerial and Decision Economics* 15, no. 1 (January/February 1994): 21–37.

79. David Marcotte, "Evidence of a Fall in the Wage Premium for Job Security," working paper, Center for Governmental Studies, Northern Illinois University, DeKalb, 1994.

80. Daniel Polsky, "Changing Consequences of Job Separation in the United States," *Industrial & Labor Relations Review* 52, no. 4 (July 1999): 565–580.

81. Richard A. Ippolito, "Toward Explaining the Growth of Defined Contribution Plans," *Industrial Relations* 34, no. 1 (January 1995): 1–20.

82. See *EBRI Data Book* (Washington, DC: Employee Benefits Research Institute, December 2005), chapter 10, table 10.1a.

83. "Independent Contractors in 2005," *Monthly Labor Review*, July 29, 2006, http://www.bls.gov/opub/ted/2005/jul/wk4/art05.htm.

84. Jonathan R. Veum, "Training Among Young Adults: Who, What Kind, and for How Long?" *Monthly Labor Review* (August 1992): 27–32.

85. U.S. Bureau of Labor Statistics, table 3: Number of hours of formal training per employee by type of formal training and industry, May–October, 1995, http://www.bls.gov/news.release/sept1.t03.htm.

86. Lisa M. Lynch and Sandra E. Black, "Beyond the Incidence of Employer-Provided Training," *Industrial & Labor Relations Review* 52, no. 1 (October 1998).

87. Jill L. Constantine and David Neumark, "Training and Growth of Wage Inequality," *Industrial Relations* 35, no. 4 (October 1996): 491–510.

88. See Tammy Galvin, "2003 Industry Report," *Training* 40, no. 9 (2003). It is difficult to say to what extent this decline is representative of a recessionary period (recovery from which is expected) or a secular decline, because it appears that the survey is no longer conducted.

89. Ann P. Bartel and Nachum Sicherman, "Technological Change and the Skill Acquisition of Young Workers," *Journal of Labor Economics* 16 (October 1998): 718–755.

90. Lucie Carrington, "Carrot or Stick?" *Training* (April 2003): 10–12.

91. *National Employers Skill Survey 2005* (London: Learning and Skills Center, 2006).

92. These two facts come from HM Treasury, "Prosperity for All in the Global Economy—World-Class Skills," Final Report, 2006, www.hm-treasury.gov.uk/media/523/43/leitch_finalreport051206.

93. Charles R. Greer, Dana L. Jackson, and Jack Fiorito, "Adapting Human Resource Planning in a Changing Business Environment," *Human Resources Management* 28, no. 1 (Spring 1989): 105.

94. Shawn Fegley, *Succession Planning: A Survey Report* (Alexandria, VA: SHRM, 2006).

95. Clifford E. Jurgensen, "What Job Applicants Look For in a Company," *Personnel Psychology* 1 (Autumn 1948): 423.

96. These data are collected by Universum, which specializes in employee branding research.

97. Peter Cappelli and Monika Hamori, "Executive Loyalty and Job Search," working paper, Wharton School, Center for Human Resources, Philadelphia, 2006.

98. Interview with the author, 2007.

Chapter 3 Appendix

1. Wolfgang Mayrhofer, Michael Meyer, Alexandre Iellatchitch, and Michael Schiffinger, "Careers and Human Resource Management: A European Perspective," *Human Resource Management Review* 14 (2004): 473–498.

2. 2006 Annual Survey Report, CIPD: London, http://www.cipd.co.uk/NR/rdonlyres/97BE272C-8859-4DB1-BD99-17F38E4B4484/0/lrnandevsurv0406.pdf.

3. K. Y. Lee, *From Third World to First* (Singapore: Singapore Press Holdings, 2000), 158.

Chapter 4

1. Diane Rothbard Margolis, *The Managers: Corporate Life in America* (New York: William Morrow and Company, 1979), 48.

2. The classic account of this process is presented in AnnaLee Saxenian, *Regional Advantage: Culture and Competition in Silicon Valley and Route 128* (Boston: Harvard University Press, 1994).

3. An exhaustive summary of the arguments about the state of the labor market for IT workers, and of the various labor market studies noted earlier, is provided in National Research Council, *Building a Workforce for the Information Economy* (Washington, DC: National Academies Press, 2000).

4. Avron Barr and Shirley Tessler, "Strategies for Survival: The Software Talent Shortage," SCIP Software Industry Study, in *Compwage's InTelligence Magazine*, March 1998.

5. Denis M. S. Lee, "Knowledge/skill Requirements and Professional Development of IS/OT Workforce: A Summary of Empirical Findings from Two Studies," paper prepared for Panel on Workforce Needs in Information Technology, National Academy of Sciences, December 9, 1999.

6. The survey results are described in Norman Matloff, "Debunking the Myth of a Desperate Software Labor Shortage," Testimony to the U.S. House Judiciary Committee Subcommittee on Immigration, April 21, 1999, updated April 8, 2000.

7. *Network World*, September 14, 1998.

8. See Peter Cappelli, "Why Is It So Hard to Find IT Workers?" *Organizational Dynamics* 3 (2001): 87–99.

9. Economist Intelligence Unit, *The CEO's Role in Talent Management: How Top Executives from Ten Countries Are Nurturing the Leaders of Tomorrow* (London: Development Dimensions International, 2006), 27.

10. Barbara Kofman and Kaitlin Eckler, "Showing Employees the Way," *Canadian HR Reporter*, June 19, 2006, 13, 17.

11. Towers Perrin HR Services, "Winning Strategies for a Global Workforce," 2006, http://www.towersperrin.com/tp/jsp/hrservices_html.jsp?webc=203/global/spotlight/spotlight_gws.htm.

12. Bruce N. Pfau and Ira T. Kay, *The Human Capital Edge: 21 People Management Practices Your Company Must Implement (or Avoid) to Maximize Shareholder Value* (New York: McGraw-Hill, 2001).

13. K. N. Gaertner and S. D. Nollen, "Turnover Intentions and Desire Among Executives," *Human Relations* 45, no. 5 (1992): 447–459.

14. Economist Intelligence Unit, *The CEO's Role in Talent Management,* 15.

15. Ibid., 27.

16. Ibid., 5.

17. See Martin J. Conyon, "Executive Compensation and Incentives," *Academy of Management Perspectives* 20, no. 1 (2006): 25–44, for evidence on compensation costs. It can be argued that some part of that additional pay was essentially free in the sense that the promise of being paid more caused the executives to work harder and produce at least that much more value. That argument depends on the notion that pay truly varies with performance, and the evidence for that position is at best mixed.

18. "Homer vs. The Eighteenth Amendment," *The Simpsons,* 1997, http://www .thesimpsons.com/episode_guide/0818.htm.

19. See, for example, William Chan, "External Recruitment and Intrafirm Mobility," *Economic Inquiry* 44, no 1 (2006): 169–184.

20. Sumon Majumdar, "Market Conditions and Worker Training: How Does It Affect and Whom?" *Labour Economics* 14, no. 1 (2006): 1–23.

21. In the language of economics, the firms are creating a *negative externality* with their lateral hires by depleting the talent development programs of their competitors.

22. Karen Higginbottom, "Low Attrition Causes Headache for IBM," *People Management* 12, no. 14 (2006): 14.

23. Leasing talent offers greater flexibility in adjusting supply to changes in demand. But again, employers pay a rather steep premium per hour for the flexibility of using leased staff.

24. In formal terms, the mismatch costs are greater when the coefficient of variability for the demand for talent (defined as the ratio of the standard deviation of actual demand over time to the mean demand over time) is greater. Because you also must forecast internal supply, there is an equivalent coefficient of variability for the supply of talent (defined as the ratio of the standard deviation of the actual supply of talent available over time to the mean demand over time). Because the two measures are largely independent of each other, the sum of the two coefficients of variation is what drives the extent of the mismatch costs.

25. An interesting account of what actually happens to individual careers when companies restructure is provided in John C. Dencker, "Corporate Restructuring and the Employment Relationship," in *Employment Relations: The Future of White Collar Work,* ed. Peter Cappelli (Cambridge: Cambridge University Press, forthcoming).

26. In operations research terms, the critical ratio is the cost of undershooting demand over the combined costs of undershooting and overshooting demand. As this ratio grows, it makes sense to deliver more talent and risk overshooting the forecast; as it falls, the reverse is true. What you need in a forecast is to see a distribution of the critical ratio times the probability of undershooting the forecast (assuming that the distribution is normal and the probabilities of undershooting and

overshooting are symmetrical) for possible future levels of talent. You then choose the supply of talent to deliver so that the probability of undershooting (the actual level of demand being equal to or greater than demand) is equal to the critical ratio.

27. It is more difficult to quantify the costs associated with overshooting because they include the developmental costs for each employee, which can be substantial especially if accumulated over the years; the costs of paying more in compensation associated with skills and competencies than the employee is producing, probably only a modest cost if compensation arrangements are not market-based; the amount of time the excess candidates must wait until they can step into the appropriate role, if at all, a number that also includes how long you think those competencies will be needed; and the costs associated with the increased probability that a candidate sitting on the bench will quit. Included in the latter can be the bumping costs associated with attempting to fill the vacancy from within. If the cost estimates include all the expenses associated with developing an employee over the years—expenditures that would be lost if that employee leaves—then the overshooting costs could be enormous. If, on the other hand, you think that an outside hire is a perfect substitute, then the costs are relatively small. That would also call into question why you are doing internal development at all for that position.

28. My colleague Paul Schoemaker offers an alternative approach, which may be easier for many people to answer: are the odds greater than a coin toss that you will overshoot demand by x percent? The question can be repeated for various values of x to pin down the probability of overshooting, and then of undershooting.

29. Vivek Gupta, interview with the author, 2006.

Chapter 5

1. Anne Barrett and John Beeson, *Developing Leaders for 2010*, Research Report 1315 (New York: The Conference Board, 2002).

2. Esther Rudis, *The CEO Challenge*, Research Report 1337 (New York: The Conference Board, 2003).

3. Shawn Fegley, *2006 Talent Management: A Survey Report* (Alexandria, VA: SHRM, 2006).

4. For illustrations, see, for example, D. T. Byrant, "A Survey of the Development of Manpower Planning Policies," *British Journal of Industrial Relations* 3, no. 3 (1965): 279–290.

5. I. Gasciogne, "Manpower Forecasting at the Enterprise Level: A Case Study," *British Journal of Industrial Relations* 6, no. 1 (March 1968): 94–106.

6. Lynn Morton, *Integrated and Integrative Talent Management: A Strategic HR Framework*, Research Report 1345-04-RR (New York: The Conference Board, 2004).

7. Mary B. Young, *Strategic Workforce Planning: Forecasting Human Capital Needs to Execute Business Strategy*, Working Group Report (New York: The Conference Board, 2006).

8. David Creelman, "Gerald Brossard—Interviews," *Workforce Management* 85, no. 5 (2005): 59–62.

9. This information comes in part from Young, *Strategic Workforce Planning*, and Andreas Karl, director of global talent development for Dow, interview with the author, 2006

10. Pat Cataldo, interview with the author, 2006.

11. Young, *Strategic Workforce Planning*.

12. Don Ruse, interview with the author, 2006

13. Matt Brush, interview with the author, 2006.

14. Valerie Murzl, interview with the author, 2006.

15. This aspect of the bullwhip problem is known as *order synchronization.*

16. Strictly speaking, this aspect of the problem is caused by the time lag between individual decisions on the supply side and adjustments in market wages, known as a "cobweb" cycle because of the pattern of the adjustment process in a graph of supply and demand.

17. Louis V. Gerstner Jr., *Who Says Elephants Can't Dance?* (New York: Harper Business, 2002), 250.

18. Interview with Mary Lauria, director of talent, Johnson & Johnson, 2006.

19. *Leadership 2012*, Research Report, Corporate University XChange, Harrisburg, PA, 2007, p. 36.

20. Matthew Guthridge, Asmus B. Komm, and Emily Lawson, "The People Problem in Talent Management," *McKinsey Quarterly* 2 (2006).

21. Interview with the author, 2006.

22. *Leadership 2012*, 36.

23. Jeffrey Cohn, Rakesh Khurana, and Laura Reeves, "Growing Talent As If Your Business Depended on It," *Harvard Business Review*, October 2005, 62–70.

24. Peter Cappelli. "Talent Management in the 21st Century: Lessons from Singapore," Working Paper for Singapore Management University's Wharton/SMU Research center, 2004.

25. There are also some differences among ministries in the ways talent is identified. The Ministry of Defense has arguably the most-sophisticated practices. For example, it borrowed from the Royal Dutch/Shell Group of Companies the practice of "current estimated potential." When a candidate is about age twenty-five, the company uses ability tests and other psychological instruments to try to predict the candidate's potential for advancement over the next decade.

26. Peter Cappelli, "Talent Management in the 21st Century: Lessons from Singapore." Working Paper for Singapore Management University's Wharton/SMU Research center, 2004.

27. George Stalk Jr., "Rotate the Core," *Harvard Business Review*, March 2005, 18–19.

28. Presentation by David Bomzer, then director of human resources for Ingersoll Rand, at the Wharton Council of Employee Relations meeting, 2004.

29. Rejecting or sidelining candidates who do not complete developmental experiences successfully becomes a self-fulfilling prophesy in that those candidates are never given the chance to see whether they could succeed in advanced positions.

Chapter 5 Appendix

1. This is in contrast to CEOs leaving for other firms; in that case, share prices tend to fall. See Rachel M. Hayes and Scott Shaeffer, "How Much Are Differences in Managerial Ability Worth?" *Journal of Accounting and Economics* 27 (1999): 125–148.

2. For a review of the evidence, see Andrew N. Garman and Jeremy Glawe, "Succession Planning," *Consulting Psychology Journal: Practice & Research* 56, no. 2 (Spring 2004): 119–128.

3. "Succession Planning," April 2006, Chartered Institute for Personnel Development (CIPD), http://www.cipd.co.uk/subjects/hrpract/general/successplan,htm.

4. Matthew Guthridge, Asmus B. Komm, and Emily Lawson, "The People Problem in Talent Management," *McKinsey Quarterly* (2006).

5. See Shawn Fegley, *Succession Planning: A Survey Report* (Alexandria, VA: Society for Human Resource Management, 2006).

6. Economist Intelligence Unit, *The CEO's Role in Talent Management: How Top Executives from Ten Countries Are Nurturing the Leaders of Tomorrow* (London: Development Dimensions International, 2006).

7. C. Brooklyn Derr, Jon P. Briscoe, and Kathy Bruckner, "Managing Leadership in the United States," in *Cross Cultural Approaches to Leadership Development*, edited by C. Brooklyn Derr, Sylvie Roussillon, and Frank Bournois (Westport, CT: Quorum Books, 2002).

Chapter 6

1. Strictly speaking, this is an example of a *bilateral monopoly*, at least in the short term. Although the employee cannot use the skills elsewhere, the employer might also be in trouble if an employee with these unique skills quits, and it might strike a deal that gives the employee some benefit to stay put. But over a longer period, the employer can always replace those skills, and the ability of the employee to hold up the employer dissipates.

2. See, for example, Mark A. Loewenstein and James R. Spletzer, "General and Specific Training: Evidence and Implications," *Journal of Human Resources* 34, no. 4 (Autumn 1999): 710–733.

3. Defenders of training and development rightly argue that investments in employees are necessary to maintain performance in the organization; without training and development, performance elsewhere in the business might decline and affect returns on other investments. Those are important considerations, albeit difficult to quantify, and should be included when you estimate the contribution of these investments.

4. This result is calculated using the famous Capital Asset Pricing Model:

$Kc = Rf + \beta x (Km - Rf)$

Where:

Kc is the risk-adjusted discount rate:

Rf is the rate of a "risk-free" investment, such as Treasury bonds (in this case set at 5 percent)

and *Km* is the return rate of a market benchmark (in this case, the company's other business investment opportunities)

5. Morgan McCall, Michael Lombardo, and Ann Morrison, *The Lessons of Experience: How Successful Executives Develop on the Job* (New York: Free Press, 1988).

6. Deloitte Development LLC, "It's 2008: Do You Know Where Your Talent Is? Why Acquisition and Retention Strategies Don't Work," 2006.

7. See Loren Gary, "Pulling Yourself Up Through the Ranks," *Harvard Management Update*, October 1, 2003.

8. Fara Warner, "Inside Intel's Mentoring Movement," *Fast Company*, April 2002, 116–120.

9. For an interesting account of how individuals manage to do something similar across organizations, see Siobhan O'Mahony and Beth A. Bechky, "Stretchwork: Managing the Career Progression Paradox in External Labor Markets," *Academy of Management Journal* 49, no. 5 (2006): 918–941.

10. Timothy Gardner, "Human Resources Alliances: Defining the Construct and Exploring the Antecedents," *International Journal of Human Resources Management* 16, no. 6 (2005): 1049–1066.

11. Ibid.

12. See www.wegmans.com/about/pressRoom/pressReleases/stJohnFisherDonation.asp.

13. Edwin Leuvan and Hessel Oosterbeek, *Demand and Supply of Work-Related Training* (Rotterdam, The Netherlands: Tinbergen Institute, December 2006).

14. D. H. Autor, "Why Do Temporary Help Firms Provide Free General Skills Training?" *Quarterly Journal of Economics* 116 (2001): 1409–1448.

15. A factor that is eroding this arrangement is the willingness of other employers to hire associates away from their current firms, creating something like a market wage for their work that is typically higher than associates' pay.

16. Interview with the author, 2007.

17. A calculation of tuition assistance as a proportion of total postsecondary expenses must be somewhat indirect: Census calculates that half of all students (including, of course, those who are not working) receive some aid, and one-third of students who received aid got some from their employer. Therefore, roughly 17 percent of all students received employer assistance. If employers paid one-third of the costs for these students, then they are paying about 5 to 6 percent of all postsecondary expenditures.

18. Peter Cappelli, "Why Do Employers Pay for College?" *Journal of Econometrics* 121, no. 1–2 (2004): 213–241.

19. Ibid.

20. Ibid.

21. Ibid.

22. Perhaps the simplest explanation is that tuition assistance is a tax-free benefit that employers offer as a form of cost-effective compensation. Employee payments for their own tuition are tax deductible only under limited circumstances (for course work directly related to their jobs), but employers can provide their employees with tuition assistance as much as $5,250 tax free. Similarly, employers can avoid paying FICA contributions on those payments that they would otherwise have to pay on compensation, arrangements known as Section 127 benefits. The Taxpayer Relief Act of 1997 kept all undergraduate tuition reimbursements tax exempt to recipients but made graduate reimbursements taxable unless they were for courses related to work, a criterion that has been interpreted broadly. But the utility of additional compensation for the workforce is greater for other employee benefits that are used by more employees, such as expanded health care. So it is not obvious why employers that are motivated to offer tax-free compensation would choose this benefit as opposed to others.

23. Cappelli, "Why Do Employers Pay for College?"

24. A similar study using data on individuals reached the same conclusion about lower turnover as did mine. See George S. Benson, David Finegold, and Susan Albers Mohrman, "You Paid for the Skills, Now Keep Them: Tuition Reimbursement and Voluntary Turnover," *Academy of Management Journal* 47, no. 3 (June 2004): 315–331.

25. Interviews with author.

26. International Foundation of Employee Benefit Plans, *Results 1993-2: Educational Assistance in the Workplace* (Washington, DC: IFEBP, 1993).

27. The effort to find the best talent and to do so early is not limited to Singapore's own students. Singapore scholarships offer educational opportunities to promising students from across Southeast Asia, with the hope that they will stay in Singapore and build their careers. This information was gathered through extensive conversations with government officials while the author was a Distinguished Visitor in Singapore's Ministry of Manpower, 2007.

28. United's objective was not so much to cut costs as to keep these five hundred new pilots out of the pilot's union (because they were not yet employees) in case the union went on strike.

29. Thanks to Jim Jacobs at the Community College Research Center, Columbia University, for these examples. Details on these and similar arrangements are at www.ccrc.tc.columbia.edu.

30. See *Digest of Educational Statistics and Measures* (Washington, DC: National Center for Educational Statistics, 2005).

31. K. A. Phillippe and M. J. Valiga, *Faces of the Future: Summary Findings* (Washington, DC: ACT & American Association of Community Colleges, 2000).

32. *Digest of Educational Statistics* (Washington, DC: National Center on Educational Statistics, 2005), table 250.

33. Interview with the author, 2006.

34. The arguments that follow are outlined in more detail in Peter Cappelli, "A Market-Driven Approach to Retaining Talent," *Harvard Business Review*, January–February, 103–111.

35. Jeremy Smerd, "Sun Healthcare Group," *Workforce Management,* March 26, 2007, 32.

36. For evidence, see Alan M. Saks and Blake E. Ashforth, "A Longitudinal Investigation of the Relationships Between Job Information Sources, Applicant Perceptions of Fit, and Work Outcomes," *Personnel Psychology* 50, no. 2 (1997): 395–426.

37. D. M. Rousseau, V. T. Ho, and J. Greenberg, "I-deals: Idiosyncratic Terms in Employment Relationships," *Academy of Management Review* 31, no. 4 (2006): 977–994.

38. Peter Cappelli, *The New Deal at Work: Managing the Market-Driven Workforce* (Boston: Harvard Business School Press, 1999), 206.

39. Ibid., 189.

40. Careful readers will recognize that rehiring these former employees does not necessarily allow an employer to capture returns from the training made previously. The reason is that the wages for employees who have been in the outside market have already risen to market levels. The payoff comes from the fact that the employer knows with as much certainty as possible that a person is a good employee who is well suited to its needs, making this a low-cost hire.

41. Cappelli, *The New Deal at Work.*

42. Details of the program are laid out in Deloitte and Touche, "Personal Pursuits: Time Off for Personal Goals," 2007.

43. "Internal Mobility," Taleo Company, 2005, http://www.taleo.com/research/whitepapers-research.php#internalMobility.

44. Psychologists refer to this statistical problem as *range restriction* because the range of the independent variable, in this case the test score, is limited in the studies compared with the true range in real life. You can make corrections that, given certain assumptions, can estimate how big this problem is, but it is essentially im-

possible to resolve the problem with statistical adjustments when the restriction is significant.

45. C. Brooklyn Derr, Candace Jones, and Edmund L. Toomey, "Managing High-Potential Employees: Current Practices in Thirty U.S. Corporations," *Human Resource Management* 27, no. 3 (Fall 1988): 273–290.

46. Interview with the author, 2007.

47. Ibid.

48. David J. Woehr and Winfred Arthur Jr., "The Construct-Related Validity of Assessment Center Ratings: A Review and Meta-Analysis of the Role of Methodological Factors," *Journal of Management* 29, no. 2 (April 2003): 231–258.

49. William C. Byham, "Bench Strength," *Across the Board*, February 2000, 35–37.

50. Ed Frauenheim, "Firms Walk Fine Line with 'High-Potential' Programs," *Workforce Management*, http://www.workforce.com/section/11/feature/24/54/84/index.html.

51. Joe Mullich, "Let Your People Go," *Workforce Management*, http://www.workforce.com/archive/article/23/95/24.php.

52. Alan Deutschman, "Building a Better Skunk Works," *Fast Company*, March 2005, 68–73.

53. Edmond J. Metz, "Designing Succession Systems for New Competitive Realities," *Human Resource Planning*, September 1, 1998, 31–37.

54.

Chapter 7

1. In European work systems, individual employees might have a designation or rank that traveled with them across jobs. Thomas A. DiPrete (*The Bureaucratic Labor Market: The Case of the Federal Civil Service* [New York: Plenum Press, 1989]) notes this distinction.

2. Cyril Sofer, *Men in Mid-Career: A Study of British Managers and Technical Specialists* (Cambridge: Cambridge University Press, 1970), 21.

3. Rosabeth Moss Kanter, *Men and Women of the Corporation* (Boston: Basic Books, 1977).

4. A description of this development is provided in Peter Cappelli, *The New Deal at Work* (Boston: Harvard Business School Press, 1999).

5. Sumner Slichter, James Healy, and Robert Livernash, *Collective Bargaining in American Industry* (Washington, DC: Brookings Institution, 1960).

6. Lin Grensing-Pophal, "The Do's and Don'ts of Recruiting from Within," Society for Human Resource Management, October 2000, www.shrm.org/whitepapers.

7. General Electric has attempted to address the problem of local managers holding back talent from the corporate office by building an assessment of such behavior into the performance appraisals of those managers.

8. Peter Cappelli, *The New Deal at Work: Managing the Market-Driven Workforce* (Boston: Harvard Business School Press, 1999).

9. New companies that never had job-posting systems use the phrase "internal job board," whereas companies that had established posting systems, typically unionized versions, tend to refer to them as "electronic job-posting systems."

10. Sharon M. Tarrant, "Setting up an Electronic Job Posting System," *Training and Development* 48, no. 1 (January 1994): 39–43.

11. Joe Mullich, "Looking Inward," *Workforce Management* 84, no. 3 (March 2005), 50–51.

12. Ibid.

13. Haig R. Nalbantian and Anne Szostak, "How Fleet Bank Fought Employee Flight," *Harvard Business Review*, April 2004, 116–125.

14. Robert Fulmer, Philip A. Gibbs, and Marshall Goldsmith, "Developing Leaders: How Winning Companies Keep on Winning," *Sloan Management Review* 42, no. 1 (Fall 2000): 49–59.

15. Andreas Karl, interview with the author, 2005.

16. "Internal Mobility," iLogos Research (a division of Recruitsoft), 2003.

17. Rado Kotorov and Emily Hsu, "A Road-map for Creating Efficient Corporate Internal Labor Markets," *Career Development International* 7, no. 1 (2002): 37–46.

18. Ibid.

19. Diane Morello, vice president, Gartner Research, interview with the author, 2005.

20. See, for example, D. Quinn Mills, *The IBM Lesson: The Profitable Art of Full Employment* (New York: Times Books, 1988).

21. David Blanchard, "How Big Blue Finds its Human Assets," *Logistics Today*, June 2006, 1–14.

22. Ibid.

23. Interview with the author, 2006.

24. Interview with the author, 2006.

25. The details of this arrangement are outlined in Peter Hagstrom, "Oticon A/S: Project 330," Case 195-140 (Boston: Harvard Business School Publishing, 1995.

26. Interview with the author, 2006.

27. Teni Mardarossian, Exxon human resources manager, interview with the author, 2005.

28. The Naviquest company has since changed its name to NavAgility and has concentrated more on helping individuals identify a standardized way to describe their competencies; see www.navagility.com.

29. Interviews with Fidelity managers, 2005.

30. Norman Tonina, interview with the author, 2006.

31. Ibid.

32. Ibid.

33. David Brown, "TD Gives Employees Tool to Chart Career Paths," *Canadian HR Reporter*, June 20, 2005, 11, 13.

34. Stan Smith, Deloitte US, interview with the author, 2006; See also Joe Mullich, "Let My People Go," Workforce Management http://www.workforce.com/archive/article/23/95/24.php. "Next Generation Initiatives: A Summary of Research Activities, Responses, Accomplishments, and Future Direction" Deloitte US, February 9, 2006 (internal company document).

35. Interview with the author, 2006

Chapter 8

1. The classic study of scientific paradigms and their effect on scientific progress is Thomas S. Kuhn, *Scientific Revolutions*, 3rd ed. (Chicago: University of Chicago Press, 1996).

2. *Leadership 2012*, Research Report, Corporate University XChange, Harrisburg, PA, 2007, 6.

Acknowledgments

The idea for this book came relatively soon after finishing my earlier book, *The New Deal at Work*, which described the breakdown of lifetime employment and the move toward more market-driven employment relationships. I thought that there must be some new model emerging that would describe how employers were managing careers and the development of talent in the context of the more open labor markets—lateral hiring and layoffs—that had already been under way for more than a decade.

I was wrong, but it took me several years to discover that. After attending lots of talent management conferences and workshops, reading through the business press, talking to employers, consultants, and other experts, I realized that most U.S. employers simply were not managing talent at all in the early part of the 2000's. Those that were did so as if they still had lifetime employment models, albeit with the obvious downside that they were losing most of their candidates to competitors.

Travels to other countries helped suggest that the U.S. approach to managing talent, whose reach remains global, was not the only one, and that employers in other parts of the world were thinking about these issues differently. I am especially grateful to Singapore Management University's SMU/Wharton Research Center for funding my investigatory study of talent management practices among Singapore companies. More recently, my research in India, especially a project supported by the National Human Resources Development Network there, has helped me see the beginnings of a different approach.

Some U.S. employers have begun to think differently and more systematically about their practices, and I am thankful to the many employer representatives cited in the text for the descriptions they shared about developments in their businesses. The candid observations of the corporate supporters of our Center for Human Resources at Wharton were especially helpful.

Mary O'Sullivan, Dan Raff, and Paul Osterman helped me with the historical and contextual parts of the book. We have arguably the best Operations Research group in the world at Wharton, and my colleagues there were especially helpful. Gerard Cachon in particular quickly got over his initial surprise that I would be interested in the fine points of research in the operations area, and he helped me see applications of operations arguments that go well beyond what I am able to describe here. Seeing the title of Gerard's book with Wharton colleague Christian Terwiesch, *Matching Supply with Demand*, was the turning point in my understanding of talent management because it suggested that the basic challenge in talent management—identifying the demand and then setting out to manage supply to just meet demand—was the same as in other aspects of business and management. John Wright played an important role in shaping the book and getting it published. Melinda Merino offered very helpful editorial advice in sharpening the arguments. Both John and Melinda were their usual supportive and enthusiastic selves throughout the process.

A number of historical studies were particularly important for me, especially Rosabeth Kanter's *Men and Women of the Corporation* and William H. Whyte's magisterial *The Organizational Man*, which offered one of the first and arguably the paradigm-defining description of the arrangements for managing careers and individuals in that now increasingly brief period when most every important influence was within the control of the firm. In the process of writing this book, I discovered that Whyte was born and raised just a few miles from here. Maybe there is something in the water that drove our interest in understanding organizational and career issues.

Index

About the Author

Peter Cappelli is the George W. Taylor Professor of Management at the Wharton School and director of Wharton's Center for Human Resources. He is also a research associate at the National Bureau of Economic Research in Cambridge, Massachusetts, and a Distinguished Scholar of the Ministry of Manpower for Singapore. He served as senior adviser to the Kingdom of Bahrain for Employment Policy from 2003–2005.

Cappelli has served on three committees of the National Academy of Sciences and three panels of the National Goals for Education. He was recently named by Vault.com as one the twenty-five most important people working in the area of human capital and by Recruit.com as one of the top one hundred people in the field of recruiting and staffing. He is a fellow of the National Academy of Human Resources. He serves on the advisory boards of several companies and is the founding editor of the *Academy of Management Perspectives*.

Cappelli's recent research examines the implications of changes in employment relations in the United States. His publications include *Change at Work* (Oxford University Press, 1997) and *The New Deal at Work. Managing the Market-Driven Workforce* (Harvard Business School Press, 1999). His work on managing retention, electronic recruiting, and changing career paths has appeared in the *Harvard Business Review*.

Cappelli has degrees in industrial relations from Cornell University and in labor economics from Oxford where he was a Fulbright Scholar.